METAFILM

METAFILM

Materialist Rhetoric and
Reflexive Cinema

Christopher Carter

THE OHIO STATE UNIVERSITY | COLUMBUS

Copyright © 2018 by The Ohio State University.
All rights reserved.

Library of Congress Cataloging-in-Publication Data
Names: Carter, Christopher, 1974– author.
Title: Metafilm : materialist rhetoric and reflexive cinema / Christopher Carter.
Description: Columbus : The Ohio State University Press, [2018] | Includes bibliographical references and index.
Identifiers: LCCN 2018002742 | ISBN 9780814213728 (cloth ; alk. paper) | ISBN 0814213723 (cloth ; alk. paper)
Subjects: LCSH: Film criticism. | Motion picture producers and directors—Interviews. | Materialism. | Rhetoric.
Classification: LCC PN1995 .C3583 2018 | DDC 791.430—dc23
LC record available at https://lccn.loc.gov/2018002742

Cover design by James Baumann
Text design by Juliet Williams
Type set in Palatino Linotype

In memory of Phillip Dwayne Carter
(1952–2014)

CONTENTS

Acknowledgments   ix

INTRODUCTION   Reflexive Materialism   1

CHAPTER 1   Refusal   21

CHAPTER 2   Mediated Mourning   49

CHAPTER 3   Material Correspondences   70

CHAPTER 4   Sound Affect   90

CHAPTER 5   Witness   111

CONCLUSION   *Un Certain Regard* (or, Four Ways of Looking Back)   137

Notes   159
Works Cited   169
Index   185

ACKNOWLEDGMENTS

THANKS FIRST to Tara Cyphers, acquisitions editor at The Ohio State University Press, for guidance and support throughout the crafting of this book. She brings an unmatched efficiency to her work, along with a kindness and communicative ease I can only call exemplary. Thanks also to Claire Sisco King and an anonymous reviewer, both of whose feedback recharged my thinking and introduced new subtleties into the manuscript. Even when the critiques were most pointed, and perhaps especially then, collaborating with Tara and her team was a rich affirmation.

Russel Durst provided similar affirmation as I joined the English faculty at the University of Cincinnati, regularly reading my work and teaching me to streamline ideas. Laura Micciche matched his generosity by providing forums for writers to share works in progress and practice rhetorical listening. I am eager to collaborate with her on Parlor Press's Writing Program Administration series beginning in fall 2017. Joyce Malek and Chris Campagna have been my allies in the Composition Office, helping me keep an eye always to the classroom, where many of the best ideas are born. Ron Hundemer has also been a fine collaborator, demonstrating an enviable attention to detail in his administrative efforts. Such colleagues keep me excited about coming to work, and their support made it possible to write this book.

Financial backing came from UC's Taft Research Center, which helped cover the publication costs of this book, and also allowed me to attend several meetings and events where I received generative commentary on its chapters. I am grateful to Taylor and Francis for permitting me to reprint portions of "Mediated Mourning: Troubled Identifications in Atom Egoyan's *Ararat*" from *Rhetoric Review* vol. 34, no. 1, and I am also pleased that portions of chapter 3 ran in *K. B. Journal* (under a Creative Commons license) in 2016. Publishing interrelated pieces in those venues strengthened my confidence in the overall project and lent momentum to later writing.

Late-stage momentum also owes to the encouragement of Jay Twomey, who prompted me to draft a book proposal that would trace the arc of my argument while establishing firm connections between chapters. His leadership as head of UC English has been deft and assured, and his attention to the professional development of the faculty merits particular praise. While I have certainly benefited from it, teacher-researchers throughout the department have experienced similar good fortune.

While relying on such extraordinary colleagues, I have also taken inspiration and reassurance from my family, and I am grateful that the job in Cincinnati brought us all closer together. Thanks to Kelly, Robert, Ellis, and Tess Sperry for their unfailing hospitality, and to my mother, Patty Carter, who led the cheer through every stage of drafting and production. She taught me a love for stories early on, whether on the page or screen. My father, Phil Carter, nurtured those same loves while modeling careful attention to how things are made. He lives in our memories as the consummate craftsman.

Finally, I thank Beth, Jonah, and Ben for giving purpose to my work, opening new satisfactions while magnifying every pleasure. Jonah has a builder's mind like his grandpa, the eye of a budding scientist, and an artist's imagination. Ben has a designer's ingenuity and a novelist's knack for building characters. Both of them are world makers—gamers who know more about screen culture than this book could ever contain. My love and profound gratitude go to Beth for what our boys have become, for keeping us all attuned to each other, for supplying the gravity that holds our world in place. She stokes our sense of adventure, helps us mature by trying new things. She is all compassion, patience, promise—the insistent stir and sway when life starts to settle. She brings me up against the limits of this genre, for mere acknowledgment could never be enough.

INTRODUCTION

REFLEXIVE MATERIALISM

> Humans are only one of many living things, and all these things long to live, and the highest form of living is freedom: a man to be a man, a cloud to be a cloud, bamboo to be bamboo.
> —Richard Flanagan, *The Narrow Road to the Deep North*

> What critical materialism encourages is an expansive, diachronic approach to analysis and rhetoric that scrupulously maps contexts not only to trace multiple historical and material forces but also to recognize people—people otherwise at risk of being diagrammed out of scenes and scopes of concern.
> —Tony Scott and Nancy Welch, from *College English*'s "Comment and Response"

A CAR HORN BLARES. The words "Chicago, 1968" appear from blackness. Cut to a foggy lens through which we see figures running toward us. The fog crystallizes into a shattered windshield.

Now we sit in the car, inspecting its interior. A seatbelt quivers in the light of an open passenger door. A man with a movie camera appears in the aperture, a sound technician close behind. They circle to the hood and kill the horn. The view widens to reveal the whole car, pieces of broken detour sign surrounding it, its chassis merged almost entirely with a stoplight pole.

The cameraman moves to the rear of the vehicle and squats. A woman who first escaped our view now hangs out the passenger door, unmoving. The lens lingers on her dress, on bits of wreckage, twisted door trim, the stained and unyielding concrete of the curb. The soundman records the post-crash hum. No traffic disturbs the intimacy.

Their business complete, the men withdraw from the vehicle, tending to their equipment. Only ninety seconds have passed, though the blend of calm and emergency slows the feel of time. The cameraman remarks, as if in afterthought, "Better call an ambulance."

So begins Haskell Wexler's 1969 film, *Medium Cool*. The scene is fictive, though the subsequent narrative crosses into the territory of documentary, as his characters move through the spaces of the 1968 Democratic National Convention (DNC) and interact with antiwar protesters outside. As the men travel from the initial wreck to the collision of ideologies at the convention, Wexler hones his skill as a cinematographer by lingering on extrahuman things: clothes, motorcycles, wine glasses, tanks, bedcovers, truncheons, kitchen tables, riot gas, and to punctuate the film's reflexivity, cameras. In the late stages of the turbulent 1960s, *Medium Cool* demonstrates preoccupation with issues that would claim crucial importance, nearly fifty years on, in the study of rhetoric.

MATERIALISMS

Inspired by the writings of Bruno Latour and Jane Bennett, a new materialist orientation toward rhetoric stresses the communicative power of objects, refusing in many cases to distinguish them from subjects. New materialists demand attention to the substance of disclosure, figuring substance not as the ground or situation from which rhetoric emerges, but as the very form and body it takes. Scholars such as Laurie Gries suggest that as soon as such forms exert consequentiality for other bodies, they participate in a becoming that is resolutely rhetorical; others, such as Thomas Rickert, locate rhetoric in the potential for becoming, the ambience that conditions all things' transformation. Conceptions of ambience, actor-network theory, and object-oriented ontology all track those transformations in ways that decenter human beings while retaining their participation in the ecological mix. Rickert includes within that ecology the coevolving of person and discourse as the world discloses itself "through affective, symbolic, and material means" (*Ambient* 162). As *Medium Cool* attends to that disclosure, it evokes the feel of things, their psychic and haptic texture.

New materialist rhetoric's attraction to the extrahuman veers from the field's anthropocentric tendencies while locating life in nontraditional places. Novelist Richard Flanagan captures the sensibility when he observes that "humans are only one of many living things, and all these things long to live, and the highest form of living is freedom" (227). He accords this longing not just to conscious organisms but also to clouds and bamboo, whose liberation lies in immanence, their determination to be nothing other than themselves.

We constrain the vitality of such phenomena, the argument runs, when we value their symbolic qualities over their substantive integrity. To appreciate that integrity, Gries encourages us to look not for meaning but for movement. In *Still Life with Rhetoric: A New Materialist Approach for Visual Rhetorics*, she takes the pulse of things by observing how they travel, where they appear, and how they change along the way. She expresses greater interest in the coevolution of bodies than any metaphoric resonance they might hold. To illustrate her long-term faith in the connection between movement and becoming, she writes of living in the Rocky Mountain West, seeing tumbleweeds get caught up in desert fencing, and walking out to free them. "This action," she explains, "was based on a belief that tumbleweeds desire to keep moving; their 'job' is always to be on the road, in flow" (71). To study rhetoric, for Gries, is to study things at work, to track their circulation.

Haskell Wexler shows similar fascination with flow in the opening scenes of *Medium Cool*. As soon as his focal reporters contact emergency services, they flee the scene as a silhouetted figure watches from an overpass. The observer's presence punctuates the wrongness of their actions, the scandal of recording the crash's aftereffects and yet leaving the woman behind. But news must be delivered. Information wants to move. Given the unending urgency, driving to the television station looks inefficient; worse yet, it limits their ability to collect more images. So they call in the bike man.

He arrives in sleek black leather, stops to gather the footage, and sets off toward downtown Chicago. The urban skyline opens up; he enters its flow. In a succession of tracking shots, we follow him over bridges, down thoroughfares, under elevated train tracks, and around corners, at times careening deathly close to cars in the opposite lane. Rather than arriving at the station, however, the scene ends with a reverse shot in which the bike man approaches. We have followed the news item for four full minutes, from production and packaging through circulation and delivery, only to find we were the intended recipients all along. But the message fails to reach us. We watch the carrier dissolve as the original blackness takes hold.

Medium Cool thus visualizes the drift of rhetoric while prefiguring new materialist doubt about the arrival of meaning. Peter Wollen voices such doubt in *Signs and Meaning in Cinema*, describing film as not "an instrument of communication but a challenge to the mystification that communication can exist" (163). Breaking faith with the "mystification" of pure idea delivery, Wexler's picture attends to the mediating apparatus whereby rhetors excise as much as they express, and to the courses whereby audiences bring idiosyncratic screens to the interpretative act. The movie associates rhetorical delivery with anxious motion, with travel along highways and back roads that lead not to closure but interruption, dissolution, and new emergencies.

As the film conveys the momentum of imagetext, it harbors reservations about its own attention to the life force of extrahuman things. With its glimpse of the woman in the wreck, the film captures the reporters equating her body with its surroundings, yet distances itself from that equivalence. While depicting an onlooker who stays behind as the information travels, it refuses an unmixed endorsement of speed or a relaxed affiliation with flat ontology. It shares Tony Scott and Nancy Welch's misgivings about people "being diagrammed out of scenes and scopes of concern" or fading into those scenes as undifferentiated things ("Tony" 589).

Undoubtedly, pursuing the motions of expressive materials teaches us how information replicates and transforms itself. But seeking life in things may proceed alongside the objectification of the human. Critique of anthropocentrism rightly questions the narcissism of the researcher, the species-identification that codes the non-self as a subordinate or tool, always ready to hand. Still, de-emphasizing persons may also mean turning from the social, leaving us little to say about injustice even when it lies plainly before us.

Critical materialism prioritizes the investigation of those injustices. As Scott and Welch define it, the school of thought involves "an expansive, diachronic approach to analysis and rhetoric that scrupulously maps contexts" while foregrounding how material culture reflects divisions of social power and vice versa ("Tony" 589). It shares Gries's interest in circulation while attending to its economics, and more specifically, who benefits in financial and political terms. Rather than only studying how things move forward along untold tributaries of the information ecology, it perceives them reaching back into the past, at once arising from and exposing histories of human conflict and enforced inequality. Not only does it linger at the scene of trauma like the silhouette on the bridge, it pursues the history of the scene and asks how we can preempt its repetition. It resists, in however limited fashion, the scene's reduction to a readily digestible commodity.

To situate *Medium Cool* at the nexus of new and critical materialisms does not mean merely interpreting the film. The movie constitutes a mode of theorizing in its own right, visualizing an earlier version of the vitality that Gries describes in *Still Life with Rhetoric,* and practicing the mapping that Scott and Welch call for in *College English.* Like the movies that figure into this book, it exemplifies how images participate in public discourse, both spurring and enacting the negotiation of controversy. Even as cinema entertains, it often performs the work that Robert Hariman and John Louis Lucaites attribute to famous pictures in *No Caption Needed: Iconic Photographs, Public Culture, and Liberal Democracy*: it helps orient "the self within civic life," it infuses "social knowledge" and "collective memory," and it offers "figural resources for communicative action" (9, 11). *Medium Cool* addresses the audience's civic orientation by probing the photographer's responsibility to his subjects when working in public space—a concern now sharpened by the age of ubiquitous camera work.

The movie refines cultural memory by documenting and dramatizing antiwar protest, African American collectivism, feminist politics, and the militarized suppression of dissent. In visualizing coalitional rhetoric, it clarifies forms of alliance and contention between the various constituencies and gives us figural means for entering the fray. And what is more, it reflects on its own techniques of mediation, examining technologies of visualization and sound design that populate the story world. That process, Robert Stam explains in *Reflexivity in Film and Literature,* yields an unruly dialectic: "It indulges in play and then pulls out of the play world. It casts a spell and then as quickly disenchants" (5). As a political metafilm, *Medium Cool* lures us into its space and then calls the lure into question; it invites identification with the labor of investigative journalism and just as powerfully provokes our alienation.

THE TEMPERATURE OF DELIVERY

The picture's contradictory signals require deft participation by viewers, many of whom find themselves arguing with the film rather than conforming to its push and pull. The elliptical character of many scenes requires watchers to supply information or draw tentative conclusions based on limited evidence. As mysteries accrue, the film's allusion to Marshall McLuhan's *Understanding Media: The Extensions of Man* takes on particular salience. In this 1964 work, McLuhan explains that

> there is a basic principle that distinguishes a hot medium like radio from a cool one like the telephone, or a hot medium like the movie from a cool one like TV. A hot medium is one that extends one single sense in "high definition." High definition is the state of being well filled with data. A photograph is, visually, "high definition." . . . Telephone is a cool medium, or one of low definition, because the ear is given a meager amount of information. And speech is a cool medium of low definition, because so little is

given and so much has to be filled in by the listener. On the other hand, hot media do not leave so much to be filled in or completed by the audience. (22–23)

Among the technologies that afford us varying degrees of involvement, McLuhan counts cinema as a hot instance that dominates the rhetorical encounter with its heavy quotient of information. Film overwhelms the visual sense, he implies, rather than inviting audience invention.

When considering *Medium Cool*'s connection to *Understanding Media*, Wexler remarks, "I don't know anything about Marshall McLuhan. I read some of the stuff, I didn't understand it at all. He was pretty smart so I gave it that title" (qtd. in Rampell). Whether or not we accept that explanation, his movie appropriates McLuhan's vocabulary while controverting his claims. Film may be high-definition, but it still leaves much to "fill in." It may flood the visual sense, but it also involves other senses in ways that are by turns commonplace and unpredictable.

Movies provide an abundance of sequenced visual details, but the significance of the details is never a given. They require viewers to undertake acts of constructive processing, some of which occurs in such routine fashion that it escapes notice. The triggering of habitual responses coheres with McLuhan's idea of "hot" rhetoric. But Wexler's movie breaks the routine while posing the witnessing of onscreen violence as an ethical problem. Such tactics suggest the imprudence of labeling an entire medium hot or cool, as instances of mediation vary widely in the interactivity they summon.

When we factor in the multimodal character of film, the temperature of delivery becomes more uncertain. The mode of sound, for example, may match the high-definition of the moving image, and still oblige audiences to demonstrate an aptitude for inference. Sounds may synch seamlessly with pictures, thus aiding their mimetic appeal. They may also contradict the visual, misalign with the image track, or transgress what dramatists such as Denis Diderot and Molière call "the fourth wall" (Pavis 154). If we consider that few audience members perceive these effects in precisely the same way, the prospect of a hot medium that bears the full burden of the rhetorical encounter appears unlikely.

Given that distinct encounters invite differing degrees of participation, no medium will produce the same experience every time. New materialist theory acknowledges variety by attending to hot and cool encounters with images, which sometimes make swift impressions and other times nudge us to linger. Lingering may involve "filling in" details so as to derive sense from the picture or it may give way to sabotage. Gries illustrates such possibilities in *Still Life with Rhetoric* by tracking Shepard Fairey's remediation of Mannie Garcia's 2006 photograph of Barack Obama. The Fairey poster's patriotic color scheme, Obama's gaze into the future, and the "Hope" script at the base of his likeness make their points with directness. The image spread quickly due to its activation of preexisting semiotic codes, appealing readily to liberal-democratic sensibilities while indicating the historical import of the United States' first African American president.

But the spread also depended on cooler responses in which prosumers recast the poster in partisan ways, ensuring that the image appeared on "more than two million websites" and in a range of national contexts by 2014 and 2015 (Gries, *Still* 1). Those instances of détournement turn Obama into Santa Claus, the Mona Lisa, Big Brother, the Joker, an assortment of zombies, and even Shepard Fairey himself. In an era of social media, it is not solely a thing's semiotics that ensure or inhibit its proliferation but the thing's utility for composing.

Given new materialists' interest in the recomposition of visual objects, they resist the type of coolness they associate with academic interpretation. Gries, for example, contends that investigating the aesthetics and design of images deflects attention from the rhetorical work they do in public settings. Along with Kevin DeLuca and Joe Wilferth, she questions importing methods for analyzing print into the realm of visual culture (*Still* 18). She differs with DeLuca and Wilferth on the value of examining circulation, especially insofar as those thinkers associate such study with deep contextualization of pictures in various historical environments.[1] She has no more interest in slow contextualization than they do, but she sees the mapping of movement as an alternative to those research practices rather than an extension. Iconographic tracking, she argues, does not get mired in the details of a single graphic or remix, but instead holds "potential to disclose how rhetoric unfolds as a complex, distributed event" (20, 106–7). Her approach would privilege the journey of the bike man to any stop along the way, the "eventfulness" (8) of transportation to any discrete interpretation. But she writes in a period that needs no bike man to mobilize information, an era where memes appear, take wildly diverse forms, and show up in broadly variant places in a fraction of the time it takes to navigate downtown Chicago.

Critical materialist theory pays similar attention to the streaming of visual rhetoric, though it holds fast to the question of who profits. The image commodity often circulates at high speed, affording hot interchanges as people operate their smartphones, drive by digital billboards, race past ads in the subway, glimpse snatches of television news in bars or restaurants. But recognizing how images help reproduce inequality takes a cooler approach. Scott and Welch enact that approach in "One Train Can Hide Another: Critical Materialism for Public Composition" by focusing on *Kony 2012*, a video in which the U.S. charity Invisible Children exposes a history of atrocities in Uganda. The video presses for the arrest of Joseph Kony, a warlord known for abducting youth and forcing them into military service. After describing the video's viral spread and its reputation for empowering young people, Scott and Welch note its value for teachers of rhetoric and writing. Classes include "students blogging about the video through Aristotle's appeals, Lloyd Bitzer's rhetorical situation, and Michael McGee's ideographs," all of which suggests a "public-writing pedagogy" that is poised to reestablish "the relevance of rhetorical education" (563).

But as the video offers those opportunities, attention to its dissemination eclipses consideration of whom the film serves. Although it appears to serve the children of Uganda and the project of securing international human rights, those prospects remain open to dispute. More certain, for Scott and Welch, are the video's advantages for charitable and religious organizations as well as U.S. military power in the region. The authors point to "the commodification of activism through sales of Stop Kony action kits," the presence of "such dubious funders as the religious-right Discover Institute," and the "dramatic widening of the U.S. military footprint in Africa since 2008" (564). Their approach shares much with Gries's in that they track the consequentiality of images, studying what pictures do rather than seeing them as texts whose internal logic is paramount. But whereas Gries foregrounds uptake and remix, Scott and Welch describe the neoliberal mesh within which those consequences occur.

Medium Cool embodies the kind of materiality that elucidates that mesh rather than quietly operating within it. It thereby exemplifies the type of film that inhabits the chapters in this book, each of which details the rhetoric of reflexive materialism in modern cinema. Reflexive materialism aligns at times with Gries's perspective and at other times with that of Scott and Welch, demonstrating their productive coexistence in some cases and sharp antagonism in others. But whether the films address image circulation as an affective, ethical, or political-economic phenomenon—or all those things at once—they show awareness of participating in the same conditions they describe.

They invite cool practices of engagement but they do not need the critic to determine their theoretical significance. They are works of theory in themselves, performing their arguments in multiple, interlocking modes rather than leaving materialist considerations to the more logocentric thinkers among us. As they perform those cases, they present materialism as a way of composing rather than assessing the already composed. The movies thus embody a self-conscious variant on Wollen's idea of cinema as "the factory where thought is at work, rather than the transport system which conveys the finished product" (164). *Metafilm* endeavors to trace such thought in action across movies in different social and geographical contexts, clarifying continuities and divergences among their versions of reflexive critique. In so doing, the book acknowledges how those movies slip past anything we might write or say about them, and how their liveliness eludes the control of screenwriters, directors, production crews, and audiences, catalyzing an agency that intersects with human decision but cannot be reduced to it.

REFLEXIVE RHETORIC

Scholars have paid limited if trenchant attention to film as rhetoric, examining the technical choices that inform movie design, the value of cinema for teaching writing, and the moving image's influence on spectator subjectivity. John Harrington's *The Rhetoric of Film* describes cinema in terms of narrative strategy, outlining how camera work aligns with character perspective, and how sound collaborates with pictures to evoke diverse emotions. It also describes how that collaboration produces a sense of temporal and spatial continuity, and how audiovisual composing techniques produce cohesive arguments. Laurence Behrens took up Harrington's work shortly after its publication, lauding its emphasis on how movies address audiences while noting its lack of attention to classical appeals. Whatever its limitations, it informed studies by Dale Adams and Robert Kline in the mid-1970s, Ulrich Wicks in the early 1980s, and Russell F. Proctor II and Ronald B. Adler in the early 1990s, all of whom saw film as a resource for teaching critical literacy and communication.

By 1999, Ellen Bishop published the essay collection *Cinema-(to)-Graphy: Film and Writing in Contemporary Composition Courses*, in which Edward Maloney and Paul Miller articulated the utility of movies for writing teachers, suggesting that they teach us to recognize narrative layering while also proffering meta-knowledge about the cultures in which movies circulate. Other contributions to the collection address the rhetorical character of documentary truth claims, representations of race in fiction and nonfiction film, and the unpredictability of reception. That unpredictability aligns with Gries's ideas about the instability of viral rhetoric, as do the chapters on how pictures inspire contradictory experiences based in viewers' ideological predispositions. The study of how pictures mediate ideology prepares the way for critical materialist analysis, though none of the essays dwells for long on class antagonisms or the economics of the film industry.

Rhetorical studies of film tend to underplay the connection of cinema to class struggle, though they give us ready ways of uncovering those issues. In *The Terministic Screen,* David Blakesley attends to the material effects of the moving image in his definition of a rhetorical perspective on film, which "usually focuses on problems of appeal in the broadest sense," each of which arises "in a context and situation that ranges from the internal world of the film to the external world of the viewer and critic" (2). Blakesley draws powerfully on the work of Kenneth Burke in his studies of film, detailing how movies produce the sense of "identification" between the "internal world" of the narrative and the "external world" of the addressee. In analyses of *Vertigo* and *The Usual Suspects,* he describes how pictures usher audiences into worlds of gendered violence and compelling misrepresentation, and how they reflect curiously on viewers' participation in the illusion. He thereby affords us a fitting framework for studying *Medium Cool,* which, as we have seen, dramatizes the production of violent news objects while troubling the ethics of their circulation.

From its opening, Wexler's movie identifies us with the scene of devastation. But it also maintains distance from the journalists who witness the disaster yet refuse to intervene. That dynamic of invitation and retreat generates what Kenneth Burke calls a "terministic screen," which refers to how a specific lexicon focuses attention on certain dimensions of a text while leaving others outside the frame. Whereas prose devises a terministic screen through verbal patterns, audiovisual media bring new layers to the concept: the literal screen "directs the attention" while metaphorically "screening" other information by filtering it or keeping it outside the frame (Blakesley, *Terministic* 2–3). Questions of what to include and exclude, what to emphasize and blur, from what angles and for how long, are all rhetorical concerns. No matter how heated the delivery, asking those questions works to cool the rhetorical interchange.

Cooler approaches to rhetoric preserve the complexity of Burke's idea of identification, which designates a contingent sharing of interests amid a range of irreducible singularities. Less directive than persuasion, identification is the precondition for moving an audience, an indication that enough common ground exists to sustain cooperation. Common ground does not mean sameness or unity; rather, it allows for and even depends on differences among interlocutors. In establishing a sense of shared territory, movies do the work of what Blakesley calls "reconstitut[ing] the subject," or reorienting viewers toward a set of spatial, ideological, and affective relations that are specific to each filmic experience (13). In a contribution to *The Terministic Screen*, James Roberts echoes Blakesley's formulation by describing how movies create "mobile and shifting subjects," whether by crafting characters or mediating our experience of them (120).

But however compelling that mediation, identification does not imply a spectator who thoroughly complies with the film's epistemology. Common ground is a space of negotiation, which, when it stalls, may strain the sense of affinity or provoke its dissolution. When films direct attention to the techniques by which they elicit assent or influence us to suspend disbelief, they threaten the fantasy necessary to maintain the rhetorical situation. Yet by at once designing the fantasy and analyzing its historical and sociopolitical implications, such movies also give us uncommon reasons to watch. By attending to the violence involved in the making and reception of film, they reconstitute the subject of cinema as materialist praxis.[2]

Reflexive materialism thereby works to frame a political collective despite the affective prevalence of the hot transaction. Affect, in the sense given us by Jenny Rice and Brian Massumi, designates a precognitive condition that binds materialities, human and otherwise, rather than residing in any one of them. The movies that occupy this book challenge the affective states that they associate with lethargy, intractability, escapism, and despair. To disturb that situation, they engage in any number of unconventional behaviors, including directly addressing the audience, fashioning movies within movies and then confusing the diegetic layers, questioning labor ethics on set, and introducing absurdity into otherwise naturalistic scenarios.

These flights from decorum often coincide with an agonistic rhetoric that calls attention to turmoil on our side of the screen, and to the histories of trauma that ground audience identification with the narrative. Such agonism not only incites wrangling with onscreen drama but also invokes a need for political action in extra-cinematic space. While the metaleptic techniques of the films can be disorienting enough, the pictures prove especially maddening when conveying their inadequacy to the problems they pose, reveling in provocation rather than imagining resolution.

But the lure of uncertainty, and the involvement in a puzzle where the objectives are unclear and the pieces change shape, teach us about not just the rhetoric of movies but the experience of vision. James Elkins clarifies the lesson in *The Object Stares Back* by describing the agency of the watched, which he figures sometimes as a kind of snare, other times as a "forest of traps," and most memorably, as an "irresistible effect" that binds viewers to objects "as if we were tied to them by little wires" (19–20). Reflecting on the rhetorical performance of a display case, he suggests that "instead of saying I am the one doing the looking, it seems better to say that objects are all trying to catch my eye" (20). The wires exert a considerable pull, which derives partly from the labors of the objects' creators and those who design the display, but also constitutes a strength that does not denote the workings of human will. Cinema tends to parallel Elkins's interaction with the exhibit, though rarely do commodities visualize the suasive apparatus through which they conjure the sense of attachment.

Such reflexive materialism seeks less to displace human agency, however, than to cooperate with it. Bruno Latour defines such cooperation as the work of the collective, which he distinguishes from sheer human solidarity by linking it to varied forms of material interactivity (*We*). This redefinition of the collective dilutes its historical association with direct action politics, but it has the advantage of disentangling transformative rhetoric from human planning. While the cooperation of materialities in the interest of transformation may entail synergy and mutual affirmation, it also involves tension and redirection, resistance and doubt.

The films in this book express such doubt in ways akin to James Agee and Walker Evans's multimodal experiment *Let Us Now Praise Famous Men*, which ensues with Evans's uncaptioned photographs of sharecroppers and their environs in 1930s Alabama, and continues with Agee's novel-length reflection on living with the farmers for a brief period. As the two men traveled south from New York City to study the effects of the Great Depression, Agee became desperately uncomfortable with the violence of their privileged gazes. Their book attempts to offset that violence in the photos as well as the prose, affording the farmers opportunities to "stare back" in ways that defy liberal objectification. "Who are you," Agee writes, "who will read these words and study these photographs, and through what cause, and for what purpose, and by what right do you qualify to, and what will you do about it" (7). The movies that motivate the chapters ahead all pose versions of those challenges, some in the same agonistic tone, others in more indirect ways. Who we are, the films imply, expresses itself in what we do about what we see.

However forcefully Agee poses his queries, he withholds answers. And however tight the relationship he and Evans posit between people and their environment, they refuse to concede equivalence between those forms of materiality, or to indulge onlookers who pretend compassion while reducing the farmers to mere news items. A lover of still and moving images alike, Agee prefigures Wexler's concerns by more than three decades, anticipating the paradoxes of each movie in the impending chapters.

THE WHOLE WORLD IS WATCHING

The intersection of intimate forms of trauma with public conflict constitutes a theme in all the films that figure into this book. *Medium Cool* gives us the earliest example of such an intersection, and an instance of how the mingling of private and public parallels the confusion of intra- and extradiegetic worlds. Near the movie's end, the journalist who covered the opening wreck helps a distraught mother pursue her runaway son. Their search soon becomes tangled in protests occurring outside the 1968 Democratic National Convention. By the time they arrive, the military has begun to impose its will, attempting to shut down conflict between police and demonstrators but escalating it instead. An army jeep rolls down the thoroughfare with barbed fencing protruding from its grill, soldiers marching on both sides of the vehicle. Police make way for the procession, galvanized by the show of force. Someone in the crowd calls out "Fuck you!" moments before an officer releases a cloud of tear gas. Coughing cuts through the mayhem, then a voice from offscreen: "Look out, Haskell, it's real!"

That warning constitutes the most jarring interruption of mimetic convention in a film that regularly destabilizes its visual illusions. Stam characterizes such technique as a form of rhetorical incivility: "To the suave continuities of illusionism, [reflexive cinema] opposes the rude shocks of rupture and discontinuity" (7). *Medium Cool* ruptures its internal cohesion by bursting the barrier between narrative space-time and that of cinematic production. As the breach denies the diegetic realm as a world unto itself, it discloses typically hidden junctures between on- and offscreen materialities.

Some version of the offscreen warning might serve as subtext for every movie in *Metafilm*. It suggests a porous boundary between what occurs in front of the lens and what transpires behind it, denying directors and cinematographers any sanctuary. But the warning reaches past Wexler to the viewer, insisting that the movie world is the one we occupy, the world where organized dissent calls forth state-sanctioned repression. Wexler admits to feeling protected by the camera even though "all of us were in great physical danger." It is only when his assistant, Jonathan Haze, remarks on the National Guard firing gas directly at the lens that the filmmaker processes those dangers (Malooley). Mediation, the scene suggests, often brings a sense of invulnerability that abates only in the face of great violence.³

But to suggest that the camera is not a buffer does not mean that audiovisual mediation is rhetorically inconsequential. Wexler underscores its consequence in an interview for *Time Out Chicago*, revealing that he added the "Look out!" line during postproduction. "We were shooting 35mm and there was no sound man there," he explains. "I'm not positive those were his exact words, but I remembered the feeling" (Malooley). A scene where Wexler appears to forgo editing and permit the protest to "break the proscenium" actually depends on editing for its effects. The feel of spontaneity is the result of craft. Recognizing such craft, however, does not require dismissing the claim "That's real!" as a deception. Discovering a composing hand behind the scene only clarifies the extent to which the "real" is always mediated, if not by camera or aural design, by the ways our bodies, habits, memories, and assumptions define our perceptions.

Rather than straining toward purity, Wexler invites a meditative approach to representation and a critique of our responses to it. Although *Medium Cool* may not share Blakesley's lexicon, it exhibits similar attention to images' potential to "reconstitute the subject" and demonstrates a rhetorical sensibility throughout. The reconstitution occurs both onscreen and off, though the movie indicates that the exigency for transformation exists with the audience. Wexler acknowledges not recalling precise details of the DNC protest experience, but he "remember[s] the feeling" and fuses picture with sound to transfer that feeling to the viewer. His movie advocates freedoms of expression and assembly by triggering the visceral feel of having those freedoms revoked. In Wexler's narrative microcosm there can be no refuge from turmoil, as the very presumption of safe distance signals an approaching threat.

We see the danger of that presumption not just in Wexler's risky camera work, but in how he ties the movie's conclusion to its beginning. In *Medium Cool*'s closing sequence, the same camera operator who covers the film's opening wreck drives away from the DNC with the mother beside him, still in search of her son. Radio reporting overlays the image, but the aural and image tracks are out of sequence. The sound occupies a future narrative moment, revealing what the picture does not show: the driver, John Casellis, in critical condition and the passenger dead. As the reporting turns to police violence against protesters, a tire blows and Casellis loses control of the vehicle. He tries frantically to steady the wheel. For an instant, the broken windshield from the film's first minute enters our visual field. He cannot right the car's path; his passenger shrieks. Wexler intercuts the action with the cracked windshield, over and over. Merging analepsis with prolepsis, the technique indicates the return of the repressed for the journalist and for media culture; more subtly, it shows how cinema disrupts temporal linearity by visualizing cycles, accelerations, lags, leaps, and unexpected foldings. Casellis's car hits a tree, echoing the original collision with a stoplight pole. The picture goes dark.

Reports of violence continue on the radio. The empty screen gives way to an image of another car, moving so lazily as to suggest slow-motion cinematography. Yet the people in the car move at ordinary speed, craning to see the smoking wreckage outside. They pass without helping. One onlooker snaps a flash photograph.

Next appears a distanced shot of the crash as the lens retreats down a canopied road. Once the shot reaches full extension, the camera pans right to expose portions of the scaffolding on which it rests. Wexler stands several yards away on another platform, operating a second camera. He turns it toward us. We zoom slowly forward until we enter his lens. Throughout the sequence, the radio blares protesters chanting in unison: "The whole world is watching."

In its most direct sense, the chant admonishes the National Guard, police officers, and federal government for the repression of public dissent. In a less obvious sense, the chant recapitulates one of the stronger motifs in *Medium Cool*, which presents people recording terrible events but declining further to involve themselves. The assertion that a mass public watches while endeavoring not to sully itself intimates the hazards of what Guy Debord called, a few years earlier, the society of the spectacle. The spectacle incorporates all visual culture into processes of commodification, displacing the prospect of agency with sensory saturation while converting images of collective resistance into marketable diversion. Casellis serves the spectacle through the early stages of *Medium Cool*, whether covering a car accident, military training, or political theater at the DNC. Late in the film he shows signs of increased compassion, but Wexler will not let us forget Casellis's initial collusion with the system wherein "the whole world" (or at least a significant portion) watches without interceding. He has transmitted the firsthand view to far-flung publics, feeding the appetite for pictures of carnage. So the cracked windshield makes a tragic return.

As the reverse zoom pulls away from the crash, the mise-en-scène resonates in uncanny fashion with another, more famous picture from 1969, Dennis Hopper's *Easy Rider*. In both movies, the protagonists find their searches cut disastrously short. And in both, key players lie dead at the side of the road, no one to tend to them. As *Easy Rider* leaves audiences dazed by a double murder on a U.S. back road, the film affords us a good view of the perpetrators, and a chilling glimpse of their disdain for 1960s counterculture. *Medium Cool* also offers a view of such disdain, attributing it to the so-called patriotism of officers and soldiers. But Wexler's film finally aims its critical eye at the audience. Whereas the final shot of *Easy Rider* rises to a bird's-eye view, accentuating the loneliness of the riders' deaths and the violence that permeates the landscape, Wexler's assertion is more probing and direct—"The whole world is watching"—as the image machine devours us.

And in that moment of direct address the chant takes on its third and perhaps most urgent meaning. Beyond its association with citizen-based countersurveillance, and its obverse association with an ineffectual populace, the film suggests that the world awaits the viewer's response. In so doing, it delineates the paradox of politically conscious metafilm: movies that express a seemingly perverse fascination with themselves, their creators, or their artistic precursors often show at least as much obsession with reception and its relation to civic agency. To recall Agee's probing inquiry in *Let Us Now Praise Famous Men,* the picture asks not just "Who are you?" who looks but also "What will you do about it?" To forgo that challenge, the film implies, is to acquiesce to the systemic violence that criminalizes dissent.

The films that populate this book attempt to denaturalize that violence. They perceive audience complicity as the hegemonic norm, and they each furnish a multimodal corollary to Stam's assessment in *Reflexivity in Film and Literature*: "It is precisely the normality of ideology that necessitates an art which makes things strange" (211). The strange rhetoric of reflexive materialism connotes a contradictory condition wherein the thing's inward turn correlates with its outward-oriented practice of exhortation. The thing's most lucid moments of self-consciousness occur when—to call up Elkins once more—"the object stares back." The return gaze invokes concerns common to new and critical materialisms. It questions the movie's immersion in currents of distribution and reproduction as well as its affiliation with rhetorical trends that reflect and mold audience expectations. Reflexive materialism in cinema does not leave the analysis of image politics to critics and reviewers; instead, the analysis infuses the composing process, the delivery of the movie, and at times the paratextual material filmmakers release on the Internet or with DVDs and Blu-Ray discs. It exposes forms of violence that are posthuman in orientation, emerging from the inchoate fusion of the organic and the technical.

That same fusion embodies the work of political action. It does so not through straightforward invitations to identify with a political position, but through clarifying the design of such invitations, sometimes in ways that validate the appeal and other times in ways that generate misgivings. Deliberate attention to the machinery of identification and estrangement takes on heightened urgency in the contemporary era, where national leaders and media outlets cultivate an information ecology that Andrew Mitrovica laments as "post-truth." To accept such a condition as inevitable may also mean accepting an era of post-evidence and post-knowledge, even post-justice. Although no film in this book fully anticipates the troubled state of U.S. democracy in 2017, all of them express anxiety about justice at local and international levels, the trauma of its absence, and the abandonment of its pursuit.

The pictures position us like the lonely silhouette at the outset of *Medium Cool*, startled into concentration as information races ahead. That information exists as part of a living system where things strive toward that "highest form of living" Flanagan terms "freedom." The freedom of rhetoric means that it eludes human control, escaping designers' intentions and confounding audiences' efforts to arrest its motion. The figure on the overpass stands baffled as the news pulls off without him; the bike man has a delivery for us but he dissolves mid-motion. In such fickle circumstances, the prospects for reflective advocacy seem bleak. Each of this book's focal films confronts that problem, attending to missed opportunities for transformative action in contexts both intimate and public. Whether troubling the Western sense of insulation from international violence, the sanitizing of historical atrocity, the repressive psychology of patriarchy, or the racism of law enforcement, the movies exhibit repetition compulsions borne of trauma.

COMING ATTRACTIONS

Metafilm's case studies expand the conversation that *Medium Cool* initiates, summoning viewers to revise their perceptual habits and undertake activist modes of intervention in the forms of injury the movies portray. The texts perform the sort of work Stam associates with Bertolt Brecht and Jean-Luc Godard, whose self-aware productions encourage us to "reflect on the violence that inhabits ourselves and our world" (184). Like Stam, Wollen stresses how texts that investigate their own materiality press the interpreter to "interrogate himself [sic], puncture the bubble of his consciousness and introduce into it the rifts, contradictions and questions which are the problematic of the text" (163–64). Those rifts differ from chapter to chapter, though they generally arise from the convergence of psychic and social traumas, wherein personal and familial conflict commingles with the violence of warfare, transnational economics, labor exploitation, and racism. The book moves from explicitly metaleptic films to less conspicuous instances, locating heightened appeals to social action in the subtler forms of reflexivity.

The first study involves Michael Haneke's *Funny Games*, which the Austrian director released as a German-language film in 1997 and then remade in the United States ten years later. A subverted thriller that initially announces its adherence to genre expectations, it later foils the same conventions it cites. Its villains track the film's running time while checking to be sure the audience enjoys the proceedings, and they even rewind and revise those proceedings when their victims gain an advantage. After invoking a relationship of Burkean consubstantiality between viewers and the family under siege, the movie engages in what John Schilb describes as "rhetorical refusal," or the deliberate transgression of discursive decorum: it spurns (1) diegetic boundaries, (2) appropriate focus during dramatic crisis, and (3) editing techniques typically used to produce and relax tension in the thriller genre. Those refusals enact reflexive materialism by coding the narrative as a fabrication while making the film's circulation a major concern of its dialogue. The critical dimension of that materialism surfaces as the narrative clarifies the protected affluence of the central characters, only to later steal that security from them. The U.S. version intensifies the critique through geopolitical recontextualization, playing on visual rhymes between the villains' "funny games" and photographs of detainment practices at Abu Ghraib.

The subsequent chapter extends the focus on geopolitical conflict by grappling with *Ararat*, Atom Egoyan's meditation on the Armenian Genocide of 1915. Centering on the fictive making of a film about the genocide, Egoyan's picture examines the motivations of people working behind the scenes. Although he affords us a range of related portraits, chapter 2 mainly concerns itself with the experiences of the imagined film director, his art historian consultant, and her son. All three characters enact forms of mourning that, while reaching toward consubstantiality with lost family members, depend on forms of narrative mediation that clarify the futility of that desire. While the characters rely on visualization technologies to call up a vanished past, those same technologies describe the void at the core of grief. *Ararat* reaffirms the characters' experience of frustrated identification, showing how ongoing Turkish denial of the genocide intensifies the already formidable burden of 1915.

Chapter 3 extends the book's concern with international violence by addressing Icíar Bollaín's *Even the Rain,* in which a Spanish film crew shoots a Christopher Columbus biopic in Cochabamba so as to obtain suitable settings and low-cost production workers. The filmmakers soon learn, however, that their indigenous employees have begun a protest against the privatization of water in their community, and that recent price hikes will inevitably lead to bloodshed. The effort to dramatize centuries-old injustices brings immersion in contemporary ones, the most prominent of which are the Bolivian water wars and the subtler of which involve labor exploitation on-set. The ensuing drama echoes Godard's "materialist variation on reflexivity" by throwing light on "the cinema's economic base and institutional infrastructure."[4] But both the movie and Bollaín's commentary express apprehension about how *Even the Rain* reaffirms that infrastructure. By bringing such tensions into the open, she takes a dialectical approach to culture, refusing along with Stam to conceive visual rhetorics "as if they were exempt from contradiction" (12). The end result does not share *Funny Games*'s technique of breaking the fourth wall, but it similarly transgresses distinctions between worlds onscreen and off.

Chapter 4 locates such transgressions in sound design as well as visuality. Investigating the composition of Paul Thomas Anderson's *Magnolia,* the chapter examines the film's movement between what Peter Verstraten describes as intradiegetic and extradiegetic sound space. Sometimes the music that we take to be extradiegetic, or part of the film's score, turns out to be intradiegetic material that the characters can hear, or a melody they make themselves. At other moments, songs we think only one character hears turn out to accompany other segments of the narrative, becoming what Halbritter depicts as a soundtrack for collective life.[5] As that leakage crosses the juncture of narrative setting and viewer space, it generates a metadiegetic rhetoric that initiates more elaborate forms of border crossing. As sound identifies characters with the audience and vice versa, it positions the audience within what Sarah Ahmed and Laura R. Micciche designate as sticky emotional relations, or ways of feeling that bind subjects as publics whether they know each other or not. In *Magnolia* those ways of feeling come charged with the trauma of child abuse, some of which is sexual, some psychological, and most borne of neglect.[6]

The idea that audiovisual rhetoric mediates trauma in unpredictable ways also resonates throughout chapter 5. The chapter features Ryan Coogler's *Fruitvale Station,* which begins with cell phone footage of police brutality on a railway platform, giving way to a collective gasp and a blackout. Like the sound in Anderson's film, that gasp enters into metadiegetic space, conveying a whirl of affect that envelops the characters and the audience without fully belonging to either group. Combined with the cut to darkness, the sound suggests bewilderment at the unprovoked gunshot, helplessness before armed police, and an unwillingness to accept either condition. It also establishes the tone for the film to come, which chronicles the day leading up to the shooting. In a crucial but underappreciated sense, *Fruitvale Station* concerns the making of an internationally resonant documentary about the toxic mixture of bigotry and law enforcement. While some critical responses assail the politics of Coogler's re-creation, others resist the reduction of *Fruitvale*'s project to mere "recreation," or artistic play, with the veneer of social conscience. That problem becomes especially pronounced when the picture's production company capitalizes on the Trayvon Martin case, as his killer's exoneration coincides with the movie's release.

Outside early screenings, Weinstein Company employees invited filmgoers to compete for a corporate gift card by discussing police brutality on the company website. New materialist criticism emphasizes how such uses of social media expand film's reach, opening opportunities for remediation. Critical materialism, on the other hand, invites investigation of how remediation serves economic interests distinct from the politics expressed through civic computing. Whereas one school of thought might track the variations of *Funny Games* as it crosses national borders in different decades, the other would probe the film's class analysis and how it interlaces with the context of its making and reception. Whereas one school might study how extrahuman actants in *Ararat* and *Even the Rain* frustrate anthropocentric views of agency, the other accentuates how those actants become saturated with social conflict. While *Magnolia* and *Fruitvale Station* demonstrate how thing-power is multimodal and decentralized, that power converges with forms of trauma that are profoundly human. That *Medium Cool*'s ending so forcefully invokes its beginning is a signal of that trauma, and a common ploy of metafilm, which deliberately provokes our discomfort with its cyclical emplotment. As exemplars of a specifically reflexive materialism, the following metafilms embody things that are alive to their own contradictions, striving toward freedoms more elusive and profound than those of market-savvy circulation.

CHAPTER 1

REFUSAL

WHETHER DEPICTING the group suicide of an affluent family, the experiences of a teenager who murders an acquaintance and frames his parents for it, or the travails of a sadomasochistic concert pianist, Michael Haneke renders bourgeois subjects as perpetrators and victims of extreme violence, almost none of which has clear motivation. While calling attention to his films as calculating constructs, he generates scenarios that can prove alienating to even the most seasoned of filmgoers. That alienation derives in part from the antagonistic vibrancy of the films, their expression of the sort of "complex and intense vitality" that Laurie Gries associates with new materialism (*Still* 8). The more accusatory movies embody a self-conscious form of materiality, expressing the very reflexivity they posit as lacking in the viewer. The movies know our expectations as spectators, they seem to declare, and flatly refuse to fulfill them.

When Haneke's *Funny Games* premiered at the Cannes Film Festival in 1997, more than one of the event's past luminaries reacted with disdain. Wim Wenders walked out of the screening and Nanni Moretti publicly expressed disapproval of the film and director alike.[1] Seen by others as a "fraud" and a "hectoring scold," Haneke continues to draw condemnation for presenting audiences with portraits of carnage while shaming them for watching (Brunette 4, 6). Even those who value his work come close to damning it with the terms of their praise: Catherine Wheatley, for example, finds the movies invigorating in their prolonged creation of "unpleasure" (30).

Given the movies' combative character, they pose problems for scholars of film rhetoric, many of whom analyze how cinematic texts sustain audiences' engagement while mediating their habits of perception. Among the more noteworthy instances of such scholarship stands Blakesley's collection *The Terministic Screen,* which grounds the study of film in Burke's theories of identification. Blakesley positions his approach as an alternative to David Bordwell's *Making Meaning: Inference and Rhetoric in the Interpretation of Cinema,* arguing that Bordwell reproduces the popular sense of rhetoric as unsubstantiated discourse that is marked more by bias or grandiose display than logical development. By contrast, Blakesley suggests that film rhetoric is composed of appeals that "[direct] our attention with the aim of fostering identification," inviting the audience's sympathetic reaction to character and event, or to the sociopolitical implications of a movie's themes and design.[2] How Haneke's texts cultivate those reactions presents a puzzle given their tendency to chastise audiences rather than invite consubstantiality with what transpires onscreen.

On first encounter, his narratives seem to forestall the processes Blakesley deems key to rhetorical criticism. The more aggressive narratives mock the affective currents through which they flow, reproaching audiences for obsession with forms of violence that, through the processes of dramatization and distanciation, confirm the viewer's security. *Funny Games* exploits that voyeurism and announces its intentions in doing so, addressing audiences in direct fashion and feigning appreciation for their complicity. And although those forms of address may feel personally intrusive, they concern themselves not so much with individual watchers as their distributed assemblage. The film is a self-aware form of life that helps create the constituency it posits; it at once invokes and participates in the Latourian "collective." By insinuating the taintedness of that collective, it appears to delegitimize the affective milieu that brings the movie and its audience into being.

Yet, even as *Funny Games* generates walkouts and denunciations, it does not entirely abandon classic strategies for generating audience affinity with character, diegetic domain, and genre. Blakesley's redaction of Burke provides a fitting lens for interpreting the movie's early scenes, which use sequenced shots of a family drive into the woods, along with unsettling musical effects, to situate its viewers in the territory of horror cinema. Such techniques foster audience compassion for the family under siege, thus depending on a trope that suffuses the history of the genre. While using long-running conventions to guide our sympathies, however, *Funny Games* goes on to violate the principles it cites, transgressing its early patterns of appeal so as to invite identification with a meta-perspective that questions the ethics of spectatorship.

The film's main monster figure prompts such questions by calling attention to *Funny Games* as a fabrication, sometimes asking the audience to speculate on the outcome of his games, other times worrying whether the movie will reach marketable length, and most memorably, rewinding and revising a scene that displeases him. Such concerns disrupt the mimetic development of the narrative so as to stress the film's materiality—its status as a crafted object, its circulatory potential, and its machine-based tractability. By so directly flouting genre standards, the film at once affirms their influence and unsettles them through the act of naming. In so doing, it reflects Haneke's composing process as a self-consciously materialist practice, which develops a critical edge as it begins to suggest correspondences between the class privilege of its central characters and those of its audience. To draw on the insights of Tony Scott and Nancy Welch, it reminds us that media circulation can only be artificially and deceptively split off from the flow of capital ("One" 569).

New materialist theory similarly tracks the flow of multimodal rhetoric, showing how things communicate as they range across social, technological, spatial, and political situations. Gries describes an especially thorough method of pursuing popular images from their early distribution to their remixed incarnations, directing scholars away from synchronic analysis of representation toward investigations of the streams through which pictures move and the exigencies to which they adapt. The case of *Funny Games* presents an anomaly, however, in that it ridicules the stream in which it is caught: by announcing the effort to adapt to its reception context, it exposes its desire to foil that expectation. Although Gries cautions against dwelling on such desires, resisting along with Kevin Michael DeLuca the privileging of "representationalism" and methods drawn from literary criticism (*Still* 18), the film's relation to the flow of filmic commerce merits our pausing to dwell for a while. Dwelling requires a respite from tracking circulation so as to consider what might account for it, beyond the admittedly astonishing distributive action of digital culture. To analyze the film's invitations to consubstantiality, and its concomitant effort to render consubstantiality repulsive, is not merely to engage in representationalism for its own sake.

Funny Games itself rejects facile ideas of representation, at once practicing mimesis and disrupting it so as to suggest counterhegemonic ways of witnessing violence.

The effect of that rejection is first to conjure an audience who harbors various expectations for how the narrative should proceed, and subsequently to punish that audience for pleasurably anticipating the fulfillment of its expectations.[3] The movie thereby enacts what John Schilb describes as a "rhetorical refusal," which deliberately "break[s] with protocol" in ways that challenge the addressee's adherence to genre (4). Making conventions plain by defying them, such refusals can be particularly disarming insofar as they violate a perceived agreement between rhetor and audience (8). Although Schilb mostly finds these violations in print texts such as dance reviews, short fiction, academic essays, and transcribed speeches, he also wonders whether rhetorical refusals might take "imagistic forms," and he encourages theorists of visual culture to watch for examples (10, 73–74).

The following examination of *Funny Games* is, at least in part, a response to Schilb's call, locating multiple instances of refusal in the film and describing them as expressions of vibrant materiality. First, the picture refuses diegetic boundaries, with the lead villain moving seamlessly between immersion in the story world and reflexive commentary on its features. Second, the film undercuts moments of potential dramatic dynamism by disposing of its protagonists unceremoniously and sometimes outside the view of the camera. Third, *Funny Games* avoids the rapid-fire montage of much contemporary fare in favor of long takes, lingering not just on moments of physical violence but on their psychic aftermath.

By focusing on loss and grief, Haneke opposes the dulling of affect that attends the circulation of violent imagery, injecting discomfort into what Gries depicts as the "rhetorical becoming" of visual material (*Still* 78). He thereby fulfills another of Schilb's criteria for rhetorical refusals by asking audiences to forgo decorum and identify instead with a more pressing principle (5). That principle is to resuscitate horror as a visceral and ethical experience rather than consent to its status as a predictable genre. Such resuscitation does not imply an imperative to abandon violent movies but instead works to incite reflection on the material security, and the confidence in safe distance, that allows viewers to treat pictures of suffering as commodities.

That appeal takes on greater urgency when situated within Haneke's corpus, which features numerous domestic scenes where televisions broadcast images of civil war, ethnic cleansing, and mass shootings, all of which constitutes the white noise of affluent existence.[4] The reflexive materialism of *Funny Games* demands our awareness of the history from which the film emerges; more specifically, it proffers a critique of class violence and militarism that depends in part on viewers' awareness of Haneke's repertoire. Given his consistent refusal to validate the social relations he portrays, his scene-for-scene remake of the Austrian *Funny Games* in the U.S. context appears no mere technical exercise.

A KNOWING WINK

To establish a backdrop for Haneke's refusals, we must recognize how he seduces audiences into identifying with patterns he will later subvert. To appreciate the significance of such identification for the film's narrative progression as well as its mediation of audience subjectivity, we do well to address Burkean rhetorical theory as outlined in *The Terministic Screen*.

Blakesley favors identification as a critical term because it is supple enough to describe rhyming perspectives and forms of implied cooperation, whether in the film's diegesis or the audience's relationship to it. But he first outlines three other approaches to film rhetoric that have their own internal consistency, and he calls these approaches "film as language," "film as ideology," and "film interpretation." Scholars who view film as language treat it as a "grammatical system of signs" that can be observed in the conventions of framing, camera movement, shot/reverse-shot structure, and various kinds of continuity editing (4). Those who address film as an expression of ideology describe how movies reflect or expose the predispositions and assumptions of the viewing culture, many of which are held unconsciously. According to such a method of analysis, movies may be "symptomatic" of ideology or endeavor to destabilize it (5). Blakesley's third category, "film interpretation," treats cinema as "a rhetorical situation involving director, the film, and viewer in the total act of making meaning," with filmmaker, text, and audience each bringing information that makes certain interpretations compelling while rendering others implausible (6). Those who study such phenomena tend to consider rhetoric a "metasystem" wherein we interpret our interpretations, all the while construing audience response as conditioned by the ecology in which it occurs (7).

Although Blakesley frames all those approaches as forms of rhetorical analysis, he gives most attention to a fourth category he calls "film identification." Drawn largely from Burke's *A Rhetoric of Motives*, the theory posits that rhetorical engagement depends on establishing a sense of shared substance—common circumstances, values, and/or aspirations—from which communication can proceed. The assertion of shared substance, or what Burke calls "consubstantiality," presumes that social subjects are inescapably divided from each other and that the motivation for dialogue is to negotiate the differences. There exists no longing for consubstantiality without preexisting division, for "there would be no need for the rhetorician to proclaim our unity . . . if we were already identical" (Blakesley, *Terministic* 7). Gries echoes Blakesley by noting that people experience consubstantiality "even as they might retain some divisions that prevent them from being totally aligned in all perspectives and actions" (*Still* 240). Films generate this provisional affiliation with characters in various ways, which may include giving a character a political cause, a mystery to solve, or a lover to seek, all while delaying the attainment of those goals. The genres in which the characters pursue the goals, whether musical, western, or film noir, condition audience expectations as to whether and how the focal figures will realize their aspirations. Genres allow variation from film to film, but there is strong enough consistency across movies that the categories maintain coherence. Insofar as we base our viewing expectations on awareness of that consistency, we identify ourselves with the genre's presumed audience.

Viewers will likely be aware of genre from the opening frame of *Funny Games*, having been lured to the film by advertisements, personal recommendations, or interest in the director or cast. But the film's adherence to genre reveals itself in measured fashion, working to invite audience identification with a few characters while slowly signaling those characters' immersion in a particular type of narrative. The movie begins with an aerial shot of a family car towing a boat along a highway, the journey scored by seemingly extradiegetic classical music. We hear voices from within the car, as people quiz each other about the title and performer of the piece and then introduce new music once the right answer has been given. As the music changes, the scene cuts to increasingly lower-angle views of the vehicle until we join its passengers, abruptly encountering a hand ejecting a compact disc and replacing it with new music. Only after ushering the audience into the characters' sound space, their game, and finally their car, does the film afford a view of the speakers, including them in a single frame that identifies us with the family unit.

The shot exhibits the pleased expressions of mother, father, and adolescent son, off on a relaxing getaway. No sooner have we taken in the family portrait, however, than the film title superimposes itself on the scene and the music shifts mid-phrase to the screaming "thrash jazz" of John Zorn and the band Naked City. The sonic shift reminds us that we have entered the world of horror, however modified, and that the family is on a trip into the woods—which often constitutes the protagonists' first and gravest mistake.

The sense of dread produced by the music gains intensity when the family stops short of their vacation home to greet a neighbor. The mother, Anna, calls from the passenger window to draw his attention, and though he acknowledges her, he stays well away and offers only the most mechanical of replies. Neither she nor Georg understands the man's lack of hospitality, but they see that he has guests and so they drive on. Those two guests, wearing summery whites and seemingly engaged in a game of croquet, appear to be the cause of his preoccupation. Underscoring the mystery, Anna asks Georg as their car nears the house: "I wonder who the two laddies were." Moments later, an electronic gate allows them entry into the driveway of their vacation home. But the camera, rather than following the car, lingers on the closing of the gate.

The uneasy atmosphere intensifies when one laddie shows up at Anna's door asking for eggs. She brings him into the kitchen while Georg and their son Schorschi rig a boat by the lake. Almost as soon as she supplies the eggs, he drops them, and when she moves to retrieve more, he knocks her cellular phone into the kitchen sink. That accident prompts our focused identification with Anna, whose patience with her visitor has rapidly thinned out. More significantly, it strengthens our alignment with the genre's audience, who recognizes the waterlogged phone as a broken connection to the outside world. That recognition presumes a form of identification by which viewers affiliate, consciously or not, with what Carolyn Miller designates "typified rhetorical actions based in recurrent situations" (159). Reaffirming Miller's ideas about genre, Gries notes that while "situation" is an inexact category, we nevertheless "recognize a situation has occurred that is comparable to a previously occurring situation based on a stock of social knowledge acquired through enculturation" (*Still* 228). The mobility and uptake of film objects depends in part on their rendering of scenarios that remix the familiar, creating suspense by adhering to or breaking with expectations, but never entirely floating free of them. By situating a broken phone in a remote dwelling, Haneke calls up convention so forcefully that we might wonder, even early on, whether the effort involves a certain irony.

The scene's tension relaxes after Anna gives her visitor the second batch of eggs and sends him off. After laughing at the encounter, she hears the family dog barking as someone enters the house. Pursuing the noise, she finds that the stranger has returned with a friend. The young men stand just inside the screen door, looking out at a German shepherd trying to get in (and convincingly playing the stock character of the animal who senses danger where others do not).⁵ Missing Rolfi's warning, Anna reactivates the stress of the previous scene by shooing him away and assuring her guests the he just "likes to play." "Funny game," replies her first visitor, as his companion shows interest in Georg's golf clubs. After grabbing a driver and ball, he sets off into the yard to test them out. The film then cuts to father and son preparing the boat while noticing Rolfi's barking. As Georg steps from the boat to investigate, he knocks his sailor's knife to the floor, raising the question of its coming significance.

The knife, the damaged phone, and the secluded location constitute tools for invention within the genre, all working to create a sense of apprehension—partly about what is to come, but more precisely, about how it will come. "We invent," writes Candice Rai, "from the weighty stuff (material, rhetorical, bodily, historical, ideological) that already exists around and resonates among us" (139). The efficacy of invention owes in part to the rhetor's "doxic knowledge: the capacity to see and make strategic use of rhetorical forces that are tethered to commonplace arguments, bodily habits, ideological valences, cultural practices, and histories of place" (139). Haneke culls material from doxic knowledge by featuring things that have mattered before in the horror genre and are likely to matter again. Yet he does so with such mounting excess that the deadly serious drama starts to hint at self-parody. We cannot be sure of the tone, for the doxic knowledge on which he draws already values excess, as the campier entries in the genre garner their cult followings through overindulgence. So while the film's first scenes identify us with and as connoisseurs, they simultaneously produce troublesome ambiguities.

Haneke augments the mood of the film by alluding to Stanley Kubrick's *A Clockwork Orange*. While not a horror movie in the classic sense, it conveys its "ultraviolence" in ways that are by turns cartoonish and naturalistic. *Funny Games* never engages in the slapstick perversity that *A Clockwork Orange* exhibits, but it does admit, with a kind of self-impressed casualness, the absurdity of its own visuals. The genealogy for this absurdity begins to assert itself when Georg returns to find Anna confronting figures dressed in the bright white of Kubrickian Droogs. Acknowledging that Anna has already provided them eight eggs, they observe that Rolfi broke the second batch, insisting that Georg's family still has four left in their carton. The lead villain's well-mannered imposition—the calm, weirdly sophisticated demeanor that masks his vicious intentions—evokes *Clockwork*'s Alex DeLarge, who has marked preferences for smashing "eggy weggs" and invading people's homes.⁶ Although the monster figures in *Funny Games* typically refer to themselves as Peter and Paul or, tellingly, Beavis and Butthead, their most ominous intertextual links are to Kubrick's Droogs. The films' interplay across three decades tends not to announce itself, but to "advene" in ways that "jut or intrude into 'the regime of the sensible'" (Gries, *Still* 69; Bennett 262). But whereas that intrusion may imbue reception with an added unease, Georg fails at first to recognize the threat. The effect is that of an oddly portentous score, available to the viewer but not the character. By the time he recognizes the validity of Anna's concern, one of the Droogs has again dipped into the golf bag, and this time for more than a practice swing.

With Georg laid out on the floor grasping his newly shattered kneecap, the sense of disquiet turns to alarm. The blow of the club replicates the sonic interruption of domestic tranquility in the film's first scene, initiating the series of "funny games" that will overwrite the security of the lakeside retreat. Whereas Oliver C. Speck contends that Haneke's characters are typically too distanced to elicit our identification (59), *Funny Games* presents a contrary case, fostering audience affiliation with the family unit by delivering on threats distributed throughout its densely allusive narrative structure. The identification grows stronger when Paul explains that during his earlier outing, something obstructed his golf swing. Once Anna catches his meaning and sets off to find Rolfi, Paul calls out clues to help her locate the body. As the audience starts to register Paul's capacity for cruelty, he addresses the camera with a conniving wink.

The film now transgresses what Stam frames as a "dominant convention" in "classical fiction film," which stipulates "that the film remain radically ignorant of its spectator and that the actor never acknowledge the camera and hence the audience" (50). As the movie demonstrates awareness of the rhetorical situation rather than straightforwardly engaging in it, the image refuses to be the simple object of our spectatorship; it announces its own subjectivity, evincing a liveliness that is at once sardonic and accusatory. However compelling that sense of vitality, Scott and Welch contend that granting the subjectivity of things tends toward mystification, disguising those things' emergence from and strengthening of human divisions of power. In an era of expanding wealth division and profit-driven international conflict, such cautionary arguments are timely and shrewd. Whether the area of study is visual rhetoric or any variety of multimodal communication, methods related to object-oriented ontology need grounding in historical materialism if thing theory is to have a power-conscious dimension.[7]

There is little doubt that Haneke, who would go on to make movies about the repercussions of French colonialism, as well as the lineage of National Socialism in Germany, holds concerns about the historical underpinnings of atrocity. *Funny Games,* in its Austrian version and American remake, proffers no exception to that tendency. His attention to histories of violence suggests that the film's chafing against commodification constitutes part of his aim. The movie does not just invite critical materialist analysis; it performs that analysis itself. Yet it does so in ways that outstrip Haneke's intentions, as well as those of the actors and film crew. By emphasizing the movie's subjectivity through Paul's knowing wink, Haneke hints at the wildness of material rhetoric, its capacity to disrupt expectations built into the rhetorical transaction. But that wink also produces effects that Haneke and his collaborators can neither control nor predict, which involve the idiosyncrasies of audience history, the uncertainty of the film's circulatory journey, and the emergence of new associations with the passage of time.

Funny Games expresses its vitality not only in its flight from human regulation but also in how it hails its interlocutors. As the picture exceeds our interpretations, it expresses a reciprocal form of influence—or, as W. J. T. Mitchell puts it in *What Do Pictures Want?,* it makes a "claim" on us (xv). David Cronenberg's *Videodrome* (1983) visualizes that claim by featuring a television set, its picture tube swelling and its shell quivering with longing, calling out to the film's protagonist like a lover. The character, Mitchell remarks, is at once "attracted and repelled" (xvi). We might also think of John Anderton in Steven Spielberg's *Minority Report* (2002), dashing through a shopping mall while animated advertisements beckon to him by name. Although Mitchell reminds us that many images "are much more discreet about the libidinal fields they construct, the deadly kisses they invite" (xvii), *Funny Games* makes a claim on the viewer that is even more overt than the Cronenberg and Spielberg examples. Whereas those movies dramatize the picture's sexualized lure, keeping it within the boundaries of the diegesis, Haneke's villain speaks straight to the narratee, whose identity he imposes on us. That imposition insinuates that we share the villain's motives—else why would we keep watching? Why would we seek out such a film in the first place?

After feeding the audience's expectations in an exaggerated way, the movie begins to refuse them. It thereby appropriates the work of the iconoclastic critic, denying his right to objectify the threatening image, identifying him with genre fanatics instead of respecting his putative difference.[8] The work of the iconoclast involves limiting or destroying a picture's power and circumscribing its capacity to act. That effort at denial, Mitchell contends, is "just as much a symptom of the life of images as its obverse, the naïve faith in the inner life of works of art" (*What* 8). While such insights extend the examination of reflexive visuality he began in *Picture Theory*, they also harmonize with new materialist rhetoric, which emphasizes the protean character of the claims pictures make on us as well as their yielding of new life.

As the movie makes its claim on us by looking back, it abandons the techniques that persuade us to suspend our disbelief, signaling the indignity of the process by welcoming our voyeurism. At that point, it may trigger what Krista Ratcliffe designates as "disidentification" or retreat from consubstantiality. Whereas consubstantiality presumes a preexisting difference that the participants endeavor to mitigate, disidentification entails an effort to maintain or even elaborate the difference. *Funny Games* takes pleasure in what we might consider a Burkean inversion: instead of forging a contingent commonality from intersubjective distinctions, it fosters desire to distance ourselves from affinities we have already conceded. It intimates our investment in the sadism it depicts, implying that the anxious rejection of those associations may expose our unconscious drives. To revisit Mitchell's point, we find ourselves "attracted" even as we are "repelled." While it may be unfair to interpret Wenders's dismissive rhetoric and Moretti's walkout in light of that dialectic, the film provides a disconcerting analysis of those who stay. While the analysis constitutes an example of Schilb's theory of rhetorical refusal, it generates its effects through three specific forms of rebuff. The following section details one category of refusal by focusing on scenes that echo Paul's wink, violating custom by breaking the fourth wall.

PAUL'S PARADOX

Paul's wink unsettles audiences by indicating the constructedness of a narrative that has, to that point, mostly masked its craft with tropes of realism. The undercutting of that rhetoric proves disorienting, for as Schilb argues, "tampering with genre involves violating a contract felt to be in place" (8). Genre sustains itself through felt experience such that interruptions have visceral consequences. Drawing inspiration from Brian Massumi, Gries describes those consequences as grounded in social experience rather than restricted to discrete persons. While bodies may inflect "unconscious perception," such perception "recognizes how the 'individual body' is 'always-already plugged into a collectivity' and moves people and other things to imitate the behaviors, feelings, and opinions of others with which they are in relation" (*Still* 63). When Paul rends the scrim between his world and ours, we react by channeling a distributed, corporeal epistemology akin to a public reflex.

But to qualify as a rhetorical refusal in Schilb's sense, tampering with genre must not violate the contract merely for the sake of transgression, but rather draw scrutiny to what passes as tacit agreement. These refusals are thus "actively aimed at persuading their audience of something," breaking with the viewing public's valued norms so as "to shape [that public's] thinking" (10). Drawing on Steven Mailloux's *Reception Histories*, Schilb claims that the aim of refusals is to change one type of addressee into another (39). With *Funny Games*, Haneke works to transform an audience schooled in horror into one discomfited by that schooling, and by the conditions that permit images of human degradation to double as objects of pleasure. He thereby opens intersectional possibilities between rhetorical refusal and reflexive materialism, showing such materialism to be a way of making an argument in multimodal form, rather than just a means of analyzing someone else's case.

Haneke's materialist critique announces itself most prominently in the film's refusal of diegetic boundaries, which occurs first through Paul's addressing the viewer and later through his ability to control the movie's diegesis. When he turns to the audience, he asks which characters they support and whether the film is satisfying to watch. Although his wink suggests confidence that the audience shares his objectives, he soon acknowledges that the rhetorical situation is hardly so certain. After betting the family that they will be dead by 9:00 a.m., he asks for viewer input: "Do you think they have a chance of winning? You're on their side, aren't you?" The insinuation that we enjoy witnessing his work gives way to the idea that we want the family to escape and will willingly endure harrowing suspense in hope of their eventual safety. So fully do our sympathies rest with the family unit, *Funny Games* implies, that the desire for the characters' escape slowly becomes a desire for retribution. Embodied viewers may well recoil at such an implication and thereby attempt to distinguish themselves from the addressee Paul envisions. But whatever the proclivities of particular audiences, the film reminds us that the logic of revenge is deeply embedded in the genre at hand.

The family's rapid descent into despair, however, threatens to short-circuit the revenge narrative. Worn down by the games, Georg implores Anna: "Don't reply anymore. Let them do what they want. Then it will be over quicker." Paul takes offense, calling him "cowardly" and announcing that "we're not up to feature film length yet." To end early would deprive Peter and Paul of their amusement, though the latter also worries that it would destroy the movie's "entertainment value." Here again the movie stresses its own materiality, specifying the aesthetic demands that condition its cultural acceptability. To live in the way that Bennett and Gries describe, and thus to have a chance at viral uptake, it needs to show awareness of basic formal expectations. The sinister humor of *Funny Games* arises from how it declares that awareness, generating suspense by citing suspense as a dramatic prerequisite.

Although the movie recognizes its accountability to such prerequisites, it also holds viewers responsible for them. When Georg says the family has had enough, Paul once more addresses the camera: "Have you had enough? You want a real ending with plausible plot development, don't you?" Such questions suggest that although we may identify with the family, we are not necessarily willing to relinquish the pleasures of narrative progression. But dramatic tension alone is inadequate, suggests Paul, as audiences also desire its credible resolution. His insistence on plausibility creates a paradox that might be amusing were the narrative itself not so grim: by evaluating the diegetic realm he occupies, he undoes the realism he aims to preserve. To use Jay David Bolter's terms, Paul undertakes a "hypermediate" rhetorical act in the interest of maintaining narrative "immediacy" (25–26). The intrusion proceeds for the sake of audience gratification, though such gratification typically depends on the unspoken quality of rhetorical design, and viewers are unlikely to take unadulterated pleasure in the film's assertion of their vicarious participation in the violence. For Paul's hypermediate defense of immediacy is not merely a defense of believability in cinema; it also serves as an accusation. Both he and Haneke recognize the potential cruelty of the desire for plausibility, especially when it means extending the suffering of characters with whom we purportedly identify. The film's rhetorical refusals partly consist of articulating audience expectations too plainly.

Granted, the history of the horror genre works to condition our desires, but that history could not exist without viewing publics' assent. In the essay "Violence and the Media," Haneke weighs in on the relationship between moving images and the social conditions in which they circulate:

> Depending on the conviction of the debaters, either the media are that objective "mirror of society," reflecting nothing but reality itself, or the permanent presence of violence in the media is what really bears responsibility for increasing violence in our daily interactions with each other.... The inconclusiveness of this inquiry is productive for both discursive positions: Both are right. (575)

Haneke's belief in a dialectical relationship between ideology and audiovisual rhetoric generally informs his views on cinema in society, which emphasize how movies position audiences and how audiences accept, resist, or otherwise address that positioning.[9] That dialectic harmonizes with what Rai characterizes as the rhetorical materialist project, which investigates "how material conditions catalyze, transport, constrain, and constitute rhetorical forces that, in turn, shape materialities" (14). The affect of fear and constant conflict informs visual culture; the feigning of violence onscreen may, on occasion, inspire concrete acts of aggression in the streets. Paul mocks the audience's perpetuation of the cycle, thereby making evident the reflective, the provocative, and the intransigent dimensions of filmic materiality.

While Paul attributes to audiences a preference for credible development, he deems the preference incompatible with narratives of escape or revenge, as the power imbalance between the family and himself is so extreme as to forbid reassuring resolutions. When events do momentarily elude Paul's control, he responds with his most aggressive transgression of the film's diegetic boundaries. After he tasks Anna with reciting a prayer backwards—which would symbolically undo her appeal for divine assistance—she grabs a rifle that lies unguarded on the table and blasts Peter into the living room wall. In disbelief, Paul rips the weapon from her hand and knocks her to the floor. But instead of turning the gun on her, he searches the room for a remote control. Finding it, he rewinds the picture to the point before Anna gains her advantage, thereby resurrecting Peter and rescinding the retribution that the film accuses viewers of wanting.[10] In what Peter Brunette calls "the most completely (and purposely) 'artificial' moment" in the film (66), Paul expands the scope of villainy by frustrating the audience's reliance on previous movie experiences to predict narrative development.

That calculated frustration involves not only the rhetorical production of a specific response, but an effort to expose the emotions that the genre typically evokes. To bring Schilb into conversation with Lynn Worsham, the film works to transform the addressee by crafting a "pedagogy of the emotions," which she describes as "primary" in that it is "both earliest and foundational" (216). Whereas she follows Althusser in situating such pedagogy in families, schools, and workplaces, the educational process also inhabits moments of leisure, and even those forms of address that proclaim their "entertainment value" while proving anything but diverting. For some audiences, the diegetic rewind may undermine the film's pedagogy by veering into the realm of absurdity. The movie's excessive interest in its own materiality has prompted an especially harsh assessment from director Jacques Rivette, who calls it "vile," "a complete piece of shit," while locating another form of significance in its connection to *A Clockwork Orange*: "Kubrick is a machine" with "no human feeling whatsoever" (Bonnaud). By attempting to reorient feeling, Haneke risks conveying his own mechanistic detachment, striking an apparently dispassionate posture toward the characters under attack—none of whom experiences the proceedings as a game, and none of whom benefits from the movie's pedagogy.

But rather than expressing his own inhumanity, Haneke's design choices recalibrate the relationship between human and extrahuman actancy. The film revels in its own "thing-power," to use Bennett's language (6), by appropriating actions normally reserved for the viewer. Speck argues that when Haneke introduces Paul's remote, the filmmaker "not only breaks the rules of the genre but of the medium itself" (31). So egregiously does the scene violate movie rules that it feels momentarily like a video game rather than a film narrative. Paul's remote allows him to play the film like a game, learning from blunders and adjusting his moves accordingly. The analogy breaks down, however, when we recognize that the decision to restart generally rests with the gamer and not a member of the story world, and especially not the character whose defeat would seem to be the objective. That the decision is Paul's reaffirms his determination to master the diegesis in a film that "makes the issue of mastery central" from its opening guessing game (Price, qtd. in Speck 157).

Although Paul may embody the director's effort to disrupt our fantasies of control, the rhetoric of *Funny Games* eludes his command as well as ours. Neither director, character, audience, reception context, nor the thing-power of the film determines its communicative potential, which exists in a constant state of becoming. Interpretations such as those offered thus far constitute forms of fleeting invention and transformation, coiled into "dynamic assemblages" whose disentangling is "all but impossible" (Gries, *Still* 70). Being implicated in the becoming of rhetoric makes its affective resonance difficult to describe in empirical terms (Gries, *Still* 63): even our private experience of the object develops within assemblages so complex and contingent that they confound explanation. A similar contingency limits the director's authority, leaving him little room to defend his project when viewers walk out or proclaim his inhumanity. But even if the director's influence only extends so far, Haneke helps create the conditions for audience reflection by composing an object that reflects on its own persuasive appeals.

Paul's rhetorical refusal cannot have its destabilizing effect, however, without first making recourse to the rhetoric of consubstantiality. Due to that rhetoric, audiences will generally want the family to survive despite strong indications against that outcome. Roy Grundmann observes that the movie thus catches us in a double bind: "taken out of its moral vacuum and brought into existential proximity with the characters, the audience wants to stay with the victims and bear witness to their suffering, but it is also told that its very spectatorship is the actual reason for this suffering" (*Companion* 28). By gradually confusing sympathy and cruelty, the film amplifies its affect of "unpleasure." It then continues that affective schooling by trivializing scenes from which we might reasonably expect dramatic intensity. The offhand draining of suspense, which enacts in miniature the structure of the film, constitutes the focus of the next section.

ANTICLIMAX

When a film invites audiences to identify with specific characters, it creates the expectation that key moments in the characters' experience will be rendered in vivid fashion, and that the narrative will provide us purposefully paced depictions of their trials and triumphs. Haneke refuses such comforts by obliterating such scenes' narrative tension instead of gradually extending or relaxing it. Defying unspoken rules, the film casually discards the possibility of the precocious youth outwitting his captors, and then similarly disposes of the "final girl" scenario in which a sole survivor escapes or defeats the movie's monster figure. Whatever the movie, audiences expect it to take seriously its own techniques of suspense, rather than to judge those techniques dull or cheap before they have fully developed. Those expectations arise from repeat triggering over many viewing experiences, which come to express and thicken the social mesh of affect (Rai 173). Deviation from established tendencies extends the film's pedagogy of emotion, which evokes the "felt contract" of genre and asks how it feels when the contract no longer holds. The film's materialism thus lies both in metaleptic craft and in toying with the physicality of affect.

Much of the film's affective work occurs though the frustration of mastery, as there exists little hope of vanquishing a monster figure who holds power to reverse and rework the movie itself. It must be remembered, however, that Paul intrudes on the diegesis so as to champion its realism. Although Paul's paradox might seem humorous, its context makes the prospect of laughter uncomfortable at best. The simultaneous production and denial of the comic is nowhere more notable than during Schorschi's death scene, which coincides with Paul's decidedly nondramatic trip to the kitchen. The scene begins after Paul puts his victims through a grueling game of "eeny meeny miny moe," then steps briefly out of the living room to get food. As the camera follows his movements, we hear a gun's report offscreen followed by the wailing of Georg and Anna. Due to the disconnection between sound and image tracks, Wheatley finds in the scene an anticlimax of form rather than narrative (91). It appears to her not a failure of the story's progression but a successful effort to supplant the urgency of one filmic event with the dullness of another. Paul, on the other hand, remains steadfastly concerned with narrative: "Have you no sense of timing?" he asks Peter. The offscreen shooting, he believes, has cheated the audience of what we want from the genre (if not what we desire for the protagonists)—namely, the chance to witness extreme acts without any perceived loss of security.

While dismissing such ostensible pleasures, the scene also foils the subplot of the child who outmaneuvers his antagonist. Haneke teases us by having Schorschi escape earlier in the film, finding his way to a neighbor's house and locating a rifle. Paul calmly tracks him down, entering the house and (in another instance of half-comic improbability) inserting *Naked City*'s theme music into the home stereo to assure his victim that he is coming.[11] Quickly cornering Schorschi, he does not fear the boy's firearm but teaches him how to cock it. The child aims and pulls the trigger only to discover that the gun is empty. Paul replies with an amused "Poof!" that mocks the boy's perseverance and the audience's vengeful desires (or at least those desires the film attributes to us). If that mockery were not disheartening enough, the scene introduces the very weapon with which Schorschi will be killed.

After the killing occurs and Paul chides Peter for bad timing, we become increasingly aware of the living room television broadcasting a professional car race, the rev and hum of which renders Schorschi's death even more distressing. While the drone reinforces the movie's tendency toward dissonant counterpoint, the repetitive quality of the race alludes to the director's representations of television in his earlier feature films.[12] Without exception, those films associate the medium with violent spectacle. In *The Seventh Continent* (1989), an entire family commits suicide by drinking poison, sitting down to watch television as they lose consciousness. In *Benny's Video* (1992), the title character reproduces the violence he witnesses onscreen, first killing a young acquaintance and then setting up his parents as the culprits. And in *71 Fragments of a Chronology of Chance* (1994), a mass murder gets absorbed into a stream of apparently unrelated but strangely equivalent television reports, some of which include the Somali Civil War, the Kurdish rebellion in Turkey, the Bosnian War, and the Troubles in Ireland. The television in *Funny Games* may not carry such direct images of violence, but given what the medium tends to signify within Haneke's corpus, the circularity of the race has particularly vicious connotations.

The television continues Haneke's pattern of casting household items and everyday paraphernalia as agents of dread. Where new materialist theory situates extrahuman rhetoric within an ecology of negotiated being, *Funny Games* and its feature-length predecessors lend that rhetoric an ominous timbre. Drinking glasses, musical instruments, and cameras become weapons; cash machines express willful defiance; telephones transmit bad news while enabling long-distance conflict among parents and children. In a kind of Borgesian anti-order, toothbrushes, showerheads, checkout stands, art supplies, wingtips, bookshelves, ping pong paddles, gasoline pumps, receipts, and medical waiting rooms precipitate psychic breakdowns.[13] Recurrent shots and camera angles reinforce the affect of redundancy. Perhaps the purest form of the argument appears at the outset of *The Seventh Continent*, as a family much like that in *Funny Games* drives into an automated car wash. The creeping movement, along with the ambient dissonance and encroachment of rollers and streams from all sides, creates the sense of being swallowed.[14] A reiteration of the car wash sequence late in the movie links routine materiality to death, first metaphorical and then breathtakingly literal. The buzz and swish of cars on the television near Schorschi's body recalls *The Seventh Continent*'s austere beginning—as well as its conclusion, in which the snow of a poorly tuned TV envelops the optical field once the family members take their own lives.

Recognizing Haneke's assessment of television thus requires engagement with work that preceded *Funny Games*. But that assessment also extends into later movies such as *The Piano Teacher* (2001) and *Caché* (2005), which associate screen fixation with forms of psychological repression that mask past conflicts or beget new ones. From a new materialist perspective, situating one work amid a director's broader output may imply a literary approach to analysis, dwelling on synchronic intertextualities rather than the uptake and reconfiguration of bustling things. This technique involves treating images "as language-like symbols that lack power unless scholars intervene with their own explanations of intention, meaning, and significance."[15] To the contrary, Haneke's movies constitute the sort of unruly objects that confound many of the interpretations analysts might offer. But the point here is to describe one kind of power, however contingent, that arises from attention to objects' convergences, the ways they flow into and out of each other. Gries's elegant meditation on rhetorical becoming yields an invitation to *"trace* and *follow* things' dynamic movement" (*Still* 19), and thus to examine their production as well as their reappearances in altered forms. Yet things may drift toward a history of prior rhetorics at the same time that they advance toward unsure futures. Attempts to trace those movements will likely always entail an effort to order the past: it appears an arbitrary constraint, then, to discount a director's prior work or historical intertexts as part of a thing's becoming. By studying how those intertexts feed into one another, we encounter cumulative arguments that might otherwise escape notice.

One such argument involves the family's affect of insulation against the perils of otherness, which household screens work to transmit and keep at a remove. Where the earlier movies delegitimize the idea of domestic sanctuary, *Funny Games* coolly crushes it. Such destruction captures Haneke's rhetorical refusal in pointed fashion, and figures into multiple scenes of which Schorschi's death is only the most prominent. His mother's death occurs in a similarly anticlimactic way, as the film once more invokes and almost simultaneously forecloses the possibility of dramatic escape. Late in the movie, when Peter and Paul take a bound and gagged Anna for a ride in the family sailboat, she notices the knife that Georg accidentally kicked to the floor the day before. As the Droogs attend to the sails, she gets hold of the knife, hoping to gain a surreptitious advantage. True to the genre, the lingering shot of the object early in the movie has proven a good indicator of its significance. But unlike many horror films, *Funny Games* rapidly empties out the dramatic potential of the object rather than capitalizing on it. Catching Anna trying to free herself, Paul remarks on her "sporting attitude" and prompts Peter to relieve her of her last hope. Viewers share her line of sight as he reaches below the frame, brings the knife into view, and tosses it into the water, rejecting her tenacity and ours in one fluid motion. He then seats Anna on the side of the boat between himself and Paul, who asks him the time. Peter replies that it is just past 8:00 a.m., at which point Paul kisses Anna on the cheek, gives her a warm "Ciao, bella," and dumps her into the lake. When Peter objects that she had nearly an hour until deadline, he replies that the boat was becoming hard to steer and that he is getting hungry.

Their subsequent snickering mocks what Carol J. Clover and Jody Keisner call the "final girl" scenario in horror. More predictable than even the heroic child, it features an intrepid woman who manages to evade a monster figure that has eliminated her family or friends. In the version preferred by such directors as Wes Craven and John Carpenter, the "final girl" not only outmaneuvers but also conquers the villain, at least temporarily.[16] By the end of such films, the monster often arises from apparent defeat in ways that reinitiate audience anxiety while foreshadowing a string of sequels. When *Funny Games* refuses those techniques, it scorns "the cathartic effect" of its genre while confronting "spectators with their own participation in the scopic act" (Wheatley 94, 87). Creating what Wheatley describes as "an aesthetic of consequence" rather than one that favors thrills (84–85), Haneke shocks audiences less with lurid depictions of violence than with protracted portraits of its aftereffects. Those aftereffects figure prominently in the next section, which locates a third expression of rhetorical refusal in the film's editing.

RHETORIC OF THE IRREVOCABLE

While Haneke subverts convention by representing explosive events in nondramatic ways, he also resists the rapid montage that governs Hollywood and independent horror alike. All of his pictures make "liberal use of the long take in which 'nothing happens'" (Brunette 2). Championed by André Bazin of the journal *Cahiers du Cinéma*, the long take became a staple of international art cinema through the middle part of the twentieth century, suggesting through its ostensibly nonintrusive character an effort to honor the ambiguous qualities of a given mise-en-scène. The technique has strong associations with neorealism, creating a sense of immediacy through seemingly uncrafted perspectives that make audiences aware of time passing. Such awareness can prove disquieting, Haneke notes, "especially if the pictures concern matters [viewers] have learned to suppress" (qtd. in Wheatley 93). While confronting viewers with abject material, extended shots often evoke a series of conflicted responses that include "boredom, anger, laughter" before giving way to contemplation (Brunette 45). The long take thus signals another way that Haneke's work alternates between immediacy and hypermediacy, immersing viewers in the uncut development of a screened event and yet, through the sheer duration of the event, calling attention to technique.

The director's early films, which not only contain numerous extended takes but also follow them with blackouts, reflect a neorealist preference for ambiguity while insisting on a meditative approach to spectatorship. Maintaining the call for contemplation while forgoing the blackouts, the most memorable long take in *Funny Games* occurs in the living room just after

Schorschi's death, as his body lies crumpled at the far right of the screen. Anna slumps next to him in a sofa chair, remaining motionless for a full minute as sounds of racing cars emanate from the blood-spattered television. With her hands and ankles bound, she cannot at first summon the will to break free. When she notices that Peter and Paul have gone, she struggles to the television to turn it off. She then saws her bonds on the edge of the TV stand, trying to avoid looking at Schorschi. Unable to cut herself loose, she decides to get a knife from the kitchen. The camera, which has not broken its gaze for four minutes, follows her hop until she passes Georg, at which point he becomes the focus. By the time Anna returns from the kitchen, his gurgled notes of distress have become a howl.

In a less self-consciously realist scene, Anna and Georg might have hobbled to the door together, slowed by his wounds but inspired toward superhuman will. Yet in Haneke's rendition, it takes a monumental effort just to get Georg to his feet. Once upright, his mostly immobilized limbs give him no way to balance himself save for placing his weight almost entirely on Anna. It is at this most precarious of moments that she registers the loss of her son and starts to sob in ways that echo Georg's earlier explosion. She then chokes off disaster and begins edging her way to the kitchen, Georg leaning on her back and shoulders. Only now does Haneke break the ten-minute take.

Given Haneke's self-consciousness, the take appears to be yet another divergence from narrative orthodoxy. But to view the scene as merely defying predictable techniques is to overlook its intervention in the culture of screen violence. While testing the audience's endurance, the scene constitutes a response to problems posed in his earlier films. By contrast to characters who witness a montage of atrocities on television and find nothing worth noting, Anna and Georg experience atrocity firsthand, relinquishing the security and privilege they once assumed as given. Unlike Paul, who holds power to reshape events, Anna and Georg suffer the condition of irrevocability, and they feel it as piercingly as any bodily wound. The scene thereby supports Brigitte Peucker's contention that affective intensity "perforates the formalist surface of Haneke's films, and it often arises from the sight of pain" (25). The wounds that absorb our attention in *Funny Games* are certainly physical, but the film mostly denies us access to those injuries as they unfold. When the camera lingers, it frames psychic wounds as they express themselves in material form. In those instances, spectators "experience the image" with the "whole body" (139). The trauma of a lost child manifests itself as the deceleration of time, the diminished capacity to support one's own weight, the inability to confront a truth that lies always at the periphery. The materiality of affect, which Gries and Rickert discover in the constant becoming of the ecological surround, derives poignancy from its relentlessness, from the unbearable distance of what *was*—perhaps hours or only moments before. In the long take after Schorschi's death, Haneke presents us with the body horror of the irreversible.

In dwelling on Anna and Georg's post-traumatic shock, Haneke invites us to identify with them as parents and people. But as with earlier appeals to consubstantiality, the sense of mutuality is neither straightforward nor complete. It coexists with the production of disgust, which the film has already taken to excess, and which reaches its climax with Schorschi's murder. Commenting on the frequency with which Haneke's pictures deal in such excess, Christa Blümlinger associates the "phenomenon of disgust" with a "field of tension between repulsion and attraction" (147). She tracks a "systematic repetition of these configurations of disgust" in his body of work, though she mainly focuses on exploitive photojournalism in *Three Paths to the Lake* (a made-for-television movie from 1976) and the linked slaughtering of livestock and human beings in *Benny's Video* (150–56). Although *Funny Games* does not figure into her analysis in an obvious way, it provides another example of the repetition that she observes, and a potentially significant intertext for her engagement with Winfried Menninghaus. Menninghaus locates disgust in the physical proximity to something we abhor, but to which we feel a subconscious pull "or even an open fascination" (6). The long take that repels audiences also arouses our deepest compassion. What both attracts and sickens is the abruptness and obstinacy of trauma, the affect of permanence in a film that flaunts its mastery of time.

Although such metaleptic flaunting may appear to be misaligned with the picture's neorealist features, both the immediacy and hypermediacy of *Funny Games* push viewers toward actively engaged responses—among the most prominent being frustration with our inefficacy before images of unexplained aggression. Insofar as we identify with the family, we may even feel that such aggression is directed toward us. We are not then so apt to see the picture as just a formal exercise in deconstructive filmmaking.

SAFE DISTANCE

From one perspective, Haneke's refusals smack of cultural conservatism, insinuating that the best approach to the genre is to avoid it. Gail K. Hart interprets Haneke's work as drawing a causal link between watching film violence and engaging in violent behavior, and she argues in response that such a link has never been verified (qtd. in Speck 132). The anti-horror bent of *Funny Games* also appears contradictory given that the movie constitutes an entry into the same genre it denounces. Yet, the idea that the film counsels abandonment of a particular category oversimplifies its rhetorical appeal. The charge is not to stop watching but rather to watch in unconventional ways, recognizing how the genre typically reinforces an affect of safe distance from onscreen events.

This chapter has thus far constructed *Funny Games* as a subverted horror movie, but given its sociopolitical concerns, audiences might question the accuracy of that designation. In light of Haneke's attention to the history of art film, with his allusions to Robert Bresson, Pier Paolo Pasolini, Jean Renoir, and Ingmar Bergman, critics might instead view *Funny Games* as an especially savage turn on their brand of rhetorical production. The purpose here is not to draw a bright line between genres, however. Adam Lowenstein notes the folly of such pursuits in *Shocking Representation: Historical Trauma, National Cinema, and the Modern Horror Film*, remarking how often the genres collapse into each other.[17] The point is rather to show, in Lowenstein's terms, how film accesses "the discourses of horror" so as to offer an indirect but pointed analysis of the attitudes that attend twenty-first-century imperialism (9).

Haneke's effort to trouble bourgeois safe distance may help account for the decision to remake *Funny Games* in the United States ten years after the Austrian original. Translating the German into English and replacing Susanne Lothar (Anna) with Naomi Watts, Ulrich Mühe (Georg) with Tim Roth, and Arno Frisch (Paul) with Michael Pitt, Haneke revised the film in ways that would presumably render it attractive to the North American mainstream. Insofar as the film refuses a particular form of spectatorship, a scene-for-scene remake in the new context implies that the later audience merits the refusal as much as (or more than) the original viewing public. Affluent U.S. audiences, in particular, have wide-ranging visual access to violence occurring "elsewhere" while often feeling sufficiently protected that it fails to produce any sense of exigency. In *Regarding the Pain of Others*, Susan Sontag detects the convergence of Western news with the visualization of distant upheaval, and describes a sensibility that presumes U.S. exemption from routine inhumanity: "That this country, like every other country, has its tragic past does not sit well with the founding, and still all-powerful, belief in American exceptionalism."[18] For many viewers, the belief in exceptionalism subtends a world-weary response to visual records of brutality and war. As with Haneke's televisions, there is devastation consistently on the screen but little, it seems, worthy of comment. *Funny Games* explodes that scenario, erasing the distance between the vacation home and the space of torture. Robert von Dassanowsky contends that *Funny Games* affords viewers no "safety net" when confronting seemingly unmotivated aggression (254). The remake, in his view, indicts a specifically American numbness to the assault. He has also edited a collection with Oliver C. Speck called *New Austrian Film,* wherein Gabriele Wurmitzer examines how *Funny Games* attacks a number of comforting myths, among which she includes the myth of domestic safety (170–73).

The family unit's sense of insulation from violence—and from complicity with that violence—inhabits many of Haneke's works, coming to define his rhetorical approach during the late 1980s and early 1990s when he crafted a sequence of movies about the "progressive emotional glaciation of Austria" (Kunzru). He highlights connections between his focal families by spreading variations on the names Anna (Anne, Ann, Anni), Georg (Georges, George, Schorschi), Eva (Evi), and Pierrot across numerous pictures.[19] In *The Seventh Continent,* the significantly named characters experience such a sense of malaise that they eventually recoil from it all, destroying their possessions and ingesting poison together. In *Benny's Video,* the comfortable Anna and Georg discover that their son has committed a murder that he cannot (or does not wish to) explain, and they aggravate the already disastrous situation by concealing the evidence. *Code Unknown* (2000), *Time of the Wolf* (2003), and *Caché* (2005) find versions of those characters grasping for psychic stability as their lives intersect with those of homeless persons or struggling immigrants, faceless stalkers or intruders in their rural getaways. The 2012 Palme d'Or winner *Amour* further demonstrates the director's fascination with shattered contentment, though this time the violence comes as a pair of strokes that leave Anne confused, unable to continue her work as an accomplished musician and piano teacher, and eventually powerless to communicate with Georges. Thomas Elsaesser and Evan Torner have amply attested to such consistencies within Haneke's oeuvre. What still deserves comment, however, is the myth of safe distance from human rights abuses that are committed elsewhere, in places removed from home and country.

For a director so interested in disturbing the presumed security of his viewers, disallowing such a distance in the U.S. context suggests a critique of nationalism. The critique might hold force in any number of geopolitical environs, but the implicit refiguring of audience in the remake signals a precise target. That the target would attain this precision, after a mostly faithful refashioning of the film, supports Gries's argument for how rhetorical objects morph as frames of reception change. The remake's attack on the logic of exceptionalism demonstrates the inter-actancy of the living image with its viewers' histories and media ecology. To use David Karjanen's terms, that ecology promulgates the sense of "something unique and 'natural' about how society and a market economy function in the United States, based on shared cultural values such as hard work, thrift, and the protection of individual liberty and private property rights" (9). Such cultural values inform a "market fetishism" that presumes economic and moral superiority to other countries while tending to confuse those forms of superiority (10). This confusion has contradictory effects insofar as it indirectly authorizes the right to oversee other countries' affairs, yet convinces the majority of the population of its safety from those countries' trials, its status as more secure and more deserving of security than places outside its borders.

The *Funny Games* remake spoils that affect, especially when set alongside the reflexive representations of media in Haneke's corpus, which denaturalize what Nicholas Mirzoeff describes as "complexes of visuality." He intends the term "complex" in a double sense, marking the interdependencies of "a set of social organizations and processes" while also referring to "the state of an individual's psychic economy" (5). As this sort of complex merges perceptual structures with institutional ones, "the resulting imbrication of mentality and organization produces a visualized deployment of bodies and a training of minds, organized so as to sustain both physical segregation between rulers and ruled, and mental compliance with those arrangements" (5). The arrangement that segregates rulers and ruled often protects the privileged from trials commonly experienced by the dispossessed, working through repetition to convince many in both groups of the ordinariness of the situation. Complexes of visuality function in material-psychological ways to reassure privileged U.S. audiences not just that violence is far away but that someone else is responsible for it.

The second *Funny Games* screened in American theaters during a period when certain national narratives of safe distance were becoming difficult to sustain. As images of U.S. soldiers torturing prisoners at Abu Ghraib circulated widely on television and the Internet, the complex of visuality that projected the mythos of national heroism came under threat. Given that threat, the relocation of *Funny Games* seems in hindsight primed to irritate the recent psychic wounds of the film's audience. To put it in Speck's terms, scenes of creative torture and humiliation "do not appear as far-fetched and divorced from reality as they used to" for many of those viewers (167). Both *Funny Games* and the Abu Ghraib photos depict people being (or having been) stripped, bound, hooded, forced into compromising positions, and generally subjected without mercy to the authority of their occupying rulers.[20] One of the movie's more revolting instances of subjection occurs when Paul compels Schorschi to play a game of "cat in the bag," covering his head with a sack while giving his parents tasks that must be accomplished to obtain his release. The scene evokes the pictures in which U.S. soldiers similarly masked their prisoners, and alludes to the now iconic photo of a hooded figure with outreaching hands connected to electrodes.

By noting *Funny Games*'s citation of the Abu Ghraib photographs, we see how the film's recontextualized rhetoric of refusal calls up a voyeuristic experience of those images, casting it as widespread and abhorrent. The pictures offer an unforgiving portrait of what Hesford describes as an "exportation of American penal culture" that participates in the "staging" of empire (*Spectacular* 65). They undertake such staging against the will of their creators, while also demonstrating an actancy that flouts the pretensions of the U.S. government and, partly and temporarily, escapes that government's control. They demonstrated viral materiality by spreading "instantaneously and globally after a *60 Minutes II* broadcast accelerated them to national consciousness" (Hauser 188). In *Prisoners of Conscience*, Gerard Hauser links the images to ancient rhetorical practices wherein a "*fantasia* of presence" summons the audience "into the torture chamber and into the terror and agony of a body in distress" (194). But accepting the invitation leads quickly to repulsion, creating a movement between consubstantiality and disidentification that is not unlike the experience of *Funny Games*. For many who encountered the pictures during the broadcast, the sense of disgust would only grow with the publication of Seymour Hersh's "Torture at Abu Ghraib" the following week. The evidence suggested not fringe behavior but rather the culture of the military prison.

Yet, however the sticky the problem, the hegemony of American exceptionalism finds ways to protect itself. Hauser acknowledges such hegemony when he explains that, for the most part, "the war we see is the war the Department of Defense (DOD) wants civilians to see" (195). To support that assessment, he recalls Judith Butler's 2009 claim that the DOD's influence on U.S. media "structured our cognitive apprehension of war. And although restricting how or what we see is not exactly the same as dictating a storyline, it is a way of interpreting in advance what will and will not be included in the field of perception" (195). Among the most powerful instances of DOD interference in image circulation stands its ban on photographs of soldiers' caskets. Given that prohibition, the leak of the prison pictures would seem to be a grave disruption to governmental framing of events, demonstrating the unruliness of things once they enter a stream of distribution and exchange. But even as those unruly things initially cut the American conscience, the pictures also give audiences a crew of villains to scapegoat as deviating from a penal order that is presumed but never shown. Exceptionalist self-righteousness transforms the images from a rhetoric of national disgrace to one of mostly isolated criminality. Thus cleansed of culpability, audiences can engage the photos in voyeuristic fashion, suspending the tension between fascination and loathing, refashioning the indictment as one more curious commodity in the information economy.

By suggesting such intertextualities, *Funny Games* censures the U.S. mainstream for conflating geographical distance with a lack of culpability. In so doing, it invites viewers to identify with a conceptual audience that some viewers may already resemble, but that differs in substance from the majority of people Haneke suspects will see the film. The director's projected audience—the one he wants viewers to become—recognizes the irrevocability of destructive acts, maintaining its alignment with the family even as the parents undergo life-altering experiences of injury and bereavement.

That vividness counters the viewer's desire to objectify the family once the film establishes the hopelessness of their escape. Such objectification regularly works as an affective pressure release, and has long been a concern of theorists focused on the coarsening effects of the visual culture industry. As early as 1936, Walter Benjamin worried that those effects often produce such "self-alienation" that the viewing public experiences "its own destruction as an aesthetic event of the first order" (242). Rejecting this machinery of aestheticization, Haneke revolts against the complex of visuality that affords viewers comforting distance from violations of human dignity. Once the spectator identifies with the protagonists, the director endeavors to foreclose recourse to aesthetic enjoyment, pressing us to experience horror as an intensity that exceeds its commodified form.

One difficulty with such rhetorical refusals, however, is that they may themselves be refused, as at Cannes in 1997. And we should remember that although the remake specifically targeted North American audiences, the movie made near six times more money abroad (Speck 15). Granted, we might explain that discrepancy as an effect of poor marketing in the States and/or the popularity of Haneke's oeuvre in European contexts. But we might just as easily posit that a film attacking American audiences for mixing insularity with bloodthirsty scopophilia plays better outside the United States than in. Or we might be tempted, as is Roy Grundmann in his introduction to *A Companion to Michael Haneke*, "to agree with consumer comments that criticized the film for being plain boring and, in fact, not (overtly) violent enough" (29). Yielding to this temptation, however, risks verifying Haneke's assessment of his audience while rendering his intervention ineffectual. Less a rhetorical refusal than a refusal to self-assess, such a response ironically insulates the viewing subject from the critique of safe distance as at best a luxury, at worst a corrupt fantasy.

CHAPTER 2

MEDIATED MOURNING

ATOM EGOYAN'S *Ararat* (2002) imagines the making of a contemporary movie about the siege of Van in 1915, addressing in powerfully reflexive ways what Marc Nichanian calls the Armenian Catastrophe. Set largely in turn-of-the-millennium Toronto, Egoyan's picture coils together various mini-narratives about people who participate in the production of a historiographic film that is also called "Ararat." The character sketches generate affective force through juxtaposition: just as one person feels obligated to dramatize scenes of genocide to venerate the dead, another maintains that such veneration cannot occur without a thoroughgoing dedication to historical accuracy. Still another asserts both the necessity and impossibility of capturing the events in narrative form. The compulsion toward narrative reflects the characters' longing for identification with lost loved ones, while the countervailing suspicion of storytelling suggests a recognition that such identification will remain elusive. By embedding the tale of the movie's production within his own film, Egoyan at once affirms cinematic representation as an expression of mourning and probes the limits of such expression.

Amid the strata of his metafilm exist portraits of three Armenian post-exiles, each from a different generation in the decades following the siege: the filmmaker Edward Saroyan, who directs the movie to honor his mother; the art historian Ani, whose lectures on Armenian painter Arshile Gorky earn her a job as Saroyan's consultant; and Ani's son Raffi, whose father died attempting to kill a Turkish diplomat. All three characters engage in a process of mediated mourning, whether for lost loved ones or a decimated nation and culture, which counters Turkish state denial and the prospect of historical erasure. That process is mediated in two senses: first, it expresses itself through production of (or interaction with) visual texts; second, those texts interpose themselves between the bereaved and the community with whom they identify. Keeping Blakesley's Burkean approach to film rhetoric firmly in mind, this chapter finds Egoyan enacting such mourning in the very process of depicting it, affirming the aspiration toward diasporic consubstantiality while also recognizing the violence of that urge.

The violence inheres in the construction of narratives that elide the measureless detail of genocidal history, and the appropriation of such narratives for purposes of therapeutic self-affirmation. *Ararat* reflects on each kind of violence and how they intermingle, while engaging in a materialist historiography that visualizes its argument by contrasting the experiences of its focal characters. As a composing practice, reflexive materialism requires situating expressive objects within temporal streams of social and political struggle, attending to how diachronic mediation helps preserve hierarchies of authority and influence, military and economic resources. Egoyan's movie enacts that approach not just by examining how "Ararat" (the film-within-the-film) helps expose those hierarchies, but also how it participates in their reproduction. It further shows how various forms of composition, whether photographic or paint-based portraiture, art criticism, or personal videography, become tangled in the dialectic of confrontation and appropriation.

Audiences appropriate the rhetoric of mediated mourning by absorbing it into a corrupt discourse of proof. That people still require proof, despite copious testimony accumulated over nearly ninety years, suggests the efficacy with which Turkish nationalists have thrown Armenian claims into doubt. In attempting to counter that silencing effort, *Ararat* enters a space wherein the doubter can still assume rhetorical legitimacy, demanding that the Armenian post-exile either identify with the oppressor's standards of evidence or remain mute. Nichanian's *The Historiographic Perversion* construes that demand as a continuation of the very horrors in question, cautioning historians to decline the injunction to prove. The final section of the chapter shows Egoyan advancing a related form of cautionary rhetoric, holding that the mediation of mourning enrolls audiences in the project of verifying the Catastrophe regardless of his own aims. That cautionary rhetoric arises largely through the film's depiction of Raffi, who undergoes airport interrogation when he returns from Armenia carrying canisters of film related to the "Ararat" project. Suspecting Raffi of smuggling drugs, a customs official requires him to authenticate his connection to Saroyan's production and, as part of his self-defense, to verify the siege of Van. Egoyan's imagetext derives structure from the border officer's queries while gradually calling into question his right to ask them. Identifying audiences with the officer's appetite for historical veracity, *Ararat* frames the interrogation as a means of reproducing power relations between Armenian subjects and Western arbiters of international "justice" who, to use Diana Fuss's phrasing, shore up privileged geopolitical subjectivity by taking a detour through otherness (2).

Frustrated as Egoyan is by such self-serving uptake, he still honors his characters' need to tell their stories. In attempting to reconstruct Armenian history from its sometimes faint material traces, they amass what Scott and Welch regard as a critical inventory ("One" 562, 564). That inventory keeps us focused on the details of systematized violence, which include the planning and undertaking of mass extermination as well as its continuing cover-up. Scott and Welch worry about the loss of such detail amid the scholarly fascination with the apparatus of delivery and the dazzling remediation of viral images. They lament the circumstances wherein "the *idea* of public conversation *becomes* the conversation," and a fixation on "clicktivism" displaces the negotiation of activist claims ("One" 564–65). Such displacement presents a pressing concern for metaleptic rhetoric in general, as the reflexive attention to design potentially distracts from the critical inventories of arguments that address social injustice. *Ararat* mostly avoids that problem, however, by devising metanarrative techniques that accentuate the substance of public debate—whether it involves forced marches, rape warfare, prisoner immolation, or blockage of humanitarian aid—and that passionately counter efforts to dissolve that substance.

While tracking how Egoyan and his crew perform those techniques, the coming argument does more than interpret a specific film; it recounts a singularly rich contribution of visual culture to the discursive nexus of Burkean rhetorical theory, the mediation of history, and the embodied experience of grief. More specifically, the argument associates representations of genocide with competing processes of identification: on the one hand, an urge toward consubstantiality with an ancestral collective; on the other, absorption by discourses that render the post-exile answerable to skeptics and audiences who appropriate narratives of atrocity for personal catharsis.

TRUE IN SPIRIT

Edward Saroyan's film-within-a-film demonstrates Armenian rhetorical agency amid the discourses of Western neglect and Turkish denial, providing resources for memory despite disregard in some quarters and efforts to block recollection in others. His movie catalyzes memory by depicting the plundering of villages, the ritual burning of women, and the torture of children, as well as through renderings of objects passed from one generation to the next—a pocket watch, a photograph, a button from a frayed overcoat. His emphasis on materiality coheres with William Guynn's sense that memory depends on the affect of tangibility: the narrative summons audience identification by means of concreteness, which in its metaphorical sense intertwines physicality and specificity (195).

Such an invitation nicely suits Debra Hawhee's sense of how identification happens, for she finds Burke's early idea of consubstantiality to be "as much postural and somatic as it is psychological and social" (*Moving* 117). Acknowledging Burke as a cunning theorist of language, Hawhee finds him also working at "the edges of language" as he addresses the corporeal character of rhetorical exchange. Saroyan's "Ararat" exemplifies corporeal appeal by triggering not just historical alertness but visceral revulsion, merging the two in opposition to niceties that would reduce genocide to an exaggeration or a preemptive strike in time of war. The production derives additional exigency from the director's awareness that the Armenians who survived the siege are disappearing along with the mother to whom he devotes his work.[1] But even as the film constitutes a resource for memory, it reminds audiences of the unattainability of consubstantiality across generations, and thus expresses the dual character of mediated mourning. Whether mourning expresses itself through film, print, digital communications, or other modes and genres, it fuses remembrance with self-consciousness about the technological constraints and forms of narrative excess involved in historical representation.

As Saroyan begins to view the scale of his subject matter as authorization for poetically charged inaccuracies, he opens to scrutiny the forms of identification his film purportedly enables. While assessing Saroyan's set design, the art historian Ani notes the prominence of Mt. Ararat in the background of Van, and insists that the mountain would not be visible from the city. When the director explains that the image is "important" nonetheless, Ani remains steadfast: "But it's not true!" With a gentleness that works almost immediately to end debate, Saroyan answers, "It's true in spirit." Holding to the felt sense of authenticity while admitting the spectral character of truth, the director allows himself the privilege of moving a mountain so long as the work of transhistorical identification gets done. That work, he recognizes, occurs in ways that are not entirely rational. The resonance that Mt. Ararat holds for many Armenians instantiates what Burke depicts as the "physical influence of an idea," which often proves more powerful than even the most finely tuned logical exposition.[2] Despite connotations of immateriality, the "spirit of truth" evokes for Saroyan the sort of validity that reverberates in the guts and bones, and that he expects will prove persuasive not just to Armenians but to the international audiences he aims to move.

His faith in the power of the mountain image indicates sensitivity to the relationship between identity, community, and the mutuality that geography evokes. Mt. Ararat provides a visual-material form of connection among Armenian people and their descendants, even if those descendants have never visited the country. In *Democracy's Lot*, Rai explains that sense of connection by first reiterating Phaedra Pezzullo's claim that "the materiality of a place promises the opportunity to shape perceptions, bodies, and lives" through its affective vibrancy. Rai then follows by suggesting that the "private" encounter with resonant geographies kindles "the creation of collective valences."[3] Yet her book forcefully demonstrates that the emotional encounter is never entirely private, and that "collective valences" infuse geographies long before we encounter them. The book also shows that those valences are always plural, as the rhetoric of place remains contested among people who claim it as home or as crucial to their identities. But whatever the disagreements, Saroyan sees the mountain as an icon of intersubjectivity, a physical manifestation of national sensibility. As a landmark it stands immobile, enduring as the generations pass, but as an image it moves, expressing the kind of nomadic vitality and psychic poignancy that Gries associates with becoming rhetorical (*Still* 79). For Saroyan, to honor that movement is to respect the spirit of truth.[4]

In his view, that spirit justifies geographical liberties and appeals to poetic license, all of which he takes to be necessary for establishing Armenian solidarity and greater global awareness in the face of historical erasure. But whereas he stresses the mountain's mobility as an image, Ani counters with its topographical steadiness. That moment of opposition signals feelings of doubt that will intensify for her as *Ararat* progresses. The dissonance arises, however, not just from Ani's eye as a trained historian and art critic but from the landscape's implacable physicality. If we follow Rickert's description of the politics of things, we notice his dealings with Latour, for whom "the word 'thing' comes to designate a hybrid actor," or a "composite of materiality and meaning" that becomes bound up with other active phenomena, both human and not, in a variety of complex assemblages ("Whole" 138). Mt. Ararat is active even in its stillness. It collaborates with Ani in insisting on grounded validity, a "truth" that is rooted in ancient geologic formations and unimpressed by artistic convenience. As Saroyan derives affective resonance from the mountain image, he capitalizes on its affordances while disregarding what Shipka calls the "constraints" of the composing object (62). That disregard has damaging rhetorical consequences, as liberties in one area of the composition may generate misgivings about the rest.

Whereas Egoyan attributes the risks of Saroyan's approach to the desire to "get the point across" (E. Wilson 118), Ewa Mazierska points out the fictional director's reproduction of Holocaust industry clichés, which include its mainly English dialogue and sweeping orchestral score (43). To such patterns we might add lavish stagings of militarized rape and brooding soliloquies by the film's central villain, Jevdet Bay.[5] Saroyan's more melodramatic techniques evoke Steven Spielberg's *Schindler's List* (1993), which attempts the sort of totalizing reproduction that Egoyan's metafilm draws into question.[6] Egoyan makes such critique explicit in his essay "In Other Words," challenging epic representations of genocide by contending that "any blockbuster attempt to amplify the event from the very private turmoil its memory provokes is to diminish—or at least to misrepresent—an essential aspect of its meaning" (qtd. in Banita 87). By invoking the "blockbuster," he questions the monetization of atrocity and the ethics of packaging images of mass murder as a popular attraction. Like Haneke, he has misgivings about rendering historical violence consumable even as his movies participate in that process. Although he does not command the budget or the audience of a Spielberg production, he still renders the unfathomable as an object of commercial exchange. As *Ararat* tears away at its own semiotic strategies, it attempts to mitigate market hegemony. But there is no clear way to escape the problem and still do the work of memorialization.

While the slippage between audiovisual materiality and corporate-capitalist materialism presents one kind of hazard, Egoyan's more prevalent concern involves the sweep of narrative, the attempt to generate an affect of summative illustration. By including Saroyan's movie within his own, he can at once evoke that ambition and distance himself from it. Like Saroyan's project, Egoyan's *Ararat* fosters viewer identification with the psychological aftereffects of genocide, but Egoyan's movie diverges from his character's by conveying ambivalence about the temptation toward grand narrative. For rhetoricians who focus on historical trauma, Egoyan's position may prove a worthwhile heuristic, as it derives its ethic from the dialectic of memorial exigency and representational insecurity, playing out the tension between the intimate need to recollect and the wariness of grounding an epic vision in "private turmoil."

(DIS)FIGURING HISTORY

Although Ani questions Saroyan's set, she typically defers to his decisions—not just because he mixes humility with a formidable reputation, but also because she shares his desire for connection to Van's early twentieth-century population. She articulates that desire through engagement with the work of Arshile Gorky, an Armenian painter who emigrated to the United States the year after his mother died of starvation due to a Turkish blockade.7 Ani repeatedly lectures on his painting *The Artist and His Mother,* suggesting that it works both to save his mother from erasure and to honor those who died in the Catastrophe. To revisit Hawhee's language, the painting mediates a somatic affinity for the absent experience of familial and communal wholeness. Either Saroyan or Egoyan (and perhaps both) accentuate Gorky's yearning for consubstantiality by depicting him at work in his studio, forgoing brushes for a moment and laying his paint-wet hands on those of his mother image, signifying with tactile urgency the mediation of mourning. Ani reproduces the gesture at the conclusion of one of her lectures, reaching up to touch the hand of Gorky's mother as it remains projected on the screen behind her. The action punctuates her attribution of sacredness to the image, which she views as "a repository of our history."

But Ani's reverence for the painting develops alongside the film's claim that historical representation distorts the events it purportedly renders accessible. When Gorky touches his mother's hands, for example, he blurs and obscures them, enacting a form of identification that is "true in spirit" and thus caught in the contradictions of virtual validity, approximate authenticity. "The visual mutilation of the mother's body," explains Georgiana Banita, is

> closely tied up with Gorky's ability to recover the past but not to have access to it—to have it but not to properly hold it. By extrapolation, the

> massacre of the Armenian people is not only obstructed by repression or amnesia, but is essentially constituted by its lack of integration into consciousness. (97–98)

Drawing on the work of Cathy Caruth, Banita suggests that trauma typically involves the subject's inability to "hold" the past or "integrate" it into self-awareness, and suggests that the pain of denied access is a defining feature of genocide. As Gorky obliterates the image of his mother's hands, his gesture ushers the audience into an experience of loss that is simultaneously personal and cultural. Poised uncertainly between Saroyan's melodrama and Egoyan's metafilm, the scene lends concreteness to the logic of frustrated recovery that informs much of the surrounding narrative. In so doing, it signals a rhetorical condition that infuses and exceeds the cinematic frame: just as the heirs of the Catastrophe attempt to call up the individual or collective with whom they would identify, the means of invocation disfigures and eclipses its object.

For Egoyan, the means of invocation is film form itself. And given the many-layered composition of his project, the status of some scenes has a disorienting ambiguity. Depictions of Gorky in his studio, for example, may be flashbacks within the metanarrative or scenes in Saroyan's interior production. The instability corroborates Maureen Turim's observations in *Flashbacks in Film: Memory and History*, which associate the rhetoric of analepsis with the elusive character of historical closure, as such rhetoric tends to accentuate contingency, limited perspective, and unreliable recall. On one hand, the portrait of the artist at work appears to convey a reality that none of the other characters can attain; on the other, the artist may just be another actor in Edward Saroyan's film-within-a-film, a sensational mock-up of the past rather than its privileged messenger. Absent the typical markers of flashback—which might include introducing the sequence with a pensive face, a dissolve, or a soft filter—the Gorky sequences pull in opposing directions. They strive toward a time that long precedes Egoyan's movie, attempting to anchor the drama to a stratum of extra-cinematic, impossibly unmediated experience; almost simultaneously, however, they admit the inescapability of mediation and the necessary erosion of any temporal grounding. The resulting tension gives Egoyan's project its narrative momentum as well as its ethical urgency. Historical visualizations cannot overcome their epistemological limitations, nor can the fallibility of memory and its mediators dispel the materiality of large-scale atrocity or the plentiful testimony that has followed.

Such testimony supplies a lively conduit between incommensurable contexts, constituting a technology of historical transmission and transformation. Insofar as that technology becomes confused with what it conveys, it exemplifies the general character of mediation. Gries brings out that character by engaging with Latour's *Reassembling the Social*, which figures communications devices as transforming relations between people rather than serving as neutral conductors. Gries rehearses one of Latour's key distinctions by contending that we deem nonhuman things "to be intermediaries rather than mediators. While intermediaries enter into diverse relations without necessarily transforming them, mediators transform, distort, modify, and so forth" ("Dingrhetoriks" 298). Neither Gorky's canvases nor Saroyan's staging can escape those distorting effects, no matter how poignantly they generate the affect of immediacy.

For Ani the terror of such distortion becomes unbearable when her stepdaughter, believing her father killed himself to escape Ani's intolerable standards, tries to slash Gorky's painting with a pocketknife. After Ani reflects on the near-mutilation of her favored repository, she decides to act on behalf of historical authenticity by interrupting one of Saroyan's enormous set pieces, which has come to represent for her the accumulation of lies that attend the "spirit" of truth. Yet the lead actor, Martin Harcourt, refuses to break character despite Ani's intrusion on a scene in progress, describing in gruesome detail the event she has entered:

> We are surrounded by Turks. We've run out of supplies. Most of us will die. The crowd needs a miracle. This child is bleeding to death. If I can save his life it may give us the spirit to continue. . . . His pregnant sister was raped in front of his eyes before her stomach was slashed open to stab her unborn child. His father's eyes were gouged out of his head and stuffed into his mouth, and his mother's breasts were ripped off. She was left to bleed to death. Who the fuck are you?

Shaming her for presuming to judge their labor, Harcourt invests the scene with the same bodily urgency she reserves for Gorky. Demanding Ani's somatic identification with what remains of a decimated family, the actor indicates that whatever her reasons for interrupting the scene, they cannot compare with Saroyan's reasons for making the film, nor can her personal trials compare with those the scene represents. The force of his speech, with its delineation of the startlingly precise violence that is often masked by the phrase "Armenian Genocide," stops Ani short while exposing the irony of her situation. Entering Saroyan's set to protest her stepdaughter's threat to Armenian historical artwork, Ani inadvertently produces a similar kind of threat. Egoyan's decision to place the actor's improvised soliloquy just after Ani's denunciation of Celia identifies both women as intruders and vandals. While Egoyan's film disrupts the logic of historical transparency, it also rejects standards of "authenticity" that demean artistic efforts to elicit the audience's connection to onscreen struggles. Ani's speechlessness before Harcourt's litany of horrors suggests that she registers the contradiction.

That speechlessness also suggests Egoyan's identification with competing perspectives on the dramatization of genocide: the conviction that responsible re-creation must attain accuracy or not appear at all, and the belief that people have an obligation to resist the suppression of history. That Egoyan's film supports both positions should not be understood as mere inconsistency. "Any one person may find herself 'split at the root,'" writes Beth Eddy in *The Rites of Identity*. "A person may have multiple and conflicting identity attachments. Because of this plurality of identifications and because human events happen over time, a logic that cannot handle multiple tracts of development simultaneously is an inadequate tool" (72). The multiplicity of the identification process, along with tensions among various corporeal and intellectual affinities, distinguishes consubstantiation from essentialist conceptions of subjectivity. According to Diane Davis's reading of Burke, "there is no essential identity; what goes for your individual 'substance' is not an essence but the incalculable totality of your complex and contradictory identifications, through which you variously (and vicariously) become able to say 'I'" (21). For Burke, socially negotiated ideas of common interest make possible the enunciation of this "I," meaning that consciousness of selfhood signals immersion in collectivity rather than the experience of autonomy. Citing Burke's claim in *Attitudes Toward History* that "identity is not individual," Davis takes him to suggest that subjectivity "is constituted via the enactment of a series of dissociated and frequently contradictory roles defined by the groups with which one identifies."[8]

That Egoyan infuses Ani's character with opposition to Saroyan's artistic license, and yet composes Harcourt's speech as a deeply felt critique of Ani's presumption, does not imply the trumping of one position by the other, but rather signals the extent to which the filmmaker is "split at the root." Working from the experience of multiple affinities, Egoyan at once endorses and destabilizes those feelings by attributing legitimacy to them at different moments in time. Ani's disapproval of the transported mountain serves, for a significant interval, to contest the liberties that might confuse the history Saroyan depicts. Harcourt's speech, at a distinct but no less striking moment, disputes Ani's right to halt the production altogether. While capturing the complexity of Egoyan's identity work, such tensions moderate the audience's attraction to the film's varied perspectives, suggesting that principled standpoints on historical representation often have compelling counterpoints. Shane Borrowman and Marcia Kmetz suggest that the unresolved play of attitudes reflects a Burkean view of experience: "For Burke the dualism of identification and division as necessary and natural components of humans being in the world was, perhaps, yet another example of the oxymoronic nature of existence itself, where truth exists beyond logic and rests comfortably among contradictions" (279). While viewers may not locate comfortable truths amid the contradictions of Egoyan's film, the experience persuades us to resist the lure of dogmatic resolution.[9]

WHO REMEMBERS THE EXTERMINATION OF THE ARMENIANS?

Like Egoyan, Ani's son Raffi wants to tell the story accurately, but he acknowledges the imperfection of his medium and perception. Haunted by his father's death, he sets off for Mt. Ararat with a small digital camera in hopes of discovering what motivated the assassination attempt while obtaining hard evidence of the genocide. Raffi's deployment of the camera, which coincides with a trip of more than 5,000 miles from Canada to Armenia, frees him temporarily from frustrations at home, thus supporting Tschofen and Burwell's claim that when Egoyan's subjects "take up the means of production . . . their conditions of uncertainty and trauma are transmuted into mobility and flexibility" (16). Audiences who become embroiled in Raffi's detective work may come to recognize another purpose for the journey, which is "to remake Saroyan's old-fashioned cinematic document into images that are less sentimental, into a more personalized vision of history that straddles the line between the sublime and its sublimation" (Banita 90). Insofar as viewers align themselves with that more subtle purpose, they share not only Raffi's but also Egoyan's resistance to "blockbuster" renditions of genocide.

By contrasting microhistory with melodrama, both the character and the flesh-and-blood composer strive toward an agency that preserves localized forms of embodiment while reaffirming collectivist ontology. As the means of visual-narrative production affords rhetorical "mobility and flexibility," it suggests the extent to which agency derives from techno-human hybridity, which presumes not a dichotomy of composers and passive tools but different degrees of material liveliness. Rickert clarifies the point by reflecting on Latour's "From Realpolitik to Dingpolitik," which designates a collectivity of "human and nonhuman actants" that forms "a sociomaterial stitch work constantly reweaving itself into new collective forms" (Rickert, "Whole" 136). Raffi's camera both records and joins that stitch work, which includes pictures of Armenian churches, a carved Madonna and child, a mountain road, a montage of delicate meadows and vast, unpopulated landscapes, all of which enfold the so-called maker of the image. In Saroyan's production, the collective encompasses generations of people experiencing extremes of joy and distress, yet it also gathers in a phonograph, paintbrushes and pencil sketches, a photographer's tripod, a soldier's lash, a horseshoe that doubles as a torture device. Egoyan's metafilm absorbs these things and much that eludes itemization, all of which recalls Paul Lynch and Nathaniel Rivers's estimation of extrahuman materiality as "nervously loquacious" (3–4). Things participate in the making of history, providing the affective resources from which narrative takes shape, inhabiting our cognitive frameworks, and hinting at mysteries we have not yet learned to formulate.

While Raffi's camera helps mobilize his struggle with Armenian history, the mobility nevertheless exists within a bounded framework, as the trip to Armenia exemplifies the compulsive response to trauma rather than a straightforward enactment of newfound agency. Raffi's movement across thousands of miles competes with an attachment to ingrained images and long-nurtured memories, each of which entails the affective stickiness Ahmed details in *The Cultural Politics of Emotion* (11). The interplay of motion and attachment, outreach and fixity, parallels the Freudian dialectic of mourning and melancholia. The effort to mitigate grief coexists with an ethical desire to keep the pain fresh, affirming the residual stickiness of the absent objection of affection. To use Dominick LaCapra's framework, it may be that Raffi does not entirely want to work through his trauma, as achieving resolution may mean breaking faith with the past:

> One's bond with the dead, especially with dead intimates, may invest trauma with value and make its reliving a painful but necessary commemoration or memorial to which one remains dedicated or at least bound. This situation may create a more or less unconscious desire to remain within trauma. (22–23)

Raffi experiences the pain of losing his father and, no less gallingly, of failing to share the sense of consubstantiality that motivated his father's self-destructive political act. To resolve such suffering, or to grieve in a way that diminishes its intensity, risks attenuating familial attachment while dishonoring those who experienced the siege firsthand. In his eagerness to avoid such circumstances, Raffi reproduces what Egoyan calls the "national myth" whereby "you can attach yourself to something to which you have no connection other than your own conception of what that space and time might provide for you." "It is a very clear way of organizing your life," Egoyan claims, "and it's also how things are fetishized" (E. Wilson 144). Raffi alerts audiences to the fetishistic character of his project even as he carries it out, acknowledging in voice-over that despite his accumulation of images, "there is nothing here to prove that anything ever happened."[10]

The presumed availability of proof nevertheless suffuses Raffi's struggle to identify with the people of Van. Given the intensity of that struggle, he reacts passionately when the language of "genocide" undergoes critique. The half-Turkish actor Ali, who plays Jevdet Bay, makes the backstage claim that war necessitates strategic violence and that stories of mass killings and deportations are probably hyperbole. When Raffi contests those assertions, Ali admits that "something" happened but continues to question Saroyan's version of events. As a concession, the reduction of the Catastrophe to *some thing* only heightens the animosity, contradicting Ali's conciliatory tone and calling into question Raffi's understanding of history and the reasons for his father's actions. Whereas new materialist theory respects the alteration of things as they appear in different places and times, such mutability proves intolerable to people for whom the truth of genocide has paramount consequence. Echoing his mother's defense of Mt. Ararat's constancy, Raffi insists on a specificity of reference that the mention of a mere "something" cannot deliver. He further notes that the practice of spreading doubt, and taking refuge in historical malleability, have long been strategies of genocidal governments.

Ali defends his position by recounting his own reading during preparations for the role. The actor's identification with Jevdet Bay alienates not only Raffi but those viewers who have come, if not entirely to accept Saroyan's version of events, to experience investment in exposing the terror of the siege. In response to Ali's assertions that terrible things happen on all sides in wartime, Raffi explains that Turkey was not at war with Armenia in 1915, and that Armenian civilians expected "to be protected" as the conflict developed. Ali asks only that they each embrace their current privileges in Canada, forgo their mutual suspicions, and most pointedly, "drop the fucking history and get on with it." Unmoved by Ali's presentism, Raffi observes that Adolf Hitler convinced his officers of the viability of the "final solution" by asking, "Who remembers the extermination of the Armenians?"—to which Ali retorts, "And nobody did. Nobody does." Such language exemplifies Ali's rhetorical approach, which merges a plea for forgetting with the conviction that allegations of genocide require incontestable proof. His implicit demand for confirmation depends on what Janet Walker views as a naïve idea of empiricism (xviii), as if the right presentation of concrete details could convince Ali that the slaughter did occur and cannot now be rationalized as wartime strategy. Such an account would feature seamless representation and certain closure, surpassing the limits of historiography itself. For Ali, these unanswerable stipulations become a kind of weapon, or at least a shield, against his own implication in unimaginable violence. Raffi's subsequent pursuit of evidence becomes more than a way of coping with his father's death; it becomes a means of addressing Ali's challenge.

Survivors of genocide commonly express dedication to a thorough accounting of atrocity, both to respond to deniers such as Ali and to assist with the process of mourning. "The basic facts about who did what to how many, when and in what way, must be set right," Paul Connerton observes. "What is wanted is the military lists, detailing who kidnapped which person, at what date, for what reason, where that person was taken, where they were killed, where they were buried. The procedure of legal rectification must be as precise as was the administrative massacre" (25). Although their dialogue occurs outside a legal context, Ali's skepticism bolsters Raffi's need to authenticate the events under discussion. Ironically, Ali displays little willingness to listen to the facts he demands, turning his back on the camera perspective that constitutes both Raffi's and the audience's line of sight, then moving away from the foreground and finally out of view.

The refusal to engage Raffi at length prefigures the nationalist tendency toward denial that inflects many Turkish responses to *Ararat*. Although the movie was never banned, it ran on national television so as to inform citizens of how Armenian filmmakers perpetuate the feud. In "'Past Not-So-Perfect': *Ararat* and Its Reception in Turkey," Özlem Köksal observes how critical rebukes of the movie appeared before it even premiered. Citing an essay by Gündüz Aktan as one example among dozens of preemptive appraisals, Köksal notes the insistence that "contrary to the claims of the movie *Ararat*, the Turks never hated Armenians" (53–54). Toward the end of his reflections, Köksal provides the lone counterexample of Turkish reviewer İsmet Berkan praising *Ararat* as an indictment of cross-cultural contempt (63). But the more prominent strain of Turkish film criticism vilified the movie in advance, later selecting scenes from within Saroyan's movie to verify Egoyan's hatred of Turks. Raffi's encounter with Ali suggests a metafilmic anticipation of such reception, showing how the process of listening breaks down before enriching either character's identity work. The dialogue deepens Raffi's desire to set history right, but gives him little idea of how to render that record persuasive.

Given the extent to which Raffi serves as focalizer for Egoyan's diegesis, the audience's experience of *Ararat* entails sharing the young man's perspective while encountering persistent invitations to affirm his motives, along with his effort to forge an identity from the kinships he claims. Eddy reads such attempts at self-making "both as the insignia that clothe us in uniform to others' eyes, either as friend or enemy, and as the fortresses that protect our most crucial first premises about our hopes, fears, and needs" (2). Trying to secure such a fortress involves situating the self in relation to others "either as friend or enemy," for to return once more to Burke, "to begin with 'identification' is, by the same token though roundabout, to confront the implications of *division*" (qtd. in Eddy 2). Although Ali is initially overjoyed to play a major role in Saroyan's movie, he comes to suspect that the director and Raffi are engaged in identity projects that position him—not just Jevdet Bay—as monstrous other. The vitriol with which he finally dismisses Raffi signals his resentment while indicating his qualms about participating in what he takes to be blockbuster exaggeration. Raffi's effort to clarify the history of Van seems to Ali an unnecessary emphasis on division when he would prefer to accept their Canadian affinities and "get on with it." When that rhetorical gambit fails, Ali brutally asserts the absence of evidence for what Raffi and Saroyan claim as truth. For Raffi, preserving "crucial first premises about [his] hopes, fears, and needs" requires obtaining that evidence for himself even if Ali refuses to go on listening. Egoyan's film enlists the audience in Raffi's pursuit while maintaining that any evidence it produces will be perspectival and filtered, even if true in spirit.

WE WILL BRING NO PROOFS

Responding to Ali's challenge risks colluding with the repressive practices that proceed in unbroken course from Van, 1915. Nichanian argues that

> the planned murder [of the Armenians] did not consist in mere killing. The planned murder consisted, however one understands this, in erasing the

death of the victims, in eradicating all traces of death and (accessorily) of murder. It consisted in killing not life but in killing death. (55)

Ali's accusations of exaggeration attest to the efficacy of such erasure while his invitation to avoid historical thinking helps perpetuate the problem. The invitation leaves Raffi no good option for reply, for to accept it means undertaking the impossible task of forgetting—the paradoxical charge of remembering to repress—while to attempt to prove genocide cedes rhetorical advantage to the heirs of those who engineered it. Egoyan's situation as filmmaker resembles Raffi's, as the director's effort to memorialize doubles as a cry for acknowledgment. Although Egoyan detests that uncertainty, and like Raffi, cannot bear those who take refuge in it, his film nevertheless gives resentful voice to doubt. As Scott and Welch outline the principles of critical materialism, they study how film and other communicative practices relate to "the rest of the social order," noting that those practices serve political and economic interests that are not immediately obvious ("One" 566). In the case of *Ararat,* some of those interests run counter to the aims of the filmmaker. But rather than just proving vulnerable to analysis that exposes those contradictions, the movie expresses its own troubled awareness of them, and thereby exemplifies cinematic rhetoric as a contributor to materialist theory. *Ararat* contends that public mourning stands susceptible to co-optation by actants whose interests depart from those of the mourner.

Beyond administering the Armenian massacre, Turkish authorities denied it the status of atrocity so systematically that, almost a century later, English-speaking subjects such as Ali and Raffi would wrangle over the appropriateness of the term "genocide" to the history they inherit. Ali admits that "something" happened but questions Raffi's framing and wonders why they must dwell on the subject. According to Connerton, such rhetoric amounts to attempted silencing,

> for the power to silence others resides not simply in the power to prevent them from talking; it lies also in the power to shape and control the talking that they do, to restrict the things they may talk about and, more specifically, the ways in which they are permitted to express their thoughts. (77)

Ali throws suspicion onto the term "genocide" by noting its failure to account for the wartime context, insisting that military strategists like Jevdet Bay perceived the people of Van as a legitimate threat. That Raffi would need to correct the misperception of Turkey and Armenia as warring nations only clarifies the extent to which the Turkish authorities succeeded in "killing death." His determination to answer Ali involves partaking, even if critically, in a discourse that so thoroughly naturalizes the strategy of negation that its strategic character disappears. When confronted with situations akin to Raffi's, Nichanian counsels a refusal to participate, echoing Maurice Blanchot's declaration that "we will bring no proofs."[11]

Egoyan's film identifies Western audiences of non-Armenian descent with the desire for proof by insinuating their alignment with the customs officer David, who meets Raffi trying to bring film canisters across the Canadian border. Suspecting that the cans contain drugs, and alarmed by airport information about Raffi's father, David detains the young man for questioning that occurs in fragments throughout Egoyan's narrative. Raffi explains that the canisters hold footage for Saroyan's movie, though the interrogation reveals that bringing them into Canada was the black-market fee for safe passage along a military road to Mt. Ararat. As David exposes various lies about the trip, he nevertheless becomes engrossed in Raffi's account of the history that informs Saroyan's movie. With compassion for Raffi comes a mounting suspicion that the canisters hold heroin, forcing David to choose between the dictates of his job and an extralegal idea of justice—one in which historical and personal trauma converge to form an exigency that trumps border security. He finally decides to release Raffi regardless of the canisters' contents, showing a remarkable and perhaps implausible sensitivity to the young man's practice of mediated mourning.

As David's suspicions give way to paternalism, audiences might be tempted to overlook the power imbalance that exists between the officer and his suspect. Unfortunately, bracketing that imbalance does more than support a generous reading of David's character. It forgives normalized inequalities and reproduces the relation of answerability that Nichanian abhors. David not only holds authority to investigate Raffi's luggage, he assumes a right to his personal and cultural histories, asking him to prove the validity of both. While the exchange has legal stakes, it also has intimate implications for David, who tends to associate Raffi with his son Philip. Crosscutting techniques early in *Ararat* suggest a strained relationship between David and Philip, which heals almost immediately after Raffi's release. Even when David expresses a desire to learn, he turns the lessons toward the resolution of domestic psychodrama rather than critiquing the system that affords him interrogator status. The appropriation of Raffi's testimony to resolve personal crisis fortifies the power relation between privileged witness and vulnerable testifier, reproducing "hierarchical scenes of self-recognition" in ways that substantiate the thinking of both Wendy Hesford and Gayatri Spivak. Hesford reads Spivak's "Can the Subaltern Speak?" as urging critics "to avoid resurrecting victims' voices in ways that replace those voices with their own, thereby neutralizing their untranslatability" (*Spectacular* 54–55). David's delayed judgment, which appears at first to respect the gulf between Raffi's experiences and his own, gives way to an impulse that insists on translation where none is possible.

The demand to translate the untranslatable doubles as the demand for proof—one to which the post-exile responds with increasing fervor as the interview proceeds. As Raffi recounts the events of 1915, he relives the traumatic experiences of apprehending (if always in limited ways) his ancestral history and losing his father to the genocide's long aftermath. The proof imperative triggers the self-lacerating act in which the "survivor" must "fabricate, all by himself, the scene, the gaze, and the event" (Nichanian 97). Given that Raffi's experience cannot equate with those of his ancestors, his condition as survivor must be understood as heritage rather than arising from direct experience of the massacre. The post-exile fabricates "the scene, the gaze, and the event" through the experience of what Marianne Hirsch terms "postmemory," or a form of vicarious remembrance passed on through oral testimony and other material rhetoric, which works to preserve crucial familial and cultural information. Whereas Hesford argues that during the delivery of primary survivors' narratives the rhetor and audience alike are implicated "in recreating the spectacle of victimization as a scene of forced recognition" (*Spectacular* 114), her claim also resonates for postmemorial testimony. David holds authority to force that testimony regardless of the pain it produces, and Raffi wants recognition of his experience through the gaze of such an authority figure—the figure of lawful passage at the international border.

In dramatizing the post-exile's pursuit of validation, *Ararat* suggests that however representative David may be of legal propriety, his position depends on conditions of geopolitical inequality that inhibit the just mediation of Raffi's border crossing. The decision to let Raffi pass despite evidence of "guilt" does not efface that inequality, but merely realizes David's power to distinguish propriety from transgression. The advantage of David's position produces the sort of communicative impasse that Hesford associates with the "crisis of witnessing"—a crisis that evokes "ruptures in identification" as well as "the impossibility of empathic merging between witness and testifier" (*Spectacular* 99). David's desire for such merging may be tainted from the outset, for as Lauren Berlant argues, "transpersonal intimacies created by calls to empathy all too frequently serve as proleptic shields, as ethically uncontestable legitimating devices for sustaining the hegemonic field" (qtd. in Hesford, *Spectacular* 190). The privileged subject's compassion convinces him of the rightness of his authority, precluding awareness of his own benevolence as institutionally sanctioned imposition.[12]

Given David's willingness to listen with care to Raffi's testimony, *Ararat* might be seen as a call to witness for Western audiences unschooled in the history of Van. Nichanian has interpreted the film in precisely that way, hinting that it requires just what Raffi desires from David, and suggesting that Egoyan wants "the world" (with emphasis on the more economically empowered sectors of the globe) to witness (96). But if Egoyan were comfortable with a clear-cut appeal to witness, or happily identified with the discourse of proof, there would be little sense in the reflexive anxiety that *Ararat* displays. That he embeds Saroyan's epic within his own movie and throws the fictional director's rhetorical decisions into question implies Egoyan's hesitancy to condense genocidal history into a mimetic text. That hesitancy implies not just his awareness of the insufficiencies of representation, but his anticipation of what Gries portrays as the "becoming" and "transformation" of material rhetoric. Whereas the principle of becoming acknowledges "the opening up of events into an unknown future," the idea of rhetorical transformation captures the contradictory ways those events "materialize in differing spatiotemporal configurations" (*Still* 86). Egoyan has no way of controlling uptake, but by dramatizing the way David probes Raffi for his own purgative purposes, the director can at least build the critique of questionable reception into his argument. Insofar as Egoyan resists the conversion of mourning into a plea for validation from those who are distanced from genocidal history, he asserts *sotto voce* that certain listeners "mobilize meaning not to upend but reinforce relations of power" (Scott and Welch, "One" 565). To trouble those relations, he invites the audience's humility before the unknowable.

Such humility, however, does not mean rejecting memorial efforts that involve researched reenactment. When Harcourt counters Ani's criticisms of Saroyan with testaments to the bravery of the production, it suggests that Egoyan cannot dismiss entirely the aspirations of the film-within-the-film. Although the confrontations between Ali and Raffi, and between Raffi and David, suggest that Egoyan resents being implicated in the production of proof, the consequences of repression are at least as troubling. Egoyan's film contests the violence of repression while exemplifying the mediated mourning it attributes to its characters: it identifies itself with diasporic collectivism while expressing the elusive quality of that experience. The admission of failed identification does not imply futility, however, as the process of mourning contests the ongoing persecution that endeavors to erase its own trail. Whatever the flaws of a filmmaker's memorializing effort, they cannot compare with the violence of such erasure. Nichanian suggests that Egoyan confers authority on Turkish nationalist positions by dramatizing the frantic response to official denial. Yet we might also interpret the film as explicating how the Catastrophe perpetuates itself through state-sanctioned incredulity. Opening that disbelief to scrutiny, the film shares Nichanian's construction of the insatiate call to prove as part of a rhetorical strategy bent on "killing death."

To ask whether the film elicits identification with the pursuit of proof, or subjects that invitation to critical examination, is to attend to its rhetorical work. For Blakesley, to study movies as rhetoric is to recognize them as "acts that dramatize and interrogate the ways people use language and images to tell stories and foster identification" (*Terministic* 8). Not only do films tell stories, however; they at times perform apprehensive investigations of their own narrative techniques. And not only do they invite our emotional engagement; they question how audiovisual rhetoric elicits the sense of shared substance among characters or between audiences and onscreen phenomena. As supple as is Blakesley's definition of film rhetoric, I would layer its focus on instrumentality—on how people use multiple modes of communication to establish rapport with their addressees—with an emphasis on another of Burke's key terms: motive. The foregoing discussion, with its elaboration of the tension between embracing the spirit of truth and pursuing absolute accuracy, clarifies some of the motives that underlie those sensibilities. Saroyan's tendencies toward melodrama arise from devotion to his mother, and the liberties he takes bespeak an effort to capture her struggle, along with the suffering of an entire population, in the compressed space-time of a feature film. Ani's resistance to his liberties derives from dedication to her husband and to Gorky, both of whom bore the weight of the Armenian genocide long after the events in Van, and both of whose ghosts compel her toward painstaking historical recovery efforts. Saroyan's and Ani's projects interpellate Raffi in such a way that he defends both but commits to neither.

As Raffi experiences the conflict between the urgency and inadequacy of narrative, he becomes embroiled in a discourse that throws the validity of the Armenian genocide into turmoil. When his interrogator is the half-Turkish Ali, the discourse yields only the further entrenchment of warring positions. When his interlocutor is a Canadian customs official, the encounter allows that official to work through familial tensions far removed from those of Raffi and the post-exilic Armenian population. In both cases, the scene of rhetorical delivery subverts Raffi's aims, trumping his post-memorial motives with those of a more powerful addressee, and exemplifying Burke's fusion of the very idea of motive with material situation. Egoyan's *Ararat* constitutes a multimodal utterance that challenges both the imperious discourse of proof and the appropriation of Armenian history for private, unrelated ends, while at the same time remaining susceptible to both practices of reception. As with any utterance, reception cannot be determined in advance. But by dramatizing responses to Raffi's narrative, Egoyan provides a sampling of the interpretations he endeavors to guard against. The anticipatory quality of his film demonstrates how deeply mediated is the process of mourning, and how weighted with ethical consequence. It also shows how cinema, even as it "dramatize[s] and interrogate[s] the ways people use language and images" to "foster identification," invites attention to the longstanding divisions of power that inhabit the filmic interface.

CHAPTER 3

MATERIAL CORRESPONDENCES

WHETHER DESCRIBING the distillation of labor into commodities or the representation of affect through objects, Kenneth Burke regularly attends to the interlaced agencies of people and their surroundings, anticipating Latour's claim that "things do not exist without being full of people."[1] This chapter uncovers varied forms of identification between human and extrahuman materiality and thus builds on scholarship that links Burkean theories of consubstantiality to the rhetoric of film (Blakesley, *Terministic*; Oktay; Perez). The argument concentrates especially on Icíar Bollaín's *Even the Rain* (2010), a Spanish film that depicts the troubled production of a movie about Christopher Columbus's arrival in the so-called new world. Bollaín's picture depicts a fictional shoot in Cochabamba, where the crew draws on lush settings and inexpensive extras to evoke the historical period without recourse to computer-generated imagery. The attractions of the location fade, however, as the actors become embroiled in protests over the city's water policies. As skirmishes escalate into a full-scale water war, the fictive director who lauds indigenous opposition to the Spanish occupation comes to subordinate present-day protests to his artistic vision. Deriving in part from Howard Zinn's *A People's History of the United States*, *Even the*

Rain establishes relations of identification between gold, water, and film so as to connect modes of imperial violence across more than five centuries.[2] Bollaín both condemns that violence and undermines any sense of safe distance from it, for even as she distinguishes her methods from those of her invented filmmakers, her metafilm calls attention to its own set location, its own dependence on the labor of underpaid extras, its own consubstantiality with the object of critique.

To note likenesses between working conditions on the set of *Even the Rain* and the conditions the movie dramatizes is to evoke what Burke calls "ambiguities of substance." The word "substance" may "designate what a thing *is*," he writes, but it "derives from a word designating something that a thing *is not*. . . . Or otherwise put: the word in its etymological origins would refer to an attribute of the thing's *context*, since that which supports or underlies a thing would be a part of the thing's context" (*Grammar* 23). To describe the substance of a phenomenon is to deal, as Burke often does, with the interdependencies of distinction and concurrence, singularity and situational entanglement. Bollaín and her fictitious director Sebastián may be substantially joined in their renunciations of Columbus's conquest, but their shared substance does not imply sameness. She distances herself from the character, after all, by juxtaposing his affirmation of sixteenth-century indigenous resistance with his more limited concern for immediate public demonstrations in Cochabamba. Sebastián's movie exists both inside and outside Bollaín's, ambiguously serving as the guts of her production and the thing it defines itself against.

Attention to ambiguities of substance, while illuminating the relation between the metafilm and its nested counterpart, gives viewers a way to understand *Even the Rain*'s articulation of material phenomena across vast historical terrain. The coming argument establishes connections between *A Grammar of Motives*, *A Rhetoric of Motives*, and Gilberto Perez's "Toward a Rhetoric of Film: Identification and the Spectator," each of which addresses relations of consubstantiality not just between rhetors and audiences but between characters and the nonliving things that populate the narrative frame. The chapter then describes identifications between the things themselves, showing how those correspondences condense the argument of the text they inhabit. To posit "correspondence" between a terror-infused substance in the Age of Discovery, the substance of the water wars, and the substance of their cinematic representation honors the Burkean idea of ambiguity, implying likeness without unity and hinting at dialogue between extrahuman phenomena. Such linkages, while distinct from those outlined by Burke and Perez, come to us similarly permeated by the social character of rhetorical exchange, and they remain every bit as grounded in living negotiation and struggle, compromise and conflict.

They remain grounded in labor that transpires amid conditions of coercion and desperate need. Recent materialist strains of rhetorical theory show varying degrees of interest in such labor, with some focusing on how the symbiotic work of human and other actants supports the emergence of viral rhetorics, and others investigating the modes of force and exploitation that attend rhetorical production. As Gries addresses actancy and virality, she connects production to "the techno-human labor involved in bringing a design into material construction" (*Still* 114). By framing work as a techno-human fusion, she asks us to understand the production of a film as an assemblage in which the audiovisual apparatus and the social collective coadapt and mutually transform. Sidney I. Dobrin shares her concern with collectivity, affirming how "posthumanist thinking acutely critiques any concept of the individual subject in light of numerous technologies, including informational and biological"; he further observes that "systems theories and complexity theories question the very possibility of an autonomous subject" (74). The various epistemologies that inform new materialism, then, proclaim the dissolution of the isolated rhetor amid the processes of machine innovation and ideological interpellation. Those ways of knowing would seem, at first encounter, to recognize the entangling of social power with the vitality of things. They would seem to concede that any techno-human rhetoric, however it streams through complex systems, has a genealogy of contending bodies.

Yet certain varieties of posthumanism tend to repress those genealogies. Dobrin, for example, gives limited attention to what he terms "activist perspectives" on the history of subjectivity, claiming that "the metaphor of power carries entirely too much baggage to be of any real use in describing the posthuman world" (76, 89). He acknowledges that the theoretical evacuation of subjectivity has uneven consequences, as some forms of embodiment have long struggled to garner the benefits associated with the concept and others have assumed those benefits as a right. *Even the Rain* brings those struggles painfully into view, specifying the ongoing inequities that Dobrin deems the concerns of a bygone period. Citing Cary Wolfe, Dobrin explains that "it is not as though we have much choice about becoming posthuman; it is upon us" (76). Rather than viewing the analysis of power as the collateral damage of a posthumanist juggernaut, however, we might ask how forms of domination and subordination continue to express themselves through the emergence of compound assemblages; further, we might consider how the drift of vibrant materiality carries forms of avarice and violence, as well as collective pursuits of dignity and decency, that have not recently come "upon us" but have intricate histories. With its articulation of people-infused things and object-laden subjects, *Even the Rain* adopts those very lines of inquiry. In so doing, it participates in a project Dobrin appreciates, despite his dismissal of the metaphor of power: N. Katherine Hayles's critique of "the very idea that information can lose its body."[3] While Hayles conveys how rhetoric, no matter how seemingly ephemeral, depends on material delivery systems, reflexive materialism identifies those systems with neoliberal ideology and global capitalism. As Bollaín and crew visualize examples of such identification, linking them to older instances of imperialist economics, they enact reflexive materialism as a composing praxis.

Cogent as is their film's association of substances, such associations nevertheless risk undercutting audience identification with the picture's political project. With such risks in mind, the argument concludes by addressing the objection that the contexts are too divergent, too particular and nuanced, to allow for parallels. Such evaluations have a degree of validity, though they tend to interpret the conceptual overlap between substances as too perfect rather than partial and ambiguous. Critical emphasis on the movie's contrivances deemphasizes its self-consciousness, for at the very moment the text most powerfully fuses the narratives of Columbus's brutality, the water wars, and the exploitation of film workers, Bollaín calls attention to *Even the Rain* as a dream structure—and one that undercompensates indigenous workers even as it censures such practices. Although Bollaín claims that her crew showed more labor consciousness than her fictional producer, she expresses concern about the formation of onset classes and the difficulty of avoiding them (DP/30). If the imagined filmmakers constituted straightforward scapegoats, viewers could leave the experience feeling cleansed of the bad faith the film depicts. But *Even the Rain* provides no such comfort, insinuating instead the audience's complicity with the power displayed onscreen. Visceral reaction to that insinuation may explain the impulse to resist the film, to seek sure division from a thing that identifies itself with us.

THE HEAVENS WEEP

However persistently we posit divisions between people and our object context, seemingly inert phenomena express consubstantiality with human labor and social interplay. Burke addresses such consubstantiality while reflecting on the ethics of Karl Marx's historical materialism, contending that

> precisely where Marxism is most often damned as *materialistic*, is precisely where it is most characteristically idealistic. Marx's most imaginative criticism is directed against the false idealism derived from the concealed protection of materialistic interests. His chapter on "The Fetishism of Commodities and the Secret Thereof" shows how the human personality itself comes to be conceived in the abstract terms of impersonal commodities. And the whole purpose of such materialist criticism is to bring about such material conditions as are thought capable of releasing men from their false bondage to materials. (*Grammar* 214)

Burke suggests that where Marx demonstrates the identification of life with profit-generating mechanism, he engages in resolutely ethical inquiry, discrediting the logic of capitalism by describing its operations in "materialistic" fashion. *Capital* details a system wherein those who control the means of production become dependent on those means, and those who labor for the overclass find themselves fastened to—worse yet, reduced to—machinery. In Burke's view, materialist criticism aims to disrupt these modes of consubstantiality by investigating their historical concealment. Such materialism contrasts sharply with forms that disregard "the *physical* body that labors within the global economy" (Scott and Welch, "One" 567). Whereas recent theoretical trends address the vigor of nonhuman things, Burke's invocation of Marx aligns with the perspective of Scott and Welch, who critique the reduction of bodies to moving parts.

They concentrate not just on the treatment of wage earners as objects but also on the identification of labor with the commodity form. Framing commodification as a type of identification requires recognizing what Yakut Oktay describes as the "flexibility" of Burke's theory, its capacity to illuminate rhetorical transactions that transpire not only in words but also "beyond language." Those transactions occur through the profit-driven motions of bodies as much as through verbal discourse or deliberate acts of persuasion. The commodity at once concretizes labor's output and represents the expropriation of that output from the subjects who produce it. Barry L. Padgett describes this expropriation as "the alienation of the laborer into the product" (7). The estranged object expresses consubstantiality with its maker, simultaneously embodying the worker's creativity and marking a separation from it. Hardly just a signal of individualized alienation, however, objectified labor condenses what Harry Cleaver calls "a set of power relations" that pervades social experience under capitalism (83). Those relations involve an apparent interdependence between subjects who control the means of production and subjects who activate those means—a perceived co-reliance accompanied by various historical antipathies, most prominently between managers and employees but also amid the strata of the rank and file. When *A Grammar of Motives* addresses the commodification of workers, it contests forms of value that are shot through with those modes of antipathy, and it defies the "set of power relations" that systematic self-estrangement sustains.

Whereas *Grammar* briefly addresses the transfiguration of social processes into commodities, *A Rhetoric of Motives* addresses the identification of people and things by examining how affect installs itself in the surround. To illustrate such identification, he imagines a novelist who, "ending on the death of his heroine, might picture the hero walking silently in the rain. No weeping here. Rather stark 'understatement.' Or look again, and do you not find that the very heavens are weeping in his behalf?" (326). However prosaic the homology between setting and a character's action, Burke memorably identifies the animate with the inanimate, carrying forward from *Grammar* the idea of a scene-act ratio. If we accept the (con)fusion of scene and act without recognizing it as one, the acceptance likely stems from our recurrent exposure to the metonymies of popular fiction, whether novelistic or cinematic.

Inventive filmmakers sometimes rely on these metonymies to unsettle viewers' assumptions. In "Toward a Rhetoric of Film," Perez locates such techniques in the films of Carl Theodor Dreyer, who gives viewers false comfort by associating characters with the fecundity of their surroundings. "Young lovers are shown walking in a meadow," writes Perez, "with flowers around them, trees, a sunny sky with a few puffy white clouds, maybe a river softly flowing in the distance. This is of course a romantic cliché. The young lovers are being *identified* with nature." In Dreyer's *Day of Wrath* (1943), the sanguine coding of nature soon gives way to tones of reproof, as the film introduces attitudes that prevailed centuries before:

> Set in seventeenth-century Denmark, the film takes us back into a Lutheran society that looked upon nature as dangerously pagan, a realm where witches roam and the devil lurks. We heirs of romanticism may admire and embrace nature, but those Lutherans would keep it at arm's length. Set in seventeenth-century Denmark but of course aimed at us who take a different view, *Day of Wrath* does not make it easy for us to decide (as Arthur Miller does in *The Crucible*) that we are right and they were wrong. Dreyer

has cunningly, unsettlingly constructed his film around the split between these two different rhetorics of nature, these two different ideologies.

Although Dreyer's audience might interpret the narrative as validating modern perspectives, Perez finds only ambivalence in the picture, which gradually shows the "natural" lovers to be engaged in acts of betrayal and incest. When viewers identify with those figures early in the movie, they bring their social contexts into conversation with those of the characters and filmmakers, with results that are never certain and at times deeply disconcerting. Whatever the effects, to watch the production of consubstantiality between agents and scenes, persons and things, involves an overlap between the contexts of diegesis and reception, all of which occasionally feels more like a violent collision than a relaxed integration.

Perez locates such a collision in Martin Scorsese's *Taxi Driver* (1976), which presents audiences with a psychological portrait so intimate as to induce claustrophobia, hailing us as sympathetic spectators while repeatedly throwing our sympathies into question. The alternation of affinity and disgust exemplifies a Burkean ambiguity of substance, as the film produces repulsion in the attempt to establish relations of commonality. For Perez, this pattern helps clarify distinctions between identification and what Murray Smith calls "alignment" and "allegiance." Alignment "describes the process by which spectators are placed in relation to characters in terms of access to their actions and to what they know and feel," while allegiance signifies "approval, taking sides with the character in a moral sense, rooting for the hero against the villain."[4] Whereas Smith believes that the term "identification" conflates alignment and allegiance, and wishes to replace the category with more exacting concepts, Perez attributes to identification meanings that alignment and allegiance cannot encompass. Of *Taxi Driver* he writes that

> even though we don't approve [of Travis Bickle], even though we don't even like him, do we not in some significant way *identify* with him? How else to explain our response to that scene . . . in which Travis, having succeeded in getting Cybill Shepherd to go out with him, chooses to take her to a porno movie? We feel acute embarrassment. This may not be exactly what *he* feels, but surely we wouldn't be feeling it if we weren't putting ourselves in his place. We don't want to be in his place, we want to get out of there, but the film leaves us no choice, and it derives its peculiar impact from the way it puts us there.

That impact depends in part on similarities in diegetic context and context of reception. Many viewers feel the embarrassment that Travis would feel were he better attuned to his rhetorical situation, because we have been interpellated by social conventions he manages to miss. More salient still, we cringe also at how the scene identifies Travis with a particular kind of material culture, as manifested in the "blue movie" house as well as the glimpses and muffled sounds of the offending film. Betsy bolts for the door not just in response to Travis's violation of social expectation, but because the film implies his intentions toward her, regardless of whether he would claim those intentions himself. Just as Dreyer's lovers become linked to nature in *Day of Wrath*, Bickle becomes identified with his surroundings in ways not easy to escape, no matter his readiness to apologize or eagerness to try another approach. In an ironic turn that contradicts his longing for a "real rain" to cleanse New York of its seedier element, the mise-en-scène of Travis's failed date embodies the vice he wishes to eliminate.

Whether figuring mise-en-scène in terms of a scene-act ratio—"the heavens weep"—or tracking the objectification of labor, Burke's theory of rhetoric involves dialogic relations between the human and extrahuman. What we encounter less frequently in Burke's work, and what will prove key to our analysis of *Even the Rain*, is consubstantiality among nonhuman objects in the diegesis. Throughout Bollaín's film, those objects express hierarchical social relations that are maintained by violence, the threat of violence, or what amounts to the same thing, the threat of resource withdrawal. Various people in *Even the Rain* decry one type of violence while performing another, giving the audience few characters with whom to ally themselves. Even if those audiences identify at first with what Burke terms the "orientation" of key figures (*Permanence* 21), we may balk when a wider view of those figures' circumstances contradicts their previously clear-cut politics. Such contradictions arise as the film frames multiple perspectives, including those of the fictional producer and director, the indigenous actors and those who hail from outside Cochabamba, the documentarian who covers the making of the biopic, the fictional Arawaks, as well as Columbus and his crew. Those perspectives all involve an orientation toward one or more of *Even the Rain*'s focal substances, though the movie destabilizes the audience's allegiance to any single standpoint. Once we identify with the critique of one substance and its concomitant social relations, we subsequently find ourselves identified with another, similarly vexed thing. The consubstantiality of things draws viewers into a process of what Perez terms "comparative ideology," a juxtaposition of contexts wherein we fuse historical analysis with critical self-consciousness, and in which we stand implicated by Gael García Bernal's reflection on the film: "In Latin America this is nothing new. This is where we come from. This New World emerged from terrible violence and ambition, which led to what we have now" (Santaolalla 202).

To suggest that Columbus's conquests gave way to contemporary forms of violence does not entail an equation of disparate historical periods. The substantial linkage of objects—and here we should remember Burke's idea of substance as ambiguous, evoking both the object and its exterior—involves acknowledging their difference as well as their likeness. Honoring such ambiguity, the next section details correspondences between substances in three different scenes. It begins by describing a segment of Sebastián's film in which the Spanish occupiers force indigenous people to pan for gold as a tax to the crown, and it focuses on the water-drenched quality of the ensuing drama. It then addresses scenes immediately before and after the panning sequence—one in which the fictional producer Costa depicts his extras as inexpensive materials and another in which Antón, who plays Columbus, alerts one of the actors to the division of labor that makes the movie possible. In specifying correspondences between substances, the three scenes set up a metacinematic dialogue between histories of "terrible violence and ambition," accentuating not their interchangeability but their resemblance.

CORRESPONDING SUBSTANCES

A key scene in Sebastián's film begins with Columbus's "Indians" immersed in water, panning for gold. A lineup of indigenous people stands just off the riverbank, presenting small globes of gold dust to agents of the Spanish crown. The agents evaluate each offering, and if one does not meet the expected weight, they send its purveyor into the forest to be clipped. The lens tightens focus, bringing into view the worried expression of a girl as she reaches the front of the line. Her father, who proceeds alongside her, finds himself quickly caught in debate over whether his offering achieves the standard. The Spanish agents decide that the globe is slightly under weight, and so apprehend him for punishment. The girl pleads for mercy as they drag her father toward the woods, his feet splashing in slow motion through pools of water that have gathered by the river. Columbus arrives on horseback as her cries reach frantic pitch, and he gazes on the bloodstained block reserved for the day's tax evaders. The men turn to him for instruction; he nods. We see the father's wrist laid out on the block, the fall of the ax. We hear his agony as the camera locks on his daughter's face.

The scene entails a variation on Zinn's *People's History*, which attributes similar circumstances to Columbus's second expedition, in which his crew enslaved people from various Caribbean islands and made concentrated efforts to gather gold in Haiti. Intent on paying back the investors who financed the "seventeen ships and more than twelve hundred men" he brought with him, Columbus established an efficient way to motivate his workers:

> In the province of Cicao on Haiti, where he and his men imagined huge gold fields to exist, they ordered all persons fourteen years or older to collect a certain quantity of gold every three months. When they brought it, they were given copper tokens to hang around their necks. Indians found without a copper token had their hands cut off and bled to death. (Zinn 4)

The trinket that designates forced compliance in Zinn's history becomes the vessel that contains the ritual offering in *Even the Rain*. Whether designated by a copper ornament or gathered in a locket, the gold remains soaked in social relations marked by national sponsorship of theft, slavery, and wholesale slaughter of native populations, much of it undertaken in the name of Christian progress. Burkean thought holds relevance to that history insofar as he tracks the accumulation of meanings in the extrahuman; to use Rickert's formulation in *Ambient Rhetoric*, Burke "advocates seeing how social drama plays through material things" (208). Although Rickert resists the symbol-using subject/inanimate object dichotomy that often informs Burke's considerations of thing-rhetoric, the idea that motive and orientation inhere in objects and environments rather than psychology constitutes an advance in theorizing communicative ecology. Zinn's book and Bollaín's movie work in different ways not just to dramatize the pursuit of a fetishized substance, but to accentuate how that substance mediates the drama that plays through it.

As *Even the Rain* examines that drama, the extras who perform in Sebastián's production find their own natural resources appropriated by outsiders claiming interest in local progress. Although Sebastián regards the extras' troubles as insignificant by comparison to the Columbus story, the prominence of water in the lineup scene connotes its correspondence with the gold of past epochs. His orientation renders him insensitive to that correspondence, but the interplay of metafilm and interior film brings the identification of substances powerfully into view—or, to make further use of the Burkean lexicon, as audiences perceive the shifting "circumference" of Sebastián's project from a conflict-ridden Haiti to the violence occurring near the film shoot, *Even the Rain* invites us to compare the substances that motivate the struggles.[5] Once early sequences in *Even the Rain* alert audiences to the privatization of water in Cochabamba, we bring that awareness to later depictions of Discovery-era violence: indigenous people panning for gold in a flowing stream, and the raucous splashing that attends the journey to the chopping block, strengthen the film's already pronounced connection between Zinn's "history from below" and contemporary forms of exploitation.

Those forms of exploitation in *Even the Rain* have their corollary in the actual Bolivian water wars, which occurred a decade before the release of Bollaín's picture. Fabrizio Cilento explains that in the late 1990s, Bolivia entered into an agreement with Aguas del Tunari, which generated "a 300% rise in consumer charges" and forced many people to spend "one-third of their income on water" (248). The price increases, along with resentment that a public utility—even the rain—could be so shamelessly commodified, led to an uprising devoted to nullifying the contract. The protests built on previously established resistance to Bolivia's Law 2029, a statute that affords external organizations rights to supply water "to centers of population with more than 10,000 inhabitants" while demanding that "local organizations such as cooperatives or neighborhood associations" respect those agreements (Assies 17). When people refused to forgo their communal wells or subjugate the ritual value of water to exchange value, Aguas del Tunari manager Geoffrey Thorpe threatened to cut off the supply to all who would not pay (24). Outraged citizens soon occupied the Plaza and set up blockades, engaging in confrontations with troops intent on quelling the protest.[6] As the events drew international attention, the government felt pressure to reconsider Law 2029 as well as the troubled corporate contract. The protests resulted in a series of concessions that included the voiding of the Aguas del Tunari agreement, revisions to Law 2029, release of imprisoned dissenters, and financial remuneration for the wounded as well as the families of the slain (Assies 30).

By situating the Columbus biopic amid such turmoil, and accentuating the water motif of key scenes, Bollaín establishes historical juxtapositions akin to Perez's "comparative ideology." As the comparison unfolds, the correspondence between gold and water proves at once startlingly apt and necessarily imperfect. Cilento praises *Even the Rain*'s "confluence of temporalities," contending that the "short circuits" between historical periods imply a charged connection between "colonialism (what went wrong) and neocolonialism (what is wrong)" (247). In both periods, powerful emissaries appropriate the resources of the local community, exacting payment from the indigenous people in the form of labor or money. Justifying their actions as tending toward native betterment, the emissaries impose an idea of order first through the violence of hegemony and then through physical terror. The "terrible violence and ambition" of the early era, to return to Bernal's observation, prefigure "what we have now."

Still, those who recognize how gold and water correspond in the film will note significant dissimilarities as well. The process of identification, as Burke insists, presumes a state of difference. In "A Note on the Writing of *A Rhetoric of Motives*," Michael Feehan maintains that Burke's idea

> differs from some psychological theories of identification in rejecting the idea that identification involves a merger so complete that the separate identities dissolve into one. Burke's identification reaches toward consubstantiality not transubstantiality.

However evocative of earlier forms of oppression, the water wars were not transubstantial with those practices, and did not, for instance, involve the ritualized maiming of people for failing to honor the demands of an occupying force. To such distinctions we should also add the most obvious, geographical discrepancy: for although Cochabamba constitutes an inexpensive option for producing the picture, it differs dramatically from the areas where Columbus made his expeditions.

Bollaín emphasizes the problem by having María, who is making a documentary of Costa and Sebastián's production, question the venue: "We're in Bolivia. It doesn't make much sense. 7,500 feet above sea level, surrounded by mountains, and thousands of miles from the Caribbean." Sebastián echoes María's critique, playfully blaming Costa for privileging budgetary considerations over accuracy. Costa explains that if money were the primary concern, they would have shot the movie in English—to which Sebastián retorts, "Spaniards speak Spanish." Even as Sebastián affirms María's position, however, she insists on linguistic divisions that neither he nor his film acknowledges. "So Spaniards speak Spanish," she interjects with amusement, "and the Taínos that Columbus found speak Quechua?"[7] Offering a version of Ani's argument in *Ararat*, she suggests that artistic license contributes to widespread misunderstandings of epochal events, and offends the sensibilities of those who know better.

Costa finds María's critique unimpressive, as his film-producer orientation predisposes him toward realizing Sebastián's vision with the least possible expense. His perspective attains clarity in a moment that precedes the taxation scene, as he recounts during a phone conversation the advantages of working in Cochabamba. "Fucking great, man. It's cheaper to get a man to sit on a light stand than to buy a sandbag," he says. "Two fucking dollars a day and they feel like kings. Throw in some water pumps and give them some old trucks when you're done and ¡listo!, two hundred fucking extras." He delivers the soliloquy within earshot of Daniel, a would-be extra whose intensity on and off set catches Sebastián's attention and wins him the role of Hatuey, who leads a revolt against the Spanish invasion. Although Costa's monologue dominates the scene in aural terms, the camera concentrates on Daniel's reaction, featuring his face in medium close-up as Costa makes his call in the blurred background. Given that the call transpires in English, he presumes that Daniel will not understand. Once Costa finishes the conversation, he approaches the actor with Spanish words of congratulations for the scenes shot thus far. Daniel responds—in English—"Fucking great, man" before explaining in Spanish that "I worked in the States for two years in construction. I know the story." Having heard Costa reduce his coworkers to sandbags, he is in no mood for compliments.

Working in the United States taught Daniel both the English he would need to recognize Costa's insult and the tendency for foreign management to treat his people as interchangeable objects. A reflexive materialist approach to rhetoric locates that objectification within a history of neoliberal economic policies, many of which permit employers to cross borders in search of inexpensive labor, creating such difficult conditions in some countries that potential workers will themselves cross borders to seek other opportunities. In *Networking Arguments*, Rebecca Dingo associates neoliberalism with "the economic philosophy that markets will always regulate themselves," and the idea that "governments and policy makers ought to promote free market capitalism and strategies such as global trade."[8] But rather than being a purely economic value system, it also presumes to govern how people "ought to act" by prizing "entrepreneurship, competition, individual choice, self-interest, and self-empowerment" (10). Promoting what Victor Villanueva calls a "bootstraps" mentality, neoliberalism premises itself on such a fair distribution of resources that anyone who lives the system's values in earnest will flourish. It cannot account for people such as Daniel—a multilingual construction worker who also proves himself a talented actor—struggling to support his family despite his immense productivity. It overlooks the ways its own values permit the privatization of resources in ways that place Daniel and his community in a death grip. Although Daniel wants to distinguish Costa from those who disregard Cochabambans' humanity, the producer's phone call accords them the same disrespect as does Aguas del Tunari, and it reflects neoliberal principles at their most cynical.

Tracking those principles across national boundaries constitutes a crucial concern for scholars studying the spatiotemporal movement of rhetoric. Whereas new materialist scholarship follows the flow and transformation of rhetorical things across vast territories, reflexive materialism aligns with the sort of work Dingo performs when illustrating "a matrix of connections between people, nations, economies, and the textual practices" that accompany processes of globalization and uneven geographical development (12). Such materialism examines the ways this matrix condenses itself into commodity form, expresses itself as the exhaustion and undercompensation of workers, and stratifies power within and between nation-states, all while representing itself as a self-regulating market that rewards personal industry. As Dingo echoes Hesford's critique of rhetorical theories that concentrate on singular nation-states and ostensibly autonomous citizen-subjects, and lauds Eileen Schell's attention to "transnational flows of capital and people," she associates circulation not so much with the virality of the communicative object as with financial movements, police and military working in the service of neoliberal order, and collective subjects who find themselves dispossessed by that order.[9] *Even the Rain* visualizes all those forms of circulation. Through the juxtaposition of Costa's phone call with the taxation scene, Bollaín and crew locate their story and the conditions of film production amid transnational currents of wealth expropriation.

By situating concerns about film labor alongside scenes of violence against indigenous peoples, Bollaín broadens the correspondence between gold and water so that it includes Sebastián's movie. Coding film as yet another substance permeated by hierarchical social relations, *Even the Rain* addresses an issue that has received limited attention in the study of cinema and in movies themselves. Danae Clark specifies this inattention in *Negotiating Hollywood: The Cultural Politics of Actors' Labor,* encouraging scholars to consider moving pictures as "quantities of congealed labour time" (83). Such consideration breaks with conventional film criticism, which highlights the relationship between image and spectator rather than the work of making movies. Although Clark praises Richard Dyer's investigations of the star system, she regards his orientation as complicit with the corporate-capitalist ideology that obscures the work of people further down the compensation ladder (xii). Taking inspiration from Murray Ross's *Stars and Strikes,* Clark reorients readers toward film extras, who usually comprise the largest percentage of actor labor (19). She admits that such labor is difficult to examine given its often "sporadic" and "undocumented" character, but she also suggests that without creative efforts to address the problem, the study of film will persist in its attention to consumption of movies while maintaining a thin view of production (5).

Despite the force of her analysis, there is no need to cordon off film labor from audience engagement, as they both contribute to what Clark describes as the work of "cultural (re)production" (14). *Even the Rain* encourages us to bridge those modes of analysis by fostering identification with the film's self-consciousness about working conditions on the set. Antón, the veteran actor who plays Columbus, embodies that reflexive appeal. After watching rushes of the taxation scene, he praises Daniel's daughter Belén for her harrowing performance, hoping aloud that Costa is paying what her acting is worth.[10] She responds with pride that she receives "a lot more than the extras." Antón makes a show of being impressed and then tells her that he will make two million bolivianos, or approximately three hundred thousand dollars, for his part in the film. Without mockery or malice, he attempts to alter her orientation toward moviemaking by describing the stark inequalities of power and pay that it involves.

The same person who helps bring Sebastián's vision of systemic exploitation to the screen shows a cunning awareness of his own participation in such a system, and also orients the crew toward the paradox in which they are caught. Although Antón's alcoholism often muddies his perspective, he proves attuned to the historical homologies that arise while filming the biopic in Cochabamba. To identify with Antón is not merely to have a sympathetic reaction to a fictional persona but to experience, in Perez's sense, a convergence of ideologies once presumed discrete. As the upcoming section will show, some viewers refuse that convergence, resisting identification with what Amy Villarejo describes as the film's "project." For such viewers, the project of demonstrating consubstantiality across epochs looks too much like conflation.

LIKE A DREAM

Bollaín's rhetorical strategy generates multiple objections, though the present section focuses on just two. One concerns the ethics of history, the other the ethics of work. To say that *Even the Rain* is susceptible to the critiques or that it withstands them is to oversimplify the film's appeal. Bollaín anticipates the resistance, grants it validity, and in quiet ways, incorporates it into her argument. Whereas in some films those techniques reflect what Stam terms a "proleptic strategy" for disarming criticism, Bollaín aims instead to signal the sweep of the problems she poses while refusing to claim impunity.[11] She hints at discomfiting complicity with the very power relations she challenges; further, she implicates us in the film's tapestry of object associations. For no matter how critical our orientation toward the modes of identification the film depicts, she insinuates our immersion in the systems of oppression *Even the Rain* calls to mind. Rather than a polemic that purports to elude neoliberal economics, the picture enacts a form of inquiry that aims to historicize that reach, to juxtapose synchronic and diachronic modes of indigenous exploitation, and to stage a dialogue with perspectives that question the movie's ethical grounding.

The first objection to Bollaín's project concerns the narrative as a whole, though it typically concentrates on just one scene. The scene begins inside Sebastián's movie as Spanish soldiers once again round up Arawaks for punishment. As the soldiers tie the men to crosses, the camera lingers on Hatuey, who refuses a final blessing from an attending priest, proclaiming hatred for the Spanish god and Spanish greed as his captors light the pyre at his feet. The indigenous community then chants "Hatuey!" as he and twelve others slowly burn alive. The next shot focuses on Sebastián whisper-chanting Hatuey's name on a hillside overlooking the action. After an interval in which his voice mingles with those of the extras, he calls "Cut!" and applauds his crew.

As Daniel and the other actors disentangle themselves from their crosses, a police vehicle arrives. Officers apprehend Daniel and prepare to transport him to prison for participating in the water protests. But before the police can leave, the extras surround the vehicle. Wearing Arawak clothing, they flip the car and free Daniel. As the police emerge with guns drawn, Costa and Sebastián intervene to protect their investment. While Costa attempts to defuse the tension, a few extras surprise the officers by seizing their weapons, allowing Daniel to escape into the forest alongside a group of actor-activists. Dazzled by the "confluence of temporalities," and the speed with which the circumference of resistance expands before his eyes, Sebastián speaks once more in the reverent tones with which he chanted Hatuey's name: "It's like a dream," he says to Costa.

When the extras come to Daniel's aid, they do so not to defend the movie but to safeguard a leader in the fight against price hikes in public utilities.[12] While fusing narrative layers as powerfully as any sequence in the picture, the scene designates the identification of gold, water, and film as Daniel comes to embody the relations of exploitation embedded in each substance. Despite the summative character of the scene, some reviewers object to what they see as *Even the Rain*'s contrivances. Comparing Columbus-era atrocities to contemporary practices of corporate greed, or worse yet, the vicissitudes of filmmaking, seems to such viewers reductive.

Whereas Burke argues that any vocabulary for representing a phenomenon involves a necessary reduction, a coding of one thing in terms of another (*Grammar* 96), some terministic screens provoke controversy insofar as they elide historical distinctions. Dismissing the movie's "obvious parallelism" (Schenker) and "earnest didacticism" (Wheeler 246), critics oppose using the idea of imperialism to equate vastly different modes of exploitation. From such a perspective, Sebastián's assertion of the dreamlike quality of Daniel's escape looks especially suspect. If it signals the realization of Sebastián's fantasy, it illustrates his narcissism. If it connotes his surprise and disbelief, it suggests his obliviousness to parallels that critics like Schenker find all too obvious.

There is, however, another way to read the line that identifies Bollaín with her fictional director. Rather than expressing Sebastián's good fortune or bafflement, it may imply an awareness of the artificiality of the historical overlap. Given *Even the Rain*'s orientation toward film production, it may be that Sebastián lets slip not only his own anxiety about historical ethics but Bollaín's as well. To say that the intermingling of histories is like a dream is to reject their interchangeability, to assert the ambiguity of their connection. Without breaking the narrative spell, the line acknowledges that the train of material associations she has worked so hard to create is an evanescent projection, a fashioning of unity out of raw contingency.

But even if Bollaín's self-consciousness helps deflect the charge that she conflates disparate events, concerns about labor on her set remain. Duncan Wheeler, who distrusts the film's pedagogical "neatness," also questions the conditions of its production, holding that "any genuinely ethical appraisal of the film would have to look at concrete information about the treatment and payment of the indigenous cast and crew, examining how the Bolivian extras were treated" (251). In a note at the end of his chapter, Wheeler cites Bollaín's claim to have paid the extras twenty dollars a day (253). Unaware of Bollaín's disclosures about actor compensation, Roger Ebert states bluntly that he "looked in vain for a credit saying, 'No extras were underpaid in the making of this film.'" It seems that the subject matter of *Even the Rain* invites an assessment criterion that rarely figures into film reviews—and, as Clark shows in *Negotiating Hollywood*, one that receives little attention in film scholarship. And what's more, that criterion becomes the Burkean God principle by which to determine the ethics of the film's project.

But Bollaín's film never purports to embody a singular solution to the multiple problems it poses. Instead, it investigates the intersection of those problems, showing the critique of labor exploitation to have an elastic circumference, which frequently subsumes those who level the critique at others. Such an investigation does not suggest, however, the equivalence of each instance of such exploitation, nor does it indicate Bollaín's concession to inevitability. In an interview with DP/30, she claims to improve on the practices of her fictional filmmakers, yet remains uncertain about the extent of those improvements. While directing, she was conscious of differences in pay between actors, between Mexican and Spanish crewmembers, and between participants from Argentina and Bolivia, acknowledging that the distinctions held potential to create "classes" on the set (DP/30). Such class formations, she notes, are "very ugly." While supporting a spirit of mutual respect among workers, she found refreshing the requests of some Cochabamban participants not for individualized payment but for community enrichment. They wanted bricks and computers for their schools, basketball goals, trucks for transporting water, and direct payment to families for using their land (DP/30; Vitagraph). Bollaín and producer Juan Gordon accommodated such requests whenever possible, although she admits the imperfection of the result, saying that some people in the community may be "annoyed with us." *Even the Rain*'s intertexts stress the film's inability to solve the problems it poses, suggesting that the ethical tensions that infused the production process linger after the movie's release.

The interviews highlight the ambiguous relationship between Bollaín's metafilm and the interior movie, hinting that however critical she is of the biopic, it is substantially one with her own text. And here we must remember that substance, for Burke, designates the identity of a thing while gesturing toward its contextual basis, subverting the border between figure and ground. Once we acknowledge the ambiguity of substance that links Bollaín's and Sebastián's projects, her narrative depictions of filmmaking take on a disquieting quality. When we return, for example, to Costa's observation that it only takes water pumps and old trucks to buy two hundred extras, we may hear Bollaín questioning whether her own offering of trucks, bricks, and school materials to Cochabamban workers constitutes just payment. Granted, such payments came in direct response to local requests, but the worry remains that fulfilling those requests provides a cheap means to achieve grand scale. While we may, with momentary safety, distinguish between the producer who compares employees to sandbags and the director who dramatizes those attitudes, *Even the Rain* establishes a troubled identification between intra- and extradiegetic rhetors. That mode of identification becomes all the clearer when we learn of Bollaín's concerns about classes forming on the set. While her description of those concerns helps disclose the conditions of the film's production, it also provides a filter for interpreting the scene in which Antón alerts Belén to pay discrepancies between actors. In the ironic sequence that finds "Columbus" pointing out the injustice of naturalized inequality, we recognize an ugliness that Bollaín strives with limited success to avoid.

As the identification of substances reaches outside the diegesis to include Bollaín's text, it brings into question situations wherein resource-rich filmmakers address injustices in contexts distant from their own. For all Sebastián's anti-imperialist sentiments, he proves more oriented toward completing his project than ensuring the well-being of his actors. And Costa, though sensitive to the plight of Daniel and Belén, cannot commit to the long project of supporting their struggle for sovereignty. Admittedly, he helps save Belén during the demonstrations, and he later expresses respect for her father along with regret about leaving the country. But he leaves the country nonetheless, and only after intimating to Daniel that he will not return. During the taxi ride to the airport, he opens a gift from Daniel—a lovingly wrapped vial of water—and gazes into the Cochabamban streets as the bustle of commerce supplants the protests. We share his perspective as the city and its people fade. Although his shift in orientation reverses that of Sebastián by moving from self-concern to compassionate action, the conjoining of verbal and visual rhetoric at the movie's conclusion suggests that such compassion does not last: Costa and Daniel say not temporary but final good-byes; the image of the city flickers and decomposes.

The film's final dissolve merges long-established conventions of film form with a nuanced representation of affect. In one way, the decomposing image signals the conclusion of the narrative, transitioning into credits and then opening onto life beyond the screening space. But in another way, the dissolve corresponds with Costa's perspective, unfolding as multimodal commentary on his sensibilities at the story's end. To interpret those sensibilities, however, is anything but a straightforward endeavor. In *The Forms of the Affects,* Eugenie Brinkema observes a scholarly trend that opposes such interpretation, coding affect as a phenomenon that is irreducible to language. Taken though she is with the sophistication of that discourse, Brinkema sees in it a certain deferral of analytic opportunity. By dwelling on the material forms that affect takes, we gain insight into shared bodily intensities as well as cinematic politics, though the forms and insights bend inevitably toward "detours, departures, unpredictable wandering" (40). In the case of *Even the Rain,* the vanishing of the Cochabamba cityscape visualizes, among countless possibilities and erratic "foldings," the imminence of leaving the place behind (48). Costa grasps the tangible embodiment of Daniel's gratitude, but the car's motion and the corrosion of the optical field connote abandonment of Daniel's cause. In such ways cinema proffers affective rhetorics that are uncommon in other media, offering sensory textures that may not fully translate into words or disclose the interiority of some autonomous subject, but nevertheless demand explication.

Those textures at the close of Bollaín's movie indicate that the activism of well-meaning outsiders all too often proves fickle. But if the movie were merely an expression of *mea culpa,* it would hold limited interest, embodying the self-fulfilling rhetoric that declares intractable the very problems it articulates. Bollaín's movie suggests that those problems will not be resolved by cinematic narrative, and that they require dedicated attention rather than one-time address. Working in the vein of Haneke, she intimates that film may be better at posing problems than solving them. The film provides a visual corollary for Rai's contention that "simply recognizing material inequality (past or present) does nothing to rectify such inequality" (137). But it also intimates, through its critique of Sebastián's egoism and Costa's unsteadiness, that other approaches are possible; like Rai, Bollaín believes that infusing images of exploitation into "the social imagination is a critical foundation for the rhetorical invention of arguments and action geared toward addressing particularly pernicious systemic inequalities" (137). Inventive viewing treats the film as a catalyst to further action, generating not just creative ways of reading imagetext but strategies for ethical living in the wake of spectatorship. Those strategies will differ for different viewers, though as *Even the Rain* implies, dissident politics in the era of transnational capital requires a sturdy commitment to collective action. If we pick up Daniel's hint, we see that it also entails bodily and economic risk, and a willingness to subject the self to violence for the sake of communal justice.

Bollaín's film concedes that few people will choose that path, thus insinuating our consubstantiality with Costa. But assertions of shared substance, as Burke reminds us, occur within conditions of intersubjective difference. How, then, can we amplify such difference? How can we insist on the ambiguity of "substance"—a term that vacillates between identity and exteriority—and thus demonstrate that even as Bollaín's portrait of abandonment interpellates us, the correspondence is neither total nor inevitable? Whatever our answers to those questions, engagement with *Even the Rain* clarifies a profound if frequently overlooked dimension of metafilmic rhetoric: the inward turn reflects not solipsism but a summons to grapple with material circumstances that exceed the cinematic frame.

CHAPTER 4

SOUND AFFECT

VARIOUS FILMS involve a reflexive approach to aural rhetoric—Francis Ford Coppola's *The Conversation* (1974), for example, with its depiction of a paranoid sound technician; David Lynch's *Blue Velvet* (1986), as it burrows into the mystery of a severed ear; Lars von Trier's *Dancer in the Dark* (2000), with its infusion of Broadway-style musical numbers into harrowing naturalism. Such instances, so divergent in premise and style, share an interest in what Bump Halbritter describes in "Musical Rhetoric in Integrated-Media Composition" as "soundtrack as a semantic partner of the imagetrack, not a subordinate" (318–19). Like those films, Paul Thomas Anderson's *Magnolia* (1999) sets sound and image in a relation of mutuality rather than hierarchy, drawing attention to its sonic composition as aggressively as *The Conversation* and disrupting its realist conventions as boldly as *Dancer in the Dark*. And more than either film, *Magnolia* fuses sound and image in ways that reimagine the idea of narrative plausibility. At once a melodramatic narrative and a work of theory, it depicts a collective trauma that is so pervasive as to seem irreparable, and then insists through unlikely conjunctions of picture and sound that recovery is nonetheless possible.

As the film conveys the effects of child abuse on characters situated near Magnolia Boulevard in California's San Fernando Valley, it draws heavily on the songs of Aimee Mann to establish linkages between those characters. Early in the movie, Mann's reimagining of Harry Nilsson's "One" performs the Burkean work of positing a precarious unity among the Valley's inhabitants while also acknowledging their singularity, their knowledge that "one is the loneliest number that you'll ever do." Those inhabitants include Stanley and Donnie, both game show whiz kids who suffer the weight of exploitative parents. They also include Claudia and Frank, one carrying debilitating memories of being molested by her game show host father, the other scarred by his own father's abandonment of Frank's cancer-stricken mother. The Valley is also home to the fathers themselves, Jimmy and Earl, both dying of cancer decades after their initial misdeeds.[1] As the narrator explains, and as Mann's music reaffirms, "we may be through with the past, but the past ain't through with us." The songs "Momentum" and "Wise Up" constitute variations on that theme, though the interplay of the two pieces suggests a refusal to accept the condition of trauma as an inescapable repetition compulsion.

Undertaking a close examination of those pieces, the coming argument clarifies how they invite audience identification with characters as well as the affective circumstances that bind them. Those circumstances constitute the social drift and scatter of rhetoric, which according to Rai, must "live in bodies, vibrate between bodies" (6). Such affective connections resonate with particular energy in Mann's "Momentum," in which what vibrates between subjects is, ironically, a sense of immobility. The song seems at first to be an external comment on the film's sprawling portrayal of psychic injury, but proves to be aurally accessible to certain participants and may even be, to use Halbritter's idiom, the "soundtrack to their lives" (319). Such techniques become even more pronounced later in the movie, as the various characters sing sections of Mann's "Wise Up," a song that initially acts like background music and then becomes a theatrical showstopper wherein performers participate in a spatially distributed but emotionally coordinated chorus. The fusion of aural and visual rhetoric in such scenes communicates what Micciche regards as the "stickiness" of emotion (1), the psychosocial linking up of subjects (and objects) as they share space and media, all the while catalyzing and constraining each other's embodied identity performances. By breaching the boundary between score and story-sound, "Momentum" and "Wise Up" suggest a stickiness that extends beyond the filmic microcosm to include the audience, including viewers in the trauma space that permeates *Magnolia*.

To describe how *Magnolia*'s sound design identifies the narrative world with that of the viewer, this chapter examines film sounds within the storysphere, those outside it, and those that muddle the division. Robynn J. Stilwell describes that last category as "metadiegetic," framing such sounds as a form of "direct address" that seems to "spill out" from the screen and "envelop the audience, creating a particularly intense connection" (197). With such direct address in mind, late stages of the argument detail how *Magnolia* comments not just on its own aural techniques but also on the rhetorical capacities of the medium itself. When the movie most resolutely defies the logic of credibility, as with the clacking, thumping rain of frogs that heralds its conclusion, it confronts dismissive viewers with a similarly resolute credo: "But it did happen." In a picture that so fully catches audiences in the sticky rhetoric of trauma, the defiance of realist convention means wrangling with the idea of the possible, and more specific, the possibility of healing. Such healing, *Magnolia* suggests, requires attunement to the ambient environment—an attunement Rickert depicts as key to social coordination and transformation. The same ambient ecologies that communicate the affect of trauma also hold resources for change, which take sonic, visual, and kinetic form as they course through the multimodal culture that hails us as publics.

THE RHETORIC OF METADIEGETIC SOUND

Cinema's sonic track helps channel audiences' experience of movies by providing access to characters' sensory worlds, allowing us to hear a setting different from our own, or providing an aural filter for those characters and settings. Peter Verstraten's *Film Narratology* distinguishes between layers of aural rhetoric, describing sounds existing within the narrative sphere as "intradiegetic" and those outside it as "extradiegetic" (154–57). Such sounds may work in concert, as when beachgoers' intradiegetic shrieks confirm the threat of the extradiegetic, anxiety-ridden strings in *Jaws* (1975). Or the layers may work at cross-purposes, as when the romantic scoring of *Dressed to Kill* (1980) gives way to abrupt sounds of terror within the narrative domain. Among its many effects, extradiegetic sound may intensify our anticipation of screen events or set us up for surprise.

However the layers collaborate, they typically aim to deepen our participation in narrative progression, shoring up identification with the story world while suspending our sense of its artificiality. Anahid Kassabian delineates such effects in *Hearing Film*, claiming that "throughout the literature on how films engage viewers (or spectators or audiences) in identification processes, there is very little mention of music. And throughout the literature on film music, there is very little work on identification processes" (13). For both orientations, an attention to the rhetorical implications of intra- and extradiegetic sound layers might begin to supply the sought-after insights.

On occasion those layers encroach on each other's territory. "Music may seem extradiegetic," notes Verstraten, "until the camera pans to a character who is just turning off a record player at the moment the music stops" (155). The transfer from one sonic layer to another may also work in the opposite direction, as music that begins in the narrative world transforms, sometimes mid-scene, into part of a film's score. Take the scene from the *Miller's Crossing* (1990) in which Leo, Albert Finney's inimitable crime lord, plays a recording of "Danny Boy" while reclining in bed with a cigar. As the record spins, he notices smoke rising through the floorboards, senses trouble downstairs, and prepares to defend himself. Assassins burst into the room to find Leo ducking under the bed, and before they can conclude their business he takes out one assailant's legs with a pistol. The other hitman thinks better of the encounter and backtracks, allowing Leo to swipe the downed man's tommy gun and slip out a window to the yard below. The camera goes with him. "Danny Boy" does not fade but rather swells as the remaining intruder gives away his position in an upstairs window, allowing Leo a clear line of fire. Leo then turns his weapon on the hapless getaway car, which crashes and explodes as the tune reaches its apex. By scene's end, Leo stands well clear of his house while the music continues as though he never left his bed. The shift from intradiegetic to extradiegetic rhetoric produces complex and contradictory effects: on one hand, the delicate, soaring melody proceeds in discordant counterpoint to the carnage that unfolds onscreen; on the other, the persistence of the song parallels Leo's unwavering cool, the subdued and terrifying efficacy with which he does his work.

As the song aligns with Leo's perspective, the music outside the house might well be the sound of his consciousness and thus intradiegetic all along. Yet, if what we perceive is Leo's memory of the tune, rather than something he literally hears during the gunfight, it places a strain on the very definition of intradiegetic sound. No one else in the narrative, after all, has access to his aural fantasy. Given that only the audience hears it in the strict sense, our analysis of the song finds itself pulled, if uncomfortably, back in the direction of the extradiegetic. Lest we imagine *Miller's Crossing* to be anomalous, Stilwell frames such sonic confusion as a common feature of film narrative. Finding examples in *King Kong* (1933), *The Killing Fields* (1984), *The Winter Guest* (1997), *The Insider* (1999), and *The Silence of the Lambs* (1991), she and her collaborator Jim Buhler note such frequent ambiguity between intra- and extradiegetic music that they require a new term to describe the "fantastical gap" between story-sound and score. This gap they term "metadiegetic."[2]

Among Stilwell's examples, the most memorable comes from *Manhunter* (1986), in which sonic cues signal the troubled identification of its detective protagonist with the serial killer he pursues. In a twelve-minute sequence near the film's end, the killer Francis Dollarhyde plays "Inna-Gadda-Da-Vida" on the stereo as he prepares to slay his victim, while the same song accompanies detective Will Graham's movements as he nears Dollarhyde's home. At the song's climactic moment, Graham hurls himself through the killer's window to stop the murder, which Stilwell interprets as bursting "through the glass wall between nondiegetic and diegetic, into the red dragon's metadiegetic lair" (199). Clever as is Stilwell's phrasing, the properly metadiegetic moments precede the shattering glass, occurring most powerfully during Graham's perspective shot as he closes in on the criminal. Only when he breaks through the window do the men coexist in intradiegetic sound space.

Whereas for Stilwell the liminal territory between story-sound and score constitutes the domain of metadiegetic aurality, metadiegesis also refers to a rhetorical register that expresses self-consciousness about the narrative from which it emanates. As "Inna-Gadda-Da-Vida" serves both as the literal accompaniment to Dollarhyde's ritual and the aural overlay for Graham's approach, it provides commentary on the power of sound to signify character convergence: detective and killer identify with the same tune, suggesting to the audience that catching a predator means becoming one, and worse yet, becoming immersed in his ways of planning and perceiving. By using sound to establish perspectival overlap between subjects while demonstrating reflexive awareness of that technique, *Manhunter* features the kind of aural rhetoric that occurs in more intricate ways in *Magnolia*. *Magnolia*'s sound structure clarifies the affect that binds seemingly dissimilar inhabitants of the San Fernando Valley, most of whose self-destructive behavior stems from relations of abuse and abandonment forged between parents and children well before the narrative.[3]

THE STICKINESS OF FEELING STUCK

Like many of Mann's songs, "Momentum" concerns the ways people's rote behaviors provide ways of coping with disappointment and heartbreak.

Fusing a whimsical melody with the rhythms of driving rock, yet featuring lyrics that range from exasperation to outright despair, it enacts the same condition it describes. In a nicely representative passage we encounter the narrator's central problem: "I know life is getting shorter / I can't bring myself to set the scene / Even when it's approaching torture / I've got my routine." The interplay of musical form and lyrics demonstrates what Cynthia Selfe describes as "rhetorically based uses of sound as a composing modality" (643) as the electric guitar and horn-heavy instrumentation meld with Mann's wistful voice to conjure the lasting effects of trauma.

The tension between the words and the musical setting, and the appropriateness of their combination, generate a form of affect that enfolds every key player in Anderson's film.[4] Some of those players engage in revealing displays—performing tirades in bars and pharmacies, engaging in cathartic dialogue in restaurants, collapsing at a dying father's bedside after years of estrangement—but the film codes those displays as emanating not from the autonomous psyche but from a collective epistemology that refuses to distinguish between knowledge and feeling. That epistemology resonates with an idea of emotion as a distributed phenomenon: to draw on Micciche's language, emotion "emerges relationally, in encounters between people," developing *"between* bodies rather than residing in them" (13). The music of *Magnolia* insists on that relationality even when the characters seem unaware of it, and it thus serves as a "semantic partner" to an imagetrack that splices scenes according to emotional intensity rather than narrative progression.

The song begins in seemingly extradiegetic fashion as police officer Jim Kurring exits his squad car to check on a noise problem at a local apartment complex. The music continues as the scene cuts to Claudia Gator snorting cocaine from her coffee table. When the camera returns to Jim climbing the stairs of her apartment building, the song dampens considerably, signaling that the music that scores his approach is now coming from behind Claudia's door. "Momentum" does not merely accompany his investigation of a disturbance; the song is itself the disturbance. When Jim knocks, Claudia frantically hides the drugs while neglecting to turn down the stereo. After an interlude in which the camera visits other events unfolding through the Valley, it returns to Claudia's apartment, she opens the door, and "Momentum" engulfs Jim. As they struggle to communicate, Mann sings: "I can't confront the doubts I have / I can't admit that maybe the past was bad / and so for the sake of momentum / I'm condemning the future to death so it can match the past." The lyrics more obviously fit Claudia's condition than Jim's, but given that the song accompanies his movements before he reaches the door, the sequence of events identifies his situation with hers. Whereas "Momentum" seems at first to serve as narrative overlay, it works in another way as metadiegetic preparation for the film's assertion of consubstantiality between characters. It exists in the fantastical gap between the story world and its exterior, and it alerts us to coming subversions of traditional categories of film sound.

While undermining the discreteness of those categories, "Momentum" exemplifies *Magnolia*'s penchant for associative rhetoric while enrolling the audience in the film's affective network. Micciche emphasizes the "stickiness" of such networks, which inform the dynamic relationships between people and their environment. Extending Ahmed's line of inquiry, Micciche holds that

> emotion resides in neither persons/objects nor the social world exclusively. Rather, emotion is dynamic and relational, taking form through collisions . . . between people as well as between people and the objects, narratives, beliefs, and so forth that we encounter in the world. (28)

"Momentum" expresses the affective field in which those collisions occur as well as the emotional performances they generate. Those performances arise in the encounters that constitute collectivity, and they interpellate and decenter subjects rather than belonging to them. Marie Thompson and Ian Biddle note the fluid character of the affective sphere in which such events unfold, but like Micciche, they also acknowledge the ways that affect can "stick" to subjects, informing the localized enactment of emotion. Drawing on work by Clare Hemmings, they attribute a dual meaning to "stick," tying it both to adherence and an inability to progress.[5] As "Momentum" draws Jim and Claudia together, it articulates the forms of corrosive routine that dominate their lives. The song, like much of *Magnolia,* is about the stickiness of feeling stuck. We first hear the song as extradiegetic music, assuming at the outset that the characters cannot hear what we hear. But as the film simultaneously locates the source of the sound in Claudia's apartment, it identifies her point of audition with ours.

It thus exemplifies the rhetorical condition Kassabian details in *Hearing Film,* where music invites identification with "fictional worlds by washing perceivers in [what Claudia Gorbman depicts as] a 'bath or gel of affect'" (Kassabian 113). That gel flows across diegetic registers, creating explicit attachments as well as unconscious affiliations between positions onscreen and off. Christina Lane observes how cinematography helps to reinforce those connections, and she uses the language of affect and music to describe the rhetorical effects: "The camera traverses time and space, yoking together protagonists and rolling like an emotional wave through each dramatic beat" (59). Tracking shots pull us in close to the characters so that "we are encouraged to identify with them" (59). As such shots synchronize with the soundtrack, visual and aural rhetorics collaborate to produce the sensory bath that brings audiences into proximity with fictional personas. As innocuous as a bath or gel might sound, however, *Magnolia*'s invitations to intimacy come suffused with grief. The affect that circulates throughout the narrative entails a stickiness that, given its association with broken relationships, may be harrowing or physically distressing for some viewers.

As the movie binds the audience to its rhetorical sphere via audiovisual cues, Anderson takes care to designate that sphere's winding complexity. For while "Momentum" directly accompanies the encounter between Claudia and Jim, an extended montage draws multiple narrative cords into the song's compass. As Jim becomes aggravated by Claudia's refusal to open the door, the song breaks off and the scene shifts to numerous events occurring at the same time. First, we visit Linda Partridge, who, after years of infidelity, falls profoundly in love with her husband Earl as he lies dying of cancer. Like Claudia, she "condemns the future to death" by numbing her pain with drugs. We next look in on Phil Parma, the nurse who cares for Earl, and who inadvertently discovers that his patient has a pseudo-celebrity son named Frank T. J. Mackey. As Claudia tries to hide her transgressions back at the apartment, Phil begins an investigative process that will bring Earl and his son together a final time. We next turn our attention to Frank, whose career consists of leading seminars for jilted men, teaching them techniques for luring women into commitment-free sex. Quiz kid Donnie, who also struggles with dysfunctional relationships, tries during the sequence to get the romantic attentions of a local bartender. Although Donnie's yearning gaze suggests his intensity of feeling, the bartender hardly notices him. Within the time that Jim waits at Claudia's door, Anderson gives us a montage of scenes that establish sticky relations among diverse characters caught in deadening routines.

Once we observe the characters' concurrent experiences, we return to the music of "Momentum" as Claudia makes adjustments to her apartment. Although we have been away from her stereo for more than eight minutes, the design of the visual sequence suggests not a departure from the song but an assertion of its descriptive range. Instead of one long-running piece that establishes identification between characters who occupy different spaces—as with "One" at the beginning of the film—"Momentum" provides a sonic frame for Anderson's interwoven subplots. It thereby corresponds with what Kassabian terms "mood music," though it shows affect to be dispersed rather than originating in the discrete subject. Kassabian tends to represent "mood" as autonomous experience yet hints at alternative possibilities:

> The very notion of mood music raises a difficult question: *whose* mood is being expressed? It may be a character in the scene, a character in the film but not in the scene (and who may or may not enter after the music has already begun), or another subjectivity altogether. (58–59)

The rhetoric of "Momentum" combines each of the scenarios Kassabian mentions: it signals Claudia's mood as she immerses herself in the music; it describes Jim's emotional situation both before and after he enters Claudia's apartment; and it designates a relation that encompasses "another subjectivity altogether"—namely, the dispersed subjectivity that permeates the narrative without the characters' conscious awareness.

"Momentum" thereby constitutes a focused expression of the rhetoric within which the assemblage of mini-narratives occurs. Framing rhetoric as the material condition for such an assemblage reaffirms the work of Rickert, who links rhetoric to the idea of ambience. "First," he explains,

> ambience is what surrounds us as material, spatial, and environmental. Second, it conveys our affective investment and emplacement within an environs. Third, ambience itself has a kind of agency, or more precisely, ambience connotes the dispersal and diffusion of agency. (*Ambient* 16)

Although Mann's "Momentum" differs from the soundscapes of Brian Eno, whose music Rickert privileges in *Ambient Rhetoric,* her songs do not merely accompany but help to constitute the surround for Claudia and her counterparts. They express the characters' affective relationships to each other and to the mise-en-scène, concentrating their social and geographical emplacement into aural form. That sonic rhetoric suggests the distribution of agency throughout the material field, amplifying the ways characters' ecology influences their presumed range of action—which is to suggest that ambience, while evoking the capillary diffusion of agency, also connotes the distribution of constraint.

"Momentum" captures not merely the stickiness of those constraints but rather how their constancy produces a paradoxical comfort, as with the consolations of old habits. Resonating in the gap between intradiegetic and extradiegetic sound, the song seems to "spill out" from the screen to "envelop the audience" in ways designated by Stilwell, destabilizing the boundary between the story world and the ambient situation of the spectator. By troubling that boundary, the film's aural design instantiates what Shannon Walters represents as a prominent feature of rhetoric in the Burkean sense. Diverging from ancient models that presume a discrete rhetor working to persuade an external audience, Burke's reformulation "merges the rhetor with the audience," rendering permeable "the line between the rhetor's body and the audience's bodies" (38–39). The audiovisual montage in *Magnolia* accentuates the porousness of bodies in ways that establish the collectivity of characters and viewers, transporting the story world's expressions of consubstantiality to the metadiegetic realm.

Such is not to suggest, however, that the film just transfers the soothing hum of stasis to the space of the viewer. On the contrary, *Magnolia* identifies itself with an affective condition that it takes to be already widespread among the film's viewer-listeners. In terms of the film's aural sequencing, the song is ours before it is Claudia's. In experiencing that song, we engage a voice that holds such prominence in the film, and that has such poetic significance, that Joanne Dillman describes it as a character in its own right (144)—a character who serves to concentrate the affective complex of *Magnolia* into sound.

Despite the sonic rhetoric of consubstantiality, Jim and Claudia's experience of connection constitutes an anomaly within a narrative that, until its final scenes, tends to dramatize missed chances for intimacy. Emanating at once from Claudia's room and the realm of the film score, the song "mimics, apes, or models the affective field in its non-locality" or, better still, multi-locality (Thompson and Biddle 16). Although not all of *Magnolia*'s key characters hear "Momentum," it gives form to their attachment, which becomes more pronounced when Mann's "Wise Up" plays later in the movie. Not only do the characters hear that song, they all sing along, fashioning a scattered unison from the ambient fund of rhetorical resources that resonates through the Valley. At that point, they most fully embody the "I-world" hybrid that Rickert depicts as the condition of communication; they most clearly manifest the "attunement," or resonance with social-material milieu, that *Magnolia* has theorized all along (*Ambient* xviii).

In the movement from "Momentum" to "Wise Up," however, *Magnolia* fashions a reflexive aurality that extends beyond the singular film-text to the medium of delivery. The next section suggests that as the narrative builds toward the choral sequence, it expresses a pronounced self-consciousness about audience expectations, at once articulating and flouting the idea of cinematic plausibility. Whereas "Wise Up" shares "Momentum's" penchant for metadiegesis, it also exemplifies metafilmic rhetoric, bringing into relief the social and psychological work that movies often perform.

THE FANTASY OF CHORAL ATTUNEMENT

Whereas "Momentum" merges up-tempo instrumentation with somber lyrics to evoke the stickiness of feeling stuck, "Wise Up" establishes a critical variation on the earlier theme: "It's not what you thought / when you first began it / You got what you want / you can hardly stand it, though / by now you know it's not going to stop / it's not going to stop / it's not going to stop 'til you wise up." The delicately chorded ballad extends the first song's sense of desperation, yet it embeds within its structure a plea to transform the situation. The song works both to designate the effects of trauma and refuse its totalizing power. Caruth frames trauma as a "psychic wound" that takes the subject unaware, generating tensions that at once demand attention and defy resolution. The simultaneous urgency of the problem and inability to solve it produce a repetition compulsion in the subject, who revisits the event(s) not only in dreams and involuntary physiological behaviors but also in social interactions and daily customs. Forceful as is Caruth's explanation, Wendy Hesford questions its insistence on repetition, suggesting that trauma theory thoroughly details the reproduction of violence while allowing little if any room for recovery. "Wise Up" advances a rhetoric of trauma that aligns with Caruth's *Unclaimed Experience* in accentuating how psychic violence expresses itself as sublime enigma. But like Hesford, Mann's narrator declines to linger in a state of aporia. The invitation to "Wise Up" suggests that the enigma of trauma, even if it does not yield satisfying answers, need not dominate the subject's life.

Magnolia's dramatis personae hear that call and articulate it for themselves by joining the chorus. Whereas Claudia introduces musical immersion by playing "Momentum" at high volume, the "Wise Up" sequence features the bulk of the cast responding to the sonic surround. As the film cuts from one musical phrase to another, each character takes a solo, bringing an abrupt if exhilarating peculiarity to a narrative that has, to that point, been poised between naturalism and melodrama. In postproduction commentary, Anderson owns the tonal shift: "I thought the best way to do that sequence was to have it creep up on you. . . . By the time it cuts to [Jimmy Gator], you've been hoodwinked into a musical number!" (qtd. in Lane 85). Although we might defend the realism of the scene by imagining the contributors to be singing along with the radio, such an interpretation falters when we concentrate on the details. The idea that everyone would tune in to the same station at the same moment presses the limits of plausibility; the idea that they would all be moved to sing is that much more difficult to believe. But even were we to accept those conditions as dramatic coincidence, there appears little realism in the suicidal, drug-addled Linda contributing a graceful phrase, and even less in the dying Earl taking what Lane calls the "song baton" (85). Given such absurdities, and recognizing that Anderson himself frames the sequence as a musical number, we must wonder what purposes the sequence serves beyond stylistic excess.

Excess may well characterize the scene, but the surfeit of style does not imply abandonment of the film's rhetorical principles. Verstraten suggests that extreme flourishes often forsake the narrative they accompany, and he notes that for David Bordwell and Kristin Thompson, lack of narrative justification for technique constitutes the very definition of excess (22, 196–97). Finding that definition too limiting, Verstraten argues that excess can serve significant narrative purposes, as when deliberately overwrought cinematography works to ironize a scene or plot. He takes Paul Schrader's *The Comfort of Strangers* as a case in point, claiming that its extravagant staging and "stately music" undermine its tale of masculine bravura and self-affirmation. *Magnolia*'s excesses, however, neither depart from the film's story of collective trauma nor invite us to distrust it. As figured in "Wise Up," those excesses enrich the film's affective rhetoric, augmenting the sense of emergency in the song's central plea.[6] They also jolt the viewer into alertness by breaking the "felt contract" of the genre, the association of such movies with specific sound composition.

Those associations come to advene in the field of reception as embodied responses "are triggered in many individuals over time," gradually becoming "linked to broader ideologies and salient rhetorical formations" (Rai 173). When Anderson incorporates deliberate excess into his composition, he inspires reactions that diverge from somatic custom, rendering us aware of both the variation and the norm. *Magnolia* thereby theorizes the rhetoric of sound in ways that diverge from much critical work on aural reflexivity in cinema. Stam, for instance, notes that sound "can be used to illusionist or anti-illusionist ends," either amplifying the "mimetic power of the medium" or working to "derealize" the image (260–61). Anderson's film forwards a third possibility by considering how a typically anti-illusionist technique—intercutting the audiovisual codes of melodrama with those of a musical—supports a kind of affective mimesis even as it defies narrative credibility.

Well before the musical number occurs, *Magnolia* prepares us to interpret excess not as irony or counter-narrative, but as evoking the intensity of lived experience. The film features a rhetorical refusal of realist conventions while insisting on its continuity with extrafilmic space. That insistence proceeds most explicitly in nurse Phil's attempts to reunite Earl with Frank by making a series of seemingly hopeless telephone calls. When Phil reaches a sales representative at Frank's business, he pleads for understanding in ways that destabilize the cinematic fourth wall:

> I know that I might sound ridiculous, like this is the scene in the movie where the guy's trying to get ahold of the long lost son, you know, but this is that scene. This is that scene. And I think they have those scenes in movies because they're true, you know, because they really happen. And you gotta believe me, this is really happening. I mean I can give you my number and you can go check with whoever you gotta check with and call me back but do not leave me hanging on this. . . . See, this is the scene in the movie where you help me out.

As Phil evokes the history of cinema as a way to persuade his correspondent to stay on the line, his monologue also constitutes a moment in which *Magnolia* reflects on its medium. At its most straightforward, the reflection asks that we forgive the scene its reproduction of an apparently exhausted trope. Rather than undercutting the would-be critic (Stam 155), it asks the audience to modify its ways of perceiving—to see the improbable not as something that divides the film world from the viewer but rather as a field of commonality. In "the scene in the movie where you help me out," the film identifies us with Phil's interlocutor, asking us to credit the fantasy of reconciliation.

Phil's soliloquy gives us a way to engage the "Wise Up" montage as a form of excess that intensifies the rhetoric of shared trauma. Like the speech, the montage proceeds in metadiegetic fashion in that it unfolds within the story world even as it offers critical commentary on that world, and like Phil's plea, it announces both its unlikeliness and its truth value. As the movie "hoodwinks us into a musical number," it asks that we accept not the verisimilitude of the sequence but the affective appropriateness of the song. It asks that we acknowledge, in Thompson and Biddle's phrasing, "the radical distributedness" of affect (16), and it encourages us to believe in psychological recovery through choral attunement. Such attunement evokes the material dimension of Burkean consubstantiality, the experience of mutual substance as shared perception. Walters stresses material mutuality in her engagement with *A Rhetoric of Motives*, reminding us that "Burke identifies the substances of identification that make two or more people 'consubstantial' as existing in 'common sensations, concepts, images, [and] attitudes,' which induce ways of *'acting-together'* among people" (40). This acting-together at once reaffirms the distribution of affect and enmeshes bodies in "a process of change and alteration" (40). For Claudia, Linda, and Jimmy, the efficacy of that process may be a question of survival.

For all Mann's invitations to "wise up," however, she offers no straightforward description of how to obtain such wisdom. The characters demonstrate rhetorical acumen by tuning into the same song, though there remains doubt as to whether they can make the change that song requests. "Wise Up" expresses the characters' intersubjectivity, though the visual framing and editing emphasize their continuing individuation. And though the piece evinces hope for reconciliation, its dominant musical theme demonstrates the compulsive behavior associated with the very condition the film addresses: each chorus repeats three times the despairing line "It's not going to stop" to a melody marked strongly by echoes and reiterations. Such representational practices invite audiences to identify with characters' sense of entrapment, their adherence to the experience of disaster and loss (Hesford, *Spectacular* 71). The song captures, through the tangling of form and topic, the stickiness of feeling stuck. Yet in its parallel emphasis on the urgency of transformation, it aligns with a dimension of Caruth's thinking that often goes unmentioned in scholarly assessments of *Unclaimed Experience*—her insistence on the therapeutic power of heeding the "plea of an other who is asking to be seen and heard," answering the "call by which the other commands us to awaken" (9). The "Wise Up" sequence connotes people's attunement to that call while refusing to assure us that characters will ever find each other. The possibility for encountering the "other" and even eroding the self/other dichotomy requires, it would seem, an additional catalyst. In keeping with *Magnolia*'s tendency toward a distinctly aural mode of reflexivity, that catalyst arrives with a thud, a screech, and then a sonic tempest.

"BUT IT DID HAPPEN"

> Rhetoric cannot be considered solely human doing.
> —Thomas Rickert, *Ambient Rhetoric* (xviii)

The sequence begins just after "Wise Up," with Jim driving the streets much as at the outset of "Momentum." We follow him through a commercial district in the evening, the camera occasionally scanning empty stores, advertisements, and street signs he passes. Just as he notices someone scaling an alleyway drainpipe, we glimpse a promotional sign with an improbable biblical reference: "Exodus 8:2." Before Jim can investigate the possible break-in, a frog crashes into his windshield with the force of a gunshot. He cries out in alarm, another frog hits the hood, and he brings the car to a shrieking stop. In the quiet that follows, he looks with puzzlement to the sky. Then begins a storm of frogs that will encompass more than six minutes of screen time while involving every major player in the drama.

That storm, which comes as an aural assault as much as an instance of magical realism, punctuates two of the ideas that arise from Mann's music: First, it lends explicit materiality to the concept of an affective field, bringing vitality to the intersubjective relation that Rickert frames as rhetoric. Second, it re-invokes the sense that recovery from psychic trauma, no matter how unlikely, is still possible—and still worth seeking even if the remedy is never total.

But to recognize how the frogs extend earlier lines of argument, we need first to address the reference to Exodus. In the New International Version of the Bible, the passage reads, "If you refuse to let them go, I will send a plague of frogs on your whole country." Although that warning has a particular urgency in the moments before the storm, repeat viewings of the film uncover varied allusions to the verse: 82 on the side of a plane that, while gathering river water to douse a forest fire, scoops up a scuba diver; the 8 and 2 that the diver/casino worker deals to a pilot/gambler in a flashback sequence; cords coiled into an 8 and 2 atop the roof from which a teenager leaps to his death, only to be shot by his mother on the way down; a weather forecast that designates, too specifically, an 82 percent chance of rain. "The frog rain's inevitability is continually forecast," Lane explains, "between the visual cracks of the mise-en-scène" (35). Many such cracks exist, with the numerical pattern establishing itself as early as the film's first minute. And most of the biblical references correspond with what the voice-over narrator calls "stories of coincidence, chance, and intersections and strange things told, and which is which, and who only knows? And we generally say, well, if that was in a movie I wouldn't believe it." Portents of a coming plague, then, accompany the film's invitations to expand the range of the plausible.

Although there are numerous ways to interpret the warning, we should remember that the frog rain follows the musical admonition to "wise up." That song gives us a way to read the conditional clause "If you refuse to let them go." Wising up means letting go of the sticky habits and coping mechanisms that only appear to alleviate suffering. Late in the film's third hour, people who are caught in the flow of momentum admit that they must get smarter, but most of them remain uncertain how to do so. And since they cannot let go of their fixations, the frogs come in torrents. But alarming as they are, they need not signify punishment. Even though Exodus depicts Moses warning Pharaoh that ongoing enslavement of the Israelites will trigger the wrath of God, the "plague" in *Magnolia* works instead as transformative intervention. During the storm, Jim forges a connection with the drainpipe-climbing "Quiz Kid" Donnie, who describes his psychological struggles for the officer and thereby manages to regain his dignity. During the same time frame, Claudia and her mother take comfort in each other, both recognizing how Jimmy's molestation of Claudia has thwarted the family's ability to communicate. Frank, who has long resented his father and stepmother, reunites with Earl at his deathbed and shows compassion for Linda after her attempted suicide. And Stanley, whose intellect has alienated him from his social and material environment, finds himself wondrously attuned to his surroundings.

As the frogs embody the bond by which Anderson identifies *Magnolia*'s ensemble, the storm ushers in mutuality that the characters have, to that point, mostly failed to achieve.[7] With a flood of percussive sound, the frogs help the characters hear the "call by which the other commands us to awaken" (Caruth 9). Lane suggests that as the camera visits each character one last time in the aftermath of the storm, the sequence *"feels* like a re-awakening." As several of the protagonists arise from a reclining position, they "appear to 'come to'" (104). There can be no guarantee that the wakefulness will last, but there at least exists the lesson that healing occurs in an emotional economy that develops between bodies rather than within them.

Insofar as the deluge jolts the characters into coordination, it yields another example of the rhetorical force of the material environment. To appreciate such force, Ehren Helmut Pflugfelder examines the writings of Latour, who has long factored the complexity of the surround into his conception of agency. Such agency arises from contact between human and nonhuman assemblages, among which Pflugfelder includes "animals, weather, political structures, institutions, ideological instantiations, laws, and other hybrid formations that exist in the 'parliament of things'" (117). The Exodus sequence in *Magnolia* renders hyperbolic the ways human and nonhuman animals find themselves thrown together by turbulent anomaly, facing pressure surges that none can predict or control. Those surges dislodge the human actants from the tedium of self-loathing, making plain their involvement in the parliament of things and contravening their sense of isolation. For most of them, the experience is terrifying. It exposes their vulnerability, interrupts their crises, and generally wrecks their plans. Yet it brings amazement to a world gone dull. And as the mesh of astonishment captures people ranged along Magnolia Boulevard, it once more transforms their separate time lines into synchrony, reaffirming the work begun in "Momentum" and continued in "Wise Up."

That rhetoric of convergence couples magical realist imagery with sonic excess. But as with earlier forms of excess, the aural intensity neither forsakes the narrative nor infuses it with irony; instead, it amplifies the idea of consubstantiality among characters to affirm the rhetorical work of Mann's songs. As frogs pound the streets, cause crashes and house fires, dive-bomb pools, shatter windows, and plummet through skylights, they trumpet the continuity of characters' seemingly separate story lines. If Mann's songs compose the "soundtrack to their lives," the hail of frogs constitutes the sound of their worlds colliding, revealing potentials to which they were not previously attuned.[8]

The film thereby attributes a therapeutic dimension to rhetorical attunement, locating prospects for addressing trauma not in autonomous will but in ambience. Rickert explains that

> in terms of materiality, ambience grants not just a greater but an interactive role to what we typically see as setting or context, foregrounding what is customarily background to rhetorical work and thereby making it material, complex, vital, and, in its own way, active. (*Ambient* xv)

Rickert disentangles communications ecologies from the idea of a discursive backdrop, suggesting that such phenomena constitute rhetoric in action. The technological apparatus, he argues, participates in discourse rather than only enabling it. For *Magnolia*'s ensemble, television constitutes the most prevalent expression of the apparatus, as the characters engage TV as producers, performers, spectators, and salesmen. Screens drone away in homes, bars, electronics stores, and green rooms. Frank Mackey's "Seduce and Destroy" advertisements, Earl Partridge's production company logo, and the pivotal "What Do Kids Know?" game show follow the characters through those spaces and many others. At times, television mediates powerful connections between characters, as when Claudia sobs after Stanley's breakdown and her father's heart attack occur on live TV.[9] At other times, print media help forge the connections, as Phil uses a pornographic magazine to find the phone number that will help reunite Earl with Frank. More subtly, Exodus 8:2 embeds itself throughout the Valley's visual culture. And as each character sings a few phrases of "Wise Up," radio asserts its continuing prevalence as a source of affective integration.[10] When the frogs arrive, they punctuate the already vital ambience that composes *Magnolia*'s rhetoric.

The frog rain thus represents affect as a decentralized locus of agency. By situating agency in social space, *Magnolia* shares some of the concerns Rickert articulates during his own analysis of film narrative. In *Ambient Rhetoric*, he examines Bryan Singer's *The Usual Suspects*, which exemplifies the power of the surround not merely to provide semiotic resources for human agents, but rather to join in discourse so as to transform the communicative situation. The film centers on detective Dave Kujan as he investigates the elusive Keyser Söze, largely by interrogating Söze's presumed accomplice, Verbal Kint. Through a combination of taunts and leading questions, Kujan insinuates that Kint has neither the boldness nor the intelligence to hide anything worth knowing. Although Kint acknowledges that disclosure may cost him his life, he provides what Kujan takes to be a thorough accounting of Söze's exploits. Shortly after Kujan releases Kint, however, he realizes that Verbal has cleverly synthesized the available means of persuasion in Kujan's workspace. In what Rickert calls

> a brilliant montage of panning and zoom shots depicting Kujan's sudden realization of the ruse while Verbal/Söze makes his getaway, the camera reveals that many of the names and events Verbal gives to Kujan in fact come from the bulletin board in the interrogation office, the desk, and even the manufacturer's name on the coffee cup Kujan uses. (96)

Lest we attribute the trick entirely to Söze's verbal dexterity, Rickert asks us to regard the room as intervening in the power relations that attend the interrogation. "The film suggests the office space itself to be a coinventor," he contends, as "the environment is always situating us in arrangements that simultaneously unleash some possibilities and foreclose on others" (*Ambient* 96). Amid this dialectic of unleashing and foreclosing possibilities, the very circumstances that temporarily entrap Söze provide the cues that enable his escape.

But *The Usual Suspects* still locates rhetorical efficacy primarily in the artistry of the human subject, the magic of the Verbal. *Magnolia* decenters the subject to a greater degree while attributing chief instances of discursive intervention to nonhuman agents. If one of Rickert's main interests lies in the dialogic activity of material ecology, and another in disarticulating rhetoric from liberal humanist models of discourse, *Magnolia* would seem to perform both kinds of work at once. Television, radio, urban advertisements, and magazines offer communication cords by which the characters might discover each other, but only some of those characters are sensitive enough to grasp them. When many of the signals go unheeded, a cataclysm comes whereby the environment's previously invitational rhetoric becomes imperative.

As relentless percussion enfolds the cast, two instances of metadiegetic rhetoric occur, one echoing the other. The first happens just after Claudia's mother races to her daughter's apartment, where they try to protect each other from apparent apocalypse. The camera pans from that embrace to a painting on Claudia's wall, then zooms toward an inscription at the base of the image: "But it did happen." The phrase exists in the liminal area between intradiegetic and extradiegetic space, serving at once as part of Claudia's décor and a comment on narrative credibility. Although that comment most obviously addresses the storm, its proximity to Claudia and Rose's embrace suggests a second, related referent. By affirming a seemingly miraculous event as well as reconciliation in the long aftermath of child abuse, the phrase invokes two versions of the same thing.

A second instance of metadiegetic rhetoric happens in the subsequent shot, which finds Stanley calmly sitting in the library, watching the downpour. "This happens," he says. "This is something that happens." Positioned throughout *Magnolia* as a prodigious intellect, and more important, a child who knows and remembers while adults flounder and repress, Stanley verifies what many others—including the film's audience—might think impossible.[11] Speaking at once to himself and to that audience, he validates the transformative agency of material rhetoric. With that act of recognition, the frogs cease their violent descent and begin instead to flutter to the ground, almost to hover, as if resisting the grim certainty of gravity.

That moment of magic, transpiring serenely at the culmination of a thunderous climax, recapitulates *Magnolia*'s defiance of the pull of trauma. As Stanley revels in the magic, his words recall Phil's metadiegetic assertion that "they have those scenes in movies because they're true, you know, because they really happen." And through that aural parallel—one that reaches back to enfold the discourse of the narrator, who assures us that "these strange things happen all the time"—we discover that the storm not only mediates psychic wounds, nor just attributes a certain truth value to the diegesis, but validates the medium itself as a means of intervention. By insisting on improbable reunions, and encounters where troubled people hear the "call by which the other commands us to awaken," *Magnolia* suggests that such things have happened before and can happen again. The film's metadiegetic reflection on plausibility thus doubles as a metafilmic rhetoric of possibility.

That rhetoric emanates at least as powerfully from the film's aural cues as from its visuals, supporting Halbritter's idea that the soundtrack is a "semantic partner of the imagetrack" rather than a subsidiary mode of communication. As a partner of the visual mode in *Magnolia*, the soundtrack frames ambience as especially noisy—pulsating, percussive, melodic. Whether in the cyclic rhythms of "Wise Up" or the splash and slap of an urban plague, it expresses an agency that exceeds and mediates the agency of the human actant. Although *Magnolia*'s idiom may differ from those of Halbritter and Rickert, the film shares their concerns, partnering sound with image in ways that dramatize how ambience permeates the rhetorical constitution of the social.

To posit shared concerns between a film and varied theorists of rhetoric is to designate film's power as an actant.[12] For even as *Magnolia* theorizes how radio, television, print, and public signs mediate affect, the film itself also participates in that mediation. Film exists as part of the communicative environment, constituting one small portion of the rhetoric that binds audiences as publics. It channels some of the emotional energy that flows between bodies, at once synthesizing prominent strains of feeling and introducing fresh complexities into the process. In ways subtle and overt, Anderson casts the film medium as fashioning collectives from an assortment of weak ties that include the human and the extrahuman. And *Magnolia*'s frame tale, which brings together chemists, killers, pilots, dealers, and alienated children, gestures toward a network of connections much larger than those in the Valley. In an inspired turn, the director films portions of that frame tale with a 1909 Pathé camera, indicating through his choice of technology (and the visual textures it creates) that the cinema's work as a bonding agent reaches back to its beginnings. Thus the metafilmic dimension of *Magnolia* expresses itself not only through characters slyly addressing the lens, or through the collision of classical and magical realisms; it inheres in the ninety-year-old mediator that works its way, against convention and expectation, into the production process.

By making its resistance to convention plain, the film teaches us how to engage with it, how to hear the harmonies between technical reflexivity and social theory. To revisit this chapter's examples, the metadiegetic rhetoric of "Momentum" and "Wise Up" prepares us to recognize the movie's most profoundly metafilmic moment, which situates cinema as part of the surround that mediates collective identity, asserting the possibility of recuperative mutuality despite the lingering effects of psychic violence.

As Alain Badiou observes, however, such mutuality exists "under threat," as projected unities verge always on flying apart.[13] As *Magnolia* theorizes film's relationship to trauma, it registers the uncertainty of its prescription. When, for example, Mann pleads in the final scene for someone to "Save me / from the ranks / of the freaks / who could never love anyone," the tune is so prevalent that we barely hear Jim making comforting promises to Claudia. Although we perceive only snatches of monologue, Claudia receives it in full clarity, smiling directly at the audience as if to invite confidence in her prospects as well as our own. Yet the smile, Élisabeth Boyer remarks, remains "haunted" by her addiction as well as "a kind of self-destructiveness, loneliness, suffering."[14] As the film suspends Claudia and Jim in the flow of Mann's song, it entangles us in the song's indeterminacy. But we must remember that their final encounter follows the film's most improbable sequence of all—an event that develops at the juncture of urban legend and miracle. That sequence, more than any in the narrative, exemplifies *Magnolia*'s defiance of the discourse of plausibility, its faith in "strange things" that "happen all the time." Through that faith it affirms the possibility, however remote, of a rhetoric that ruptures the play-loop of trauma.

CHAPTER 5

WITNESS

IN THE EARLY HOURS of January 1, 2009, officer Johannes Mehserle shot Oscar Grant in the back on a train platform at Oakland's Fruitvale Station. Grant died later that morning. Multiple camera phones captured Mehserle firing the shot as white officers pinned the twenty-two-year-old African American man to the concrete. The footage catalyzed protests that contributed to police dismissals and the resignation of the Bay Area Rapid Transit (BART) police chief. A jury assigned Mehserle a two-year prison term, though he only served one (Jones).

In 2013, film director Ryan Coogler released *Fruitvale Station*, a feature-length docufiction based on painstaking study of the amateur video, Grant's cell phone records, and interviews with his family (Labrecque). Coogler highlights the phone footage in the film's opening minutes, leaps backward to dramatize Grant's last day, and then re-creates the killing in the movie's final third. While jarring enough in its own right, the film stirred particular unrest for its intersections with the 2012 shooting of another unarmed African American youth, Trayvon Martin. His killer, neighborhood watch patrolman George Zimmerman, was exonerated on

July 13, 2013—one day after the New York premiere of Coogler's film and two weeks before its national release (J. Rhodes).

Some commentators note the film's capacity to "give context to the predicament in which Trayvon Martin found himself," while others observe the film distributor's propensity to exploit connections between the cases, and still others describe the convergence of the movie premiere and the Zimmerman verdict as "eerie" (Lee; Tatko-Peterson; Brooks). In the years since *Fruitvale Station* appeared, that convergence has lost its uncanny quality, as racist law enforcement has obtained immense prominence in the mediasphere. Rather than only reaching back to the Martin case, the movie feels predictive, even prophetic, in its attention to police brutality and the power of images to incite protest.

Yet the anticipatory quality of the film coexists with a reflexive rhetoric that calls attention to its own representational strategies. Where earlier films in this book exemplify metafilmic rhetoric by engaging in sardonic forms of audience address, portraying the process of moviemaking, or clouding the distinction between intradiegetic and extradiegetic sound, *Fruitvale Station* does so by establishing a mutually constitutive relationship between documentary and fictive narrative. Although it may not track the activities of film crews—as do *Ararat* and *Even the Rain*—it similarly exemplifies reflexive materialism as a composing practice, rendering in detail the concrete conditions of production for a brief but internationally significant documentary.

Merging documentary with imaginative reenactment, Coogler participates in a tradition that Gary D. Rhodes and John Parris Springer trace to the infancy of cinema. What they term "docufiction" includes such exemplars as *Life of an American Fireman* and *The Great Train Robbery* (both 1903), and has always included a metafilmic dimension. Stella Bruzzi clarifies that dimension by suggesting that "the spectator is not in need of signposts and inverted commas to understand that a documentary is a negotiation between reality on the one hand and image, interpretation and bias on the other" (qtd. in Green 72). To punctuate the point, Green contends that documentary is itself "a form of metatext" that permits us "to observe the world and the mediation of the world at once" (72). *Fruitvale Station* emphasizes the worldly urgency of resistance to police brutality by leading with cell phone video, but also suggests the partiality of that footage in the sense of its incompleteness and its perspectival character. The phone images underscore that character by including viewers of the shooting in the foreground of the mise-en-scène, many of them calling out for restraint and gasping in unison when Mehserle pulls the trigger. Inviting us to identify with that audience's experience of embodied panic, the film's early sequences persuade us to watch ourselves watching, to participate in a process of reflective witness whose ethical snares gain intricacy as the film shifts from documentary to fictive re-creation.

That shift amplifies the value of the camera footage by establishing the local backdrop for its creation while foreshadowing the familial and social consequences of the shooting. It also makes a forceful argument for the right to document police behavior. That right encompasses what Mirzoeff calls "the right to look," yet features optical perception as but one mode in the experience of embodied encounter. The following discussion of *Fruitvale Station* begins by situating the right to look amid other sensory claims, portraying confrontational politics as multimodal and physiologically distributed. While the film frames countersurveillance as a form of networked embodiment, it creates an effect akin to what Wendy Hesford terms "fissures" in the "observational gaze," or self-conscious moments that "give viewers an opportunity to think about their role as witnesses" (*Spectacular* 184–85). That orientation compels us to consider both the ethical demands that witnessing makes and the constraints on meeting those demands.

Such constraints recall Scott and Welch's Marxian materialism insofar as they are at once corporeal, technological, political, and historical. Docufiction may perform communicative work beyond anything its creators plan, but it never ranges entirely free of the body politics that accompany its making and reception. While new materialism concentrates on how image rhetoric spreads in rapid, wide-ranging, and unpredictable ways, reflexive materialist theory considers how that spread reinforces and expands inequalities of power and resources. It works to ensure that the fascination with virality, whether in citizen video or the creative variations of remix culture, does not displace an analytical, even activist orientation toward the social relations through which rhetoric circulates.

After showing how the movie exposes power relations and supports the audience's right to document them, this chapter suggests that recording the slaying of Oscar Grant means confronting the rhetorical reproduction of race in a purportedly postracial society.[1] The film locates wardens of the social order on a platform—the boarding area turned performance stage—and presents the repercussions of African American nonconformity to the will of whiteness. When bystanders raise their cameras, they destabilize a process that police attempt, sometimes with great violence, to cordon off and control.[2] In recounting the failure of that control, the movie questions how viewers participate in the reproduction of race and how we might intervene in its performance.

The chapter's final sections further dwell on audience intervention by addressing the film's reception, which, while generally laudatory, poses concerns about artistic license and market cooptation of the film's activist rhetoric. The sections suggest that docufictional re-creation, which necessarily fails to embody the substance of its subject, risks devolving into a rhetoric of "recreation," or entertaining diversion, that gestures toward social transformation while augmenting the prosperity of the film's distributor. In re-creating Grant's last day, Coogler gives us an intimate perspective on the man and his family while hinting that the perspective is always flawed, and thus deflects the idea that his narrative provides an untainted window on the past. *Fruitvale Station* amplifies its mediating role by making prominent use of over-the-shoulder tracking shots, at once aligning us with the standpoints of varied characters and keeping those characters in view as rhetorical constructs. Coogler also draws attention to mediation by taking liberties with the story, some of which elicit charges of melodramatic excess (Ryan; K. Smith, "*Fruitvale Station* Is Loose"). While his narrative choices deepen the urgency of reflective witness, they may inadvertently undermine the activist impulses the film aims to stir.

Those impulses may also subside when viewers discover the specifics of the film's marketing campaign, which encourages them to visit its social media platform and offers an American Express gift card to a winning participant (Brownell). In the monetization of social justice appeals, we encounter the slippage from politically charged re-creation to profitable recreation, and we thereby discover the readiness with which neoliberal rationality works to delimit civic intervention. We see the ways that multimodal composing, even as it invites reflection on the ethics of its circulation, can serve what Scott and Welch depict as "extradiscursive interests" for whom finance outweighs other concerns ("One" 566). Amid the swell of infotainment, the proliferation of such rationality suggests another territory on which the Oscar Grant and Trayvon Martin cases converge, and another way in which *Fruitvale Station* poses urgent problems for witnesses and social movement rhetors.

THE RIGHT TO DOCUMENT

The film opens by troubling the distinction between fictive and documentary rhetoric, juxtaposing dramatization with a limited rendering of the real. The movie's dialogue commences in darkness, with the voices of Michael B. Jordan (who plays Grant) and Melonie Diaz (playing his girlfriend, Sophina Mesa) conversing about New Year's resolutions. She swears to avoid carbohydrates; he plans to stop selling marijuana. Coogler cuts to footage of the actual Oscar Grant arguing with police on the station platform. The confrontation intensifies; officers shift from verbal to physical force, wrestling Grant to the concrete and kneeling on his neck. The crowd, which has expressed agitation throughout the scene, becomes frantic, some challenging the authority of the cops and others pleading for de-escalation. Grant writhes beneath the weight of the police as Mehserle rises and draws his weapon. A muffled pop breaks the din, followed by a pulse of silence, a collective intake of air. With the gasp the screen goes black, returning us to the visual space of Oscar and Sophina's resolutions and signaling sensory overload.

The cut to black fuses at least three material-discursive realms: the space of reenactment, the documentary space of shocked silence, and the realm of the extradiegetic audience.[3] In the intersection of the blackout and the gasp, there inheres the conundrum of interior and exterior addressees who find themselves positioned both as helpless and refusing helplessness. That problem stands among the more pressing paradoxes associated with the rhetoric of reflective witness. By situating international audiences as witnesses, Coogler's appropriation of the amateur images involves us in what many police authorities aim to conceal. After initially rejecting the idea of using the footage due to its ubiquity in Bay Area news, he decided it might educate a broader range of publics: "I knew that footage like the back of my hand," he says, "but more people from around the world had no idea about this story. It made sense for them to see that footage and see what happened to Oscar. . . . There's no CGI in that, in what they did to that young man. That's the real deal."[4] Coogler features the documentary images so as to invite "people from the around the world" to share the Fruitvale bystanders' contradictory sense of defenselessness and determination to intervene.

The exigency of that invitation attains more precision later in the film, as the re-creation of the platform melee shows police blocking the bystanders' view, snatching at their phones, and calling for the train to pull away. The scene coheres with what Mirzoeff exposes as centuries-old modes of subjection, which echo in officers' command to "move on, there's nothing to see here." "Only there is," Mirzoeff remarks, "and we know it and so do they" (1). *The Right to Look* insists that enacting the unauthorized gaze already constitutes a form of political resistance. The clip of citizen video, which emanates from an onlooker's perspective and includes onlookers in the frame, exemplifies such resistance while also raising the question of its transformative potential. *Fruitvale Station* honors those who take the risk of looking, though it hints that looking connotes an incipient rather than self-sufficient form of agency. A fixation on the apparatus of delivery and reception, Scott and Welch warn, may mean valuing "form," "speed," "reach," and the "idea" of engaged discourse over what the discourse expresses, and may thus divert "attention from substance to style" ("One" 564). When Mirzoeff defends the right to look, he does so not to praise the drift of visual ideas, but to oppose surveillance practices that serve the "extradiscursive interests" of whiteness, nationalism, and capital.

The sustainability of such opposition depends on the circulation of affect as a rhetorical resource. Rather than devising abstract reasons to resist the regime of visuality, the video shows how it feels to watch authoritarian violence, and how it feels when the aggressor attempts to deny others the right to look. Lilie Chouliaraki associates such production of feeling with citizen journalism, which participates in a "valorisation of ordinary witnessing." That witnessing juxtaposes the "empiricism of facts" with the "empiricism of emotion," she argues. Here "it is not the verification and analysis of sources but the immediacy of experience that counts as news—and it is this experience that now endows journalism with a new moralising force" (308). Drawing on the work of Chris Atton, she explains that whereas television news presumes a public "we" that is moved by rhetorics of objectivity, "the witnessing of post-television journalism constitutes its publics by claiming to be precisely that 'we': ordinary witnessing is about people who 'are being represented by themselves'" (308). Self-representation through witnessing does not involve the displacement of rationality by emotion, however, but rather contests the boundary between logical and affective persuasion. To register in our bones the injustice of Mehserle's act, and to resent officers' attempts to obscure the view, hardly constitute irrational responses to events on the Fruitvale platform. Those responses proceed in part from awareness of historical surveillance of African Americans, and from the lightning-quick recognition of causal incongruity—given that nothing Grant does merits such punishment. The screen blacks out at the moment of aporia: we have witnessed an event that defies explanation and one whose rationale is staggeringly plain. The idea that such witnessing could be ordinary, or that in recording the slaying we might "represent ourselves," only heightens the terror.

Documenting the event links the act of looking with a host of perceptual experiences, communicating an especially strong relationship between sound and affective intensity. We feel the crowd's anxiety in its pleading for fairness; we feel its shock with the gun's report. Most profoundly, we feel people's awe in the gasp that accompanies the blackout. That gasp invites what Steph Ceraso designates "multimodal listening"—the kind that ripples through the body while eluding, at least in part, governance by the analytical faculties. Ceraso codes sound as more than a "semiotic resource" (114), tying multimodal listening to Debra Hawhee's idea of a "mind-body complex," which "learns and moves in response to a situation rather than through the application of abstract principles" (Hawhee, *Bodily* 10). To assert the right to document, rather than just the right to look, is to recognize the embodiment of persuasion and assume the power to move an audience through corporeal address.

The shared inhalation in the video moves us toward identification with the platform bystanders. Intradiegetic sound fuses with extradiegesis in a space that neither fully owns; as with varied scenes in *Magnolia*, that space belongs to what Robynn Stilwell characterizes as "metadiegetic" aurality, which temporarily confuses score and character perception, tightening our relationship with character while drawing our attention to film as multimodal composition. It hails us as an audience caught in an affective swirl: astonishment before absurdity, frailty before armed power, and a rejection of both conditions. The intensity of that mix helps account for the video's rapid circulation, or what Gries depicts as the contagion of rhetoric once it taps into a well of feeling (*Still* 87). Viral documentary embodies affective identification, deriving its stickiness from sound as much as picture.

With *Fruitvale Station*, multimodal identification effaces the sense of safe distance that typically characterizes the viewing experience. It reminds us, in Emily Dianne Cram's words, of how "our bodies are vulnerable—to touch, to violence, to care, and to disgust" (430). It further reminds us that "collective witnessing begs a consideration of the ethical stakes of this public drama and how it is that we can live to be vulnerable with others as citizens." But as the metadiegetic gasp signals our exposure to the abuse of power, and the constraints on our capacity to resist, it also accentuates how some subjects are more susceptible to violation than others. The documentary's sonic rhetoric draws the audience into the scene, yet cannot proffer a trans-substantial relation with either Grant or the Fruitvale bystanders—which is to say, the film's sound demonstrates the dual role of mediation as at once connecting people and confirming their difference.

Mediation thus has affinities with Burkean identification, which describes common interest between subjects while acknowledging their material specificity. That experience of common interest occurs not always as intellectual realization but as bodily response, or to revisit Hawhee's *Moving Bodies*, "somatic" consubstantiality (117). Ceraso recognizes the uncertainty of such consubstantiality as she reflects on multimodal listening, suggesting that "a sound does not necessarily affect all bodies in the same way every time (or at all), and not all bodies experience sound similarly either" (115). The sound of the gunshot and the inhalation resonate differently for people gathered at Fruitvale Station, and that difference intersects with the racial and experiential backgrounds of the auditors. Those who have experienced the terror of racist policing firsthand will hear the sounds in ways unmatched by those who have not, and none of us can share the particularity of those sounds for the Grant family. A reflective approach to witnessing grants the political value of somatic consubstantiality while remaining alert to the violence of conflating perceptual knowledge.

The work of linking embodied experiences while maintaining their singularity does not end with witnessing, but extends to victims of police brutality on which *Fruitvale Station* implicitly comments. While the film's release eerily coincided with the Zimmerman decision, it also evokes the violence visited upon Rodney King, whose near-death experience was recorded more than a decade before the ubiquity of camera phones, and whose subsequent treatment by the justice system prompted mass demonstrations in Los Angeles. The film shares further commonalities with brutality cases that have transpired since its release, some of which include the manhandling and subsequent death of Sandra Bland, the strangling of Eric Garner, and the shootings of Tamir Rice, Walter Scott, Eric Harris, Samuel Dubose, Alton Sterling, and Philando Castile (to name only a few). In a turn of events at least as unsettling as the film's release date, the deputy who shot Harris used the same defense as Mehserle when accounting for his actions: he meant to grab his Taser but drew his sidearm instead. For all the prescience of his film, Coogler could not have foreseen the particularity of such cases.

As the somatic rhetoric of *Fruitvale Station* gains complexity in the years after its release, it supports Hariman and Lucaites's case that images participate in public discourse in ways their creators do not anticipate, thus exemplifying the new materialist emphasis on object agency. New materialist thinkers tend to imagine agency, to use Gries's terms, as "a distributed enactment of entangled things intra-acting with phenomena," producing transformations that cannot be traced to a single actor nor preemptively limited in their capacity to spark other changes in the communications ecology (*Still* 6, 78). *Fruitvale Station* kindles activism centered on the Grant case while also becoming entangled with later cases. Like the viral images Gries examines, it "becomes rhetorical in divergent ways as it circulates with time" (*Still* 14). The sounds that follow Grant's shooting, while referencing a history of violent, racialized arrests, continue to connote corporeal shock at their recurrence well after the convergence of the Grant and Martin stories.

The circumstances of Grant's, Harris's, and Scott's deaths have especially haunting similarities, and demand to be considered in relation to each other. The fact that all three men were shot in the back, only to be handcuffed as they lay dying, also deserves recognition as an indicator of the chronic character of police violence, and an instance of the self-destructive repetition that typifies social trauma (Caruth; LaCapra). But it compounds the violence to reduce one case to another, or to overlook people's singularities as we note the rhymes of their final moments. The risks involved in comparison evoke what Scott and Welch describe as "the tension between the felt need to act immediately and the concurrent need to be as informed as possible" ("One" 575). The exigency for determined protest and countersurveillance derives, in part, from the repetition of unbearably interlinked scenarios: the recognition of structural injustices demands associative thinking. The exigency for reflection, on the other hand, derives from awareness of hidden complexities and the perils of oversimplification; it involves a desire not to exacerbate existing wrongs or introduce new ones in the act of intervention.[5] So while the film suggests substantial ties to cases that precede and follow its release, it leavens those connections with reflective emphasis on the singular embodiment of its focal character.

That sense of embodiment derives weight from the documentary footage that constitutes the movie's first visuals. *Fruitvale Station* enacts a form of metafilmic communication insofar as it dramatizes the circumstances that attend the clip's production, but it also enacts metafilmic rhetoric by validating the clip's existence, its power not just to exemplify countersurveillance but to spark further acts of citizen videography while generating public mourning and protest. Both the metafilm and the interior documentary embody what Gries depicts as "active, creative, and dynamic forces that co-constitute collective change" (*Still* 67). But amid their creativity and dynamism, the objects also promote the right to document injustice as it occurs, insisting on social actancy as a crucial dimension of the transformative process.

Therein lies the value of considering *Fruitvale Station* as extended analepsis, a flashback of such scope that it temporarily engulfs the present tense, creating the sense that anything might happen.[6] In that technique resides the affect of possibility, the evasion of telos unfurling with the pulse and thrum of potential. Yet, at the same time, we know the outcome. The sense of unpredictable becoming collides, again and again, with the early footage of Grant's slaying. That shaky, poorly lit footage establishes the backdrop against which the action develops, while at the same time having a historical concreteness to which other scenes in the movie can only aspire. The flashback's delicately placed images of police officers, moving trains, and sudden violence rhythmically intervene so as to keep us attuned to the inevitable. But the seeming immediacy of the flashback, and its sense of gradual, undirected disclosure, reminds us that things could have been otherwise. Thus the melancholic structure of the film harbors a countermovement toward mourning—a faith, however warrantless in the early twenty-first century, that a different social trajectory is attainable.

That conviction takes on particular urgency given state and local efforts to constrain civic camerawork. Police have a history of deliberately blocking bystanders' views, confiscating their phones and memory cards, and destroying their cameras, all in the interest of restraining the vitality and virality of the image.[7] Texas State Representative Jason Villalba and Arizona Senator John Kavanagh have produced bills aiming to regulate the distance at which filming can legally occur. And in an alarming pair of events in California and Texas, officers shot Danny Sanchez and Antronie Scott after allegedly perceiving the suspects' cell phones as handguns. Sanchez underwent surgery for a leg wound; Scott's injury proved to be fatal.

As such cases combine to create a hostile climate for citizen videographers, there arises a need to defend the rhetorical value of their work. *Fruitvale Station* mounts that defense by situating a documentary clip within a narrative that clarifies the injustice of the shooting, signals its profound impact on Grant's friends and family, and represents videography as a form of activist testimony. The documentary testifies, among other things, to the ways law enforcement reproduces race in public space. The moving image renders the zone of everyday travel, the site of ordinary social circulation, as the stage on which power incriminates itself.

STAGING RACE

The rhetoric of race unfolds in tandem with that of imaging, policing, and imaging *as* policing. Photography and cinematography reify race while also giving witness to that reification. In *On the Sleeve of the Visual*, Alessandra Raengo tracks such objectification from lynching photos to mixed media installations, slave pictures to postmodern film, showing how those phenomena strive to concretize an idea of bodily categorization while simultaneously working to expose that striving. Inspired in part by the thinking of Coco Fusco, Raengo remarks that "photography has lent materiality to race because it has provided a visual technology that has further sutured race to the body" (27). She attends especially to pictures of the ritualized murder of African Americans, which disclose the "epidermalization" of power relations as one of the "social functions of photography" (27). Among the many examples of lynching photos that align the viewer's perspective with that of the pictured assembly, she locates an extraordinary image of a crowd with a victim's silhouette superimposed upon it. The displacement of the gaze, for all its inconsistency with the typical composition of such photos, still participates in what Raengo terms "the inescapable racialization of the visual" by bringing "into stark relief a picture of whiteness as terror and terrorizing" (24–25). Race mediates regardless of whether we focus on violator or violated, infusing the security of the purportedly unmarked watcher and inflecting the blackness of the shadow. Raengo describes race as a "meta-image" governing the general experience of visuality, suggesting that it pervades not just moments of crisis but people's routine modes of perception (26). Yet the subverted photo of a lynching also expresses a metafilmic dimension in its concentration on audience, subjecting the body of onlookers to historical countersurveillance.

The photo indicts those onlookers as complicit with murder and participating in the performative reproduction of race. In the revealingly titled *Pulled Over: How Police Stops Define Race and Citizenship*, Charles R. Epp, Steven Maynard-Moody, and Donald P. Haider-Markel investigate how policing figures into that performance, arguing for a shift in focus from individual actors to the structure of the production. They detail the problem of investigatory stops in the United States, which mobilize racial stereotypes while circumventing accusations of profiling.[8] Epp and his colleagues contend that police pull racial minorities over at approximately twice the national average, though when it comes strictly to speeding violations, officers target African Americans and whites at roughly the same rate (2, 14). The authors hold that many of the stops (for something other than speed) derive from suspicion of wrongdoing rather than observable transgression of law—suspicions that draw on implicit racist scripts while (re)defining race in the process.

Those who show resentment toward that process regularly find themselves searched or even handcuffed (2–3). Epp and company tie those practices to a white supremacist strain in the history of law enforcement, reading the conventional warning "Don't get smart with me!" as consistent with the performance of racial authority.[9] Such an interpretation resonates with Mirzoeff's reflections on visuality and incarceration, wherein he finds that the caution against "eyeballing" prison guards reaffirms the presumed unilateralism of the look (8, 167). *Pulled Over* attributes that unilateralism more to the capillary flow of racial assumptions than to the bigotry of single agents, though the authors lament outright bigotry as well.

Officers engaged in race-related investigatory policing must disguise their intentions if they are to maintain compliance with proper procedure. That is, they cannot detain a motorist or pedestrian without evidence that the subject has broken a law. So police cite a pretext such as a malfunctioning taillight or failure to signal when the objective is to uncover a more significant crime. Campaign Zero, a Black Lives Matter initiative that aims to curb police violence, describes such activity as "broken windows policing," and makes eliminating the practice a top priority.[10] The exigency for its abolition comes not just from its dishonesty but also from the frequency with which it leads to disaster. After University of Cincinnati officer Ray Tensing killed Samuel Dubose, for instance, he claimed to have stopped the suspect for failing to exhibit a front license plate, though body-camera footage shows him questioning Dubose as to whether he owns the car and whether his license has been suspended (Malcolm; "Samuel"; Horn and Sparling). That same year, Prairie View policeman Brian Encinia accosted Sandra Bland—tackling her, threatening to "light her up" with his Taser, and escorting her to the prison where she would later die—before attributing the stop to Bland changing lanes without a signal (Hennessy-Fiske; Stanton). When Daniel Pantaleo strangled Eric Garner on a Staten Island sidewalk, the supposed impetus for the interrogation was the suspect's history of selling loose cigarettes ("Eric"; Goldstein and Schweber). In each case, the meta-image of race mediates the officer-civilian interaction and the public interpretation of candid videos. The fact that those videos led to the brief imprisonment of Tensing and the firing of Encinia suggests the material-political influence of countersurveillance and reaffirms the right to document. The associated fact that Pantaleo escaped indictment demonstrates the persistence of whiteness as a relation of terror.

Coogler's docufiction exposes that terror by re-creating events preceding the camera phone footage, visualizing the moment when an officer pulls Grant off the train and positions him against the station wall. The reenactment of their subsequent interaction draws on extensive interviews and analysis of cell phone records, which offer a view of how policing, to return to Epp and company's phrase, "defines race." Officers perform that definition in selecting whom to interrogate, in the length of time they detain the suspect, and through the violence of the inquiry. Although the dramatization of the train ride home reveals that Oscar participated in a fight while aboard, it represents his participation as self-defense and raises concerns about the patrol singling him out for rough treatment. Given the diversity of people riding the train and of those involved in the scuffle, the pronounced attention to Grant stages race for witnesses on and off the platform, for those who see the event firsthand and those who encounter it on video and film.

The images show Grant requesting explanation from the officers, one of whom punches him for his boldness. He responds by activating his camera phone, triggering directives by patrolmen to put it away. In *Accountability by Camera,* Douglas A. Kelly describes the tension between police repression of videography and official policies that oblige noninterference with citizen camerawork. When set alongside Brad W. Smith and Malcolm D. Holmes's *Race and Police Brutality,* Kelly's work reinforces the idea of image repression as a systemic problem that is bound up with law enforcers' efforts to protect themselves from outside scrutiny. Rejecting the idea that only "bad apples" engage in such practices, Kelly puts forward a series of case studies that reflect "historical patterns" that characterize "police culture" (7). As the Grant case suggests, the history of that culture cannot be divorced from the staging of race, though the documentation of its performance has accelerated in the age of nearly omnipresent photography.

The metafilmic narrative of Grant's detainment codes the camera phone as an enabler of social connectedness as the police attempt to sequester him. Sophina manages to contact him via cell phone even as the police forbid its use. The proscription of the phone indicates the officers' awareness of the volatility of the object, their sense that what it generates refuses their control. Although they contest Grant's right to return the gaze, they also evince anxiety about the camera's association with rapid transmission, or in Gries's terms, its connotations of "far-reaching, unforeseeable consequentiality" (*Still* 91). In the brief time that Oscar speaks with Sophina, he explains that the officers are harassing him, provoking her outrage as she waits outside the station. An officer warns him once more against using the phone, and Grant then rises from his sitting position to reason with his interrogators. The police read his movement as a signal of aggression, which leads to rapid escalation of violence and swelling protestation from the crowd.

In what may strain credibility for some viewers, one of the onlookers is the fictive Katie, whom Grant met earlier at a local grocery store. Overhearing her express uncertainty about preparing fish for dinner, Grant introduces himself and offers assistance. Showing his flirtatious streak—a near-constant source of irritation for Sophina—he puts his new acquaintance in contact with his grandmother, whom he sees as the final authority on the subject. The scene might be interpreted as an effort to thicken Grant's character by hinting at his infidelities, especially given that Coogler does not evade the subject's less gratifying traits, dwelling on his years in jail, his drug dealing, and his explosive temper. But more significantly, Katie's reappearance helps reinforce the idea of the cell phone as a means of outreach—a motif advanced by Oscar sending birthday texts to his mother and organizing a BART trip to see New Year's fireworks with friends. When Katie raises her camera at Fruitvale, she refuses to let the police isolate Grant from a network of compassionate affect. And when the officers attempt to take her phone, she eludes their grasp while steadfastly enacting her right to document.

Katie thus resists, in a limited way, a form of violence that is at once epistemological and corporeal. When Raengo represents whiteness as "terror and terrorizing," she invokes hangings, mutilations, and murder, but she also calls up the structures of perception that catalyze those events. It is those structures that inform the investigatory stops that Epp and others detail, and those structures that led toward the killing of Trayvon Martin. In Grant's case, those structures govern not only his selection and detainment but the way police construe his actions during questioning. When Grant reacts to their misunderstandings with confused anger, the officers force him to the ground. They then demand that he show his hand, even though his arm is trapped beneath his body. Although compliance requires Grant to wriggle his arm free, the movement looks to his captors like an effort to draw a weapon. Paranoia and standard operating procedure fuse, leaving no opening for negotiation. When even acquiescence takes on the hue of menace, the prospects for dialogic rhetoric crumble; suasion and violence become indistinguishable.[11]

As Coogler depicts the breakdown of dialogic possibility, he gives his audience a behind-the-scenes view of the staging of race. We should understand race not as an object, however, nor as an isolable dimension of the mise-en-scène, but rather as a form of rhetorical processing, a material-historical synthesis of construction and reception. Mitchell takes us partway to that understanding by describing race as a *"medium"* or "intervening substance," suggesting that it is "something we *see through,* like a frame, a window, a screen, or a lens, rather than something we *look at*. It is a repertoire of cognitive and conceptual filters through which forms of human otherness are mediated" (*Seeing* xii). By describing race as a substance that intercedes between interpreter and object, he captures the thickness of affect in which the idea circulates, the almost tangible quality of its interposition between subjects. Yet, as Burke reminds us in *Grammar*, the sharing of substance entails a certain ambiguity, signaling residual disunity at the very moment of intersubjective contact. If race is a medium, it is one that people must continually activate and even re-create so as to persuade themselves of its actuality. If we relate such mediation to drama, race inheres not just in the staging apparatus but in the performance itself. When Mehserle fires on Grant, he responds to scripts that long precede the decision. But in making that decision, he refines the medium—which is to suggest that shooting an African American man for trying to comply with orders, and thus proving unable to perceive the man outside the frame of malice, constitutes a performative remediation of race.

When incorporating that remediation into his film, Coogler amplifies its resonance by giving us access to sensory details that the documentary does not capture. He provides a devastating example for Mitchell's claim that race is "not exclusively a *visual* medium" but rather one that "engages all the senses and signs that make human cognition, and especially *recognition*, possible" (*Seeing* xiii). The emphasis on recognition suggests that the substance of race intervenes in thinking as much as seeing, and that thinking is a recursive, embodied endeavor. If Ceraso's "multimodal listening" connotes corporeal intensities that link the ear to the limbs and internal organs, Mitchell's conception of medium inflects epistemology as similarly grounded in sensation. Whereas Coogler's initial reframing of the documentary film leads to an assertion of sensory aporia, his rendering of the shooting late in the film insists on protracted, multimodal contact with the staging of race. The cinematic close-ups accentuate the panic in Grant's eyes, the bewilderment as the blood begins to flow from his mouth. We hear his voice throughout our bodies when he pleads, "I got a daughter." As we watch Sophina hoping for Grant to emerge from the interrogation, we share her dread. As Grant's mother, Wanda, reflects that she coaxed him to take the train to avoid traffic and trouble, we feel the irony as if a blow. Different addressees will respond to such scenes in dissimilar ways, so the aim here is not to delimit their affective potential. But whatever discerning audiences feel during those moments, they experience the cognition and *recognition* of race.

Recognition carries forward the sensory history from which it arises and adds new layers to that history. Alluding to Wittgenstein's *Philosophical Investigations*, both Raengo and Mitchell note that seeing cannot escape mediation; it is only ever "seeing *as*" (Raengo 1, 14; Mitchell, *Seeing* 13). If we frame other senses as similarly schooled by history, we might posit that feeling is always feeling *as*, perception always an act of creation. Through deep contextualization of Grant's death, *Fruitvale Station* puts the transitive character of perception on display, the way it manufactures a threat through the mobilization of stereotypes. And in subjecting perception itself to audience analysis, the movie demonstrates the theoretical value of metafilm. To reassert Green's insights from *Docufictions*, such images allow us "to observe the world and the mediation of the world at once" (72). Not only does the genre open feeling and knowing to investigation, it holds out the possibility for alternative forms of recognition, some of which inhere in the reactions of the platform bystanders.

Staging race as a form of mediation at once accentuates the deep-rootedness of embodied performances and indicates their revise-ability. While this staging constitutes a reflexive rhetorical strategy, it also orients itself toward "what happens once rhetoric has been produced and initially distributed" (Gries, *Still* 47). It thus invites a consequentialist style of analysis that addresses the film's life beyond the space of the theater. As the next section shows, such uptake ranges well beyond the goals of the director, which, in the case of *Fruitvale Station*, fit uneasily with the goals of the distributor. Emphasizing the creative character of perception yields insights about the circulation of racial ideology, but also about the idiosyncrasies of reception, which sometimes undermine the agency of the designer.[12] By opening perception and reception to multimodal inquiry, metafilm brings into focus the affective conditions for communication, and thus the rhetorical situation in which identification does or does not occur. Even though visuality may be a key dimension of that situation, rhetoric flows through singular and social bodies, geopolitical environments, and the technologies with which we claim the right to document. Claiming that right, however, may subject the rhetor to standards of presentational purity that no medium can bear. The rest of this chapter details how Coogler's sensitivity to that contradiction permeates the film's cinematography. It further shows how the movie, despite its contributions to social movement rhetoric, becomes identified with the rhetoric of neoliberalism. To use Scott and Welch's language, the film circulates within an "economy of exchange values" that emphasizes political commitment yet reduces it to discourse on the Weinstein website, conflating the idea of activist movement with a marketing campaign ("One" 564).

RE/CREATION

The commodification of *Fruitvale Station* generates distress in part because it violates the film's rhetoric of mourning. After promoting image-driven activism with its inclusion of phone footage, it supports collective grieving by incorporating documentary images at the film's end. Those images feature Sophina, Oscar's daughter Tatiana, Wanda, and a congregation gathering around the station to remember Grant's life. Jeff Labrecque sees Coogler's film as an extension of that remembrance:

> There's no memorial for Oscar Grant at the Fruitvale BART station, though there is a mural across the street and several throughout Oakland. Coogler's movie has become his de facto memorial, reminding people of what happened, why it didn't need to happen, and just how we might better treat complete strangers who are trying to get home to their loved ones, just like us.

Labrecque specifies audiences' identification with Grant's vulnerability, and with the ways everyday travel can render us subject to armed authority. Yet *Fruitvale Station* also clarifies the uneven distribution of such vulnerability, calling for organized witness in response to what Cram describes as "a history of non-response to bias crimes" (416). When so many instances of police brutality have given way to silence in the United States, she contends that "public images of grief become a political imperative" (416). The image object incites responses that reaffirm the agency of its designers while also constituting a form of political life that exceeds anything those designers foresee.

In outstripping the intentions of its makers, the film acts not just as a catalyst for deliberation but also as a participant in the conversation. A "de facto memorial," it frames mourning as an act of remembrance and a call to action. What that action might entail depends on the addressee, though the film presses for legal justice in the Grant case and promotes further citizen documentary in his name. As Cram addresses forms of grief such as *Fruitvale Station*, she regards holding vigil as a "civic performance enabled by the rhetorical dynamics of visuality, a ritual of devotional watching so that names will not be vanquished by the silences of memory" (412). Coding community commemoration as resistance to historical erasure, she suggests that vigils' "symbolic and corporeal demands constitute rich possibilities for civic and cultural transformation, particularly when seeing and being seen as a citizen is at stake" (412). Insofar as the movie-as-memorial promotes citizenship, it supports Hariman and Lucaites's contention that popular images mediate collective identity.[13] It suggests a particular version of such identity in which the collective includes not only human embodiment but the modes, materials, and Latourian "actants" that communicate mourning (Latour, *We*). *Fruitvale Station* participates in the collective while probing the limits of visual rhetoric for intervening in persistent problems. While the documentary may have helped ensure Mehserle's sentence, the sentence was light and he only served a portion of it. As similar acts of videography have merged mourning with activism in the years since Grant's death, they show police using excessive force against nonthreatening or unarmed suspects, yet escaping punishments even as lenient as Mehserle's. We need only consult the cases of Eric Garner, Tamir Rice, and Marlene Pinnock for examples.[14]

Fruitvale Station emphasizes the injustice of such cases less through lengthy disparagement of law enforcement than through meditation on Grant's lived experience, the movements and contradictions of his final day. Stephanie Zacharek writes that "Coogler dramatizes Oscar's last day by choosing *not* to dramatize it: The events unfold casually, without any particular scheme." That seeming spontaneity gives us "some sense of Oscar's time in prison" while suggesting that he "could be evasive, if not downright dishonest, with his loved ones. The idea isn't to turn Oscar Grant into a martyr; it's simply to shrink the distance between him and us." The shrinking of distance exemplifies once more the process of Burkean identification, which diminishes the space between subjects but never eradicates it. Coogler underscores this quality in his comments on the movie: he wants audiences to "have an inkling of the connection the family has" with Grant (Alloway). People tend to "open up the paper and see people like Oscar dying, and they don't think twice about it. I want this film to be something that can make those people think twice" (J. Rhodes). Consultation with the Grant family informed Coogler's depiction of Oscar, and everyone involved knew the resulting portrait would likely be painful to see. It is the painful moments, however, rather than just Grant's vibrancy and charm, that give audiences an "inkling" of how his family related to him, and that help preserve Grant's specificity against the effects of spectacle.

As the film develops that specificity, it represents Grant as an affectionate father and son, though one who struggles to keep a job, experiences intense surges of anger, and often blames others for his failings. When he addresses those failings, he sometimes makes difficult situations worse. In one instance, he proves unreliable as a grocery store employee but pleads for another chance. When the manager reveals that he has already hired a replacement, Grant reacts with threats: "You want me selling dope? You need me outside waiting for you to get done?" Later, he recalls his mother visiting him in prison and recounting the incarceration's effects on Tatiana. Oscar resents the bluntness of Wanda's delivery, accusing her of never supporting him. As she rises to leave, he demands a parting embrace. Prison guards prevent his attempt to follow her, leading to humiliating violence in the visitation room. Such scenes show how unflinching Coogler's rhetoric of re-creation can be.

No matter how resolute that rhetoric, however, it cannot close the distance between the audience and the diegetic realm. As with *Ararat*, *Fruitvale Station* embodies a form of mediated mourning wherein audiovisual technology affords the chance to merge grief with politics yet simultaneously marks the chasm between the bereaved and the lost. It also enforces the distinction between those most immediately affected by Grant's death and those who stand in solidarity. Whereas the materiality of the filmic interface helps define such differences, Coogler accentuates them with the film's cinematography. A memorable example occurs when Grant picks up Tatiana from day care, with the camera following his actions in a fluid tracking shot. Rather than adopting an omniscient perspective that overtly distinguishes itself from Grant's sight line, the lens stays just behind him, echoing his point of view and replicating his forward motion through the building. In one way, the shot gives us a sense of Grant's anticipation as he approaches his daughter, permitting us to identify with the most satisfying moments of his day. In another way, it keeps him in view and prohibits conflation of our perception with his.

A similar shot occurs in the hospital lobby after the shooting, as Wanda approaches the front desk seeking news of her son's condition. The tracking motion builds up a different kind of anticipation this time, filling the watcher with dread even though the outcome is certain. And yet it also suggests that our dread cannot correspond with Wanda's, nor can we know the particularity of her pain when she receives word of his death. As we follow her down the hall to see his body, the camera stops short, signifying through growing distance that portion of grief that remains unshareable.

Fruitvale Station's rhetoric of re-creation frames the impossibility of transubstantial unity between subjects as a feature of relational ethics. The camera reminds us of the limits to intersubjective understanding while at the same time inviting us to dwell with otherness and respect difference. Hesford contends that representing trauma often clarifies the inadequacies of communication, showing the futility of narrating violence in all its fullness, along with the outright undesirability of the audience knowing that violence. She attributes those communicative challenges to the "crisis of witnessing" (*Spectacular* 99). Yet she also takes issue with the rhetoric of crisis, inviting people to value the nontransferability of traumatic knowledge across experiential boundaries. She ratifies an "ethics of witnessing" that, in the words of Kelly Oliver, avoids "the assimilation of all differences into sameness" (qtd. in Hesford, *Spectacular* 48). On one hand, such ethics involve recognizing the untranslatability of trauma; on the other, they entail a hesitancy to mold unfamiliar material into a reaffirmation of self. *Fruitvale Station* gives us intimate access to another's story while hinting that much of it eludes even the most sensitive of audiences.

Reflective witness requires knowing the limitations of identification as we attempt to fashion principled forms of solidarity. Although Hesford warns against treating self-consciousness as sufficient means of countering "persistent objectifications of the other," she sees it as necessary for working toward "ethical engagements" (*Spectacular* 203). Stumm locates such engagements in Oliver's multilayered definition of witnessing, which includes "eyewitness testimony," acknowledgment of "that which cannot be seen," and acceptance of the "infinite encounter with otherness" (767). As Stumm addresses the legal and theological connotations of the term, she brings out yet another stratum of meaning that is indispensable to an ethics of reflective witness: "being present" to the other with whom we collaborate, being "response-able" to the vulnerable interlocutor. *Fruitvale Station* calls us to witness with its footage of the "Justice for Oscar Grant" vigil in the film's closing moments. It keeps us attuned to the characters' unknowable experience with its creative camera work, and yet insists on our response-ability to those characters through its reintroduction of documentary rhetoric at the end.

In one way, featuring eyewitness footage at either end of the drama tethers filmic re-creation to the continuing exigency of the Grant case. The images of protest insist on witnessing as a form of coalition with people who await "not our recognition but our participation in their struggles" (Esmeir 1545). In another way, the docudrama raises suspicions that such coalitional rhetoric might subordinate factual accuracy to affect. Docudrama typically implies that onscreen events occurred "much like" they did in reality (Lipkin, Paget, and Roscoe 23), which serves both as an assurance and an equivocation.[15] Coogler's film heightens the tension between document and drama by proceeding as flashback, which promises an "inside view" of "what really happened."[16] The film cannot give us that view, and announces its inadequacy to the task.[17] And yet docudrama emboldens some audiences to ask the impossible, and in some cases, to accuse the filmmakers of political maneuvering if the narrative departs from firsthand records.

One scene that has prompted such charges involves Grant nursing a dog that has been hit by a car. In a *Huffington Post* interview, Coogler acknowledges that he drafted the scene based on Grant's love of pit bulls, and accepts that audiences have opposing reactions to it: "It's a very polarizing scene. Some people get the intention and it's their favorite scene in the movie. Some people hate the whole movie because of the scene" (Tatko-Peterson). Coogler explains that he meant less to exalt Grant than to disturb connected forms of cultural labeling:

> You never hear about a pit bull doing anything good in the media. . . . And they have a stigma to them . . . [so that] in many ways, pit bulls are like young African-American males. Whenever you see us in the news, it's for getting shot and killed or shooting and killing somebody—for being a stereotype.

The explanation shows Coogler resisting stereotypes that apply to himself as well as Grant, and it discloses yet another motive for visualizing the particulars of Grant's last day. Those particulars defy the psychically ingrained images that Mehserle carried with him onto the Fruitvale platform, the very images that informed his deadly misreading of Grant's physicality.

Despite such rhetorical significance, Kyle Smith dismisses Coogler's rationale as "garbled and unsatisfying." "The film's implicit plea that all human lives are special and deserving of basic dignity is a compelling one," he writes. "But should a film about politically charged events that happened only four years ago simply fabricate incidents for dramatic effect?" (*"Fruitvale Station* Is Loose"). Finding further fault with a scene in which Grant pours a bag of marijuana into the ocean, Smith distrusts the idea that "an established criminal" will abruptly change his behaviors, and insinuates that Mehserle had reason to fear Grant was armed ("*Fruitvale Station* Tells Some"; "*Fruitvale Station* Is Loose"). The marketing of the film deflects such inquiry, Smith suggests, as he excoriates a poster for featuring "Grant with hands clasped in an almost saintly pose" ("*Fruitvale Station* Tells Some"). In two different reviews, Smith argues that the filmmakers and distributors sentimentalize the event, leaving little doubt as to protagonist and villain.

With such sentimentality comes the destabilization of re-creation (as represented by Coogler's fidelity to interviews and phone records) by the rhetoric of recreation (or the privileging of entertainment over historical mimesis). Even as the film generates an affect of authenticity through its seemingly unstructured sequencing, it trades on conventions of melodrama to deepen the pathos of Grant's death. Smith reads those deviations as activist misrepresentation, questioning whether Grant truly experienced police brutality at all. He contends that the ethical lapses involve not just theatrical invention but the omission of information, such as the facts that Grant had a history of illegal handgun possession and resisting arrest. The movie also ignores eyewitness testimony that Mehserle announced his intention to use a Taser shortly before the fatal shooting, and showed signs of distress after he pulled the trigger. Given those details, Smith interprets the shooting as accidental: "His slaying was not intended, and the videos of the actual shooting don't support a claim of outrageous policing. Grant's death was no more pregnant with lessons for society than if he had been hit by a bus" ("*Fruitvale Station* Is Loose"). Moving from a critique of artistic license to a dubious rejection of the film's premise, Smith's analysis exemplifies how the mixture of re-creative and recreational rhetoric can provoke counterargumentative excess.

Such backlash bears out Gries's case that the circulatory effects of visual rhetoric are emergent and erratic: the thing distances itself from its creators and rebels against fixed judgments (*Still* 57, 97–98). But as Smith engages with the visual object and draws his specific conclusions, he must ignore a host of material concerns, including the way race governs the interrogation, shaping the selection of suspect and the intensity of the questioning. He must bracket the hegemonic coding of Grant's skin and clothing, treating as fictive what Raengo portrays as the "epidermalization of power." For Mehserle participates in the staging of race whether or not he intends to do so. When the police warn Grant against recording their actions, they protect the already racialized unilateralism of surveillance. When they attack him for rising to request an explanation, they construct that motion as a threat to the authority of whiteness. Mehserle's decision to draw a weapon, whether Taser or handgun, arises from the operation of race as medium.[18] That operation infuses Mehserle's actions but also establishes their backdrop; it emanates from historical systems rather than the autonomous subject. If there is a viable critique of Mehserle's incarceration, it would address how, in Burkean parlance, the sentence scapegoats him for violence that is structural in character.

OUTSIDE THE METREON

The structural character of legal violence becomes all the plainer when we consider how the movie's release coincided with the Zimmerman decision. Grant and Martin suffered the consequences of formal and unofficial policing routines—customs so well established that even a non-officer, after stalking and shooting an African American teenager, can plead self-defense, convincing a jury that he was only upholding law and order. Erik Lomis, head of theatrical distribution for the Weinstein Company, noticed the relevance of the jury's decision to *Fruitvale Station,* but claims no plan for the film's limited release to accompany the verdict. "It's not going to hurt us," he admits. "But we're not saying, 'If you're upset about the Zimmerman case, go see this'" (Lee). Although the studio distances itself from capitalizing on public unrest, a series of articles appeared after the film's release noting the company's proven attunement to the "zeitgeist," as affirmed by the broad attention to the Zimmerman/Mehserle nexus on Twitter and Instagram (Brooks; Kaufman; Lee). The collision of cinematic and journalistic material intensifies the flow of ideas related to race and law enforcement, opening the way for hashtags such as #IAmFruitvaleStation while also sparking public demonstrations. An especially memorable Instagram features Octavia Spencer, who plays Wanda, calling for immediate dialogue: "Being a part of *Fruitvale Station,* you really want to be the impetus of much needed discourse about our humanity and how we interact with each other" (Lee). With young African American men dying senselessly in different parts of the country, and killers receiving little to no punishment, the zeitgeist seemed to bend toward confrontation with structural racism.

Regardless of whether we accept Lomis's assertion that the studio did not aim to benefit from the Zimmerman decision, the Weinstein Company's ability to "ride the zeitgeist" depends in part on the agency of visual objects. New materialist theory refuses "any bifurcation of humans and things, culture and nature, object and subject," all dualisms that fail "to acknowledge the ontological hybridity that constitutes reality" (Gries 5). *Fruitvale Station* troubles the subject/object dichotomy by interacting with other images of racial animus, from Raengo's lynching pictures to the Rodney King beating to portraits of Emmett Till and Trayvon Martin. It thereby demonstrates the metonymic vitality of viral circulation and the capacity of organic materials to form lively assemblages.

Reflexive materialism similarly attends to the vitality of nonliving things, but presumes that a system of vexed social relations suffuses object agency. Such an approach helps clarify how re-creation and recreation, mourning and commerce, tend to cohabit the same visual object at the same time, rather than occurring as pure, mutually exclusive types. Spencer's Instagram plea for "discourse about our humanity" proclaims the urgency of witness, and insists that spectatorship serve to initiate dialogue rather than take its place: the digital object constructs looking as a beginning rather than a political end. Yet Chouliaraki reminds us how readily "stories that focus on witnessing as horror, 'appropriating' the sufferer as someone who shares our own humanity, may lean towards a commodified sentimentalism that reduces witnessing to voyeurism" (306). The same social media moment that encourages a transition from watching to deliberation relies on language that promotes sociocultural stasis, recoding alterity as uniformity. When the Weinstein Company incorporates *Fruitvale Station* into an "I AM" campaign, which aims to foster identification with victims of social injustice, the effort underplays difference in the interest of saccharine universality.

While such practices serve the motive of corporate self-promotion, the film's opening night at San Francisco's AMC Metreon 16 laid that motive bare. As people left the theater, Weinstein employees handed them business cards featuring images of Michael B. Jordan and Ariana Neal (who plays Tatiana) along with the *Fruitvale Station* hashtag; on the reverse side, the card invites viewers to visit the company website and "Commit to end social injustice in the name of Oscar Grant" (Brownell). The word "Commit" commands the visual space of the card, and appears again in block capitals at the end of the website address. The subsequent text explains that by participating "you could win an American Express gift card" (Brownell). Concern for justice, it seems, synchronizes with branding and the affirmation of market logic, complete with sponsorship by a formidable credit card company and the prospect of a financial windfall. The neoliberal appeal to self-interest simultaneously counsels investment in the social; the exigency for disrupting structural racism intermeshes with a humanitarianism that is largely egocentric. Like the rhetoric of the film, the rhetoric of the business card remediates those contradictory motives. The materiality of the object may exceed the communicative purposes of its creators and addressees, but the object also absorbs and shapes those purposes, which is to suggest that materiality is inescapably historical.

As we have seen, the commodity form exemplifies the object that bears its own history, concretizing the labor of its makers while embodying their separation from the value they generate. Even as the commodity carries traces of its past, it foregrounds its market appeal so as to efface the social relations that bring it into existence. In chapter 3, we investigated how *Even the Rain* counteracts the seamless process of commodification by exposing the modes of value expropriation inherent in moviemaking. *Fruitvale Station* similarly unsettles its own marketization, but does so by addressing the politics of circulation rather than worker exploitation. By beginning with phone footage and transitioning to an earlier time, Coogler historicizes citizen video in ways that attune viewers to the particulars of the Grant case and thereby amplify the video's political potential. Commodification of that video, and by extension his own film, endangers the activist energies the Weinstein Company purportedly promotes.

That problem finds expression in *Los Angeles Times* reporter Chris Lee's experience outside the Metreon, contemplating the "Commit" card as "protesters took to the streets in nearby Oakland to protest Zimmerman's acquittal." Although Lee dwells only briefly on the convergence, his reporting raises the question of whether the card and the political assembly are mutually reinforcing or divergent. Both respond to the exigency of witness; both construe spectatorship as an early stage, rather than the mature expression, of political agency. Yet street protest distinguishes itself by enacting the very counter-gaze for which it calls, and by assuming the risk of public collectivity in the face of a police apparatus that has proven itself profoundly dangerous to resistant subjects. Through vulnerable collectivity, it defies the one-sidedness of the look and the racialized regulation of sense experience. It exhibits the characteristics of social action as defined by Kristie Fleckenstein, who claims that any effort worth the name must enact, in determined yet compassionate ways, the collective's ethical principles during the course of public persuasion. Deviation from those principles, whether to attract members or frustrate adversaries, fractures the integrity of the undertaking (5–6). Although social media may support fine-grained analysis, it does not, in this instance, involve so tight a fit between the means and ends of persuasion. At their best, the two forums would support each other, but the promotion of the "Commit" site heightens the threat of digital commodification, deriving exchange value from the Grant and Martin cases whether Lomis would admit it or not.

Insofar as reflexive materialism opposes the dehistoricizing tendencies of spectacle, it potentially invigorates long-term movements against structural racism. Images can enliven those movements, but only insofar as they pose relevant problems, expand the political collective, and cultivate the sort of "commitment" that embodies an obstinate threat to the status quo. Coogler recognizes that the efficacy of that threat depends on its stubbornness and longevity. While *Fruitvale Station* affords viewers a compelling viewing experience, it creates "fissures in the observational gaze" so as to disrupt egoistic satisfaction in spectatorship, reminding watchers of the drama's linkage to matters of immediate import. Like *Medium Cool* more than forty years before, *Fruitvale Station* risks joining the protest it documents. It blends vigil with political struggle, while insisting that those acts must outlast the screening if the screening is to be worthwhile.

The case of *Fruitvale Station* thereby signals a limitation to studying rhetorical circulation for circulation's sake, and instead invites attention to the affective circuits through which ideas flow, and how affect mediates embodied power relations. For Raengo as for Mitchell, those relations are "epidermalized." For Mirzoeff, they are inescapably economic. *Fruitvale Station*'s rhetoric of reflexive materialism addresses both kinds of power at once while visualizing a distributed form of counterpower. It codes citizen videography as a filter and catalyst for activism, proclaiming the right to document not as an abstract principle but as something we claim through performance. In a sensory economy so perverse that African American compliance with authority looks like furtive aggression, the multimodal production of direct and sustained resistance constitutes the only means of ethical witness, the only form of social action worth the name.

CONCLUSION

UN CERTAIN REGARD (OR, FOUR WAYS OF LOOKING BACK)

> [The world] is being lost to the systems. To the transparent networks that slowly occlude the flow of all those aspects of nature and character that distinguish humans from elevator buttons and doorbells.
>
> —Don DeLillo, *Zero K*

> Mediators have finally told us their real names: "We are beings out there that gather and assemble the collective just as extensively as what you have called so far the social, limiting yourselves to only one standardized version of the assemblages; if you want to follow the actors themselves, you have to follow us as well."
>
> —Bruno Latour, *Reassembling the Social: An Introduction to Actor-Network-Theory*

IN A CLASSIC INSTANCE of movie suspense, a locomotive rushes toward a child who cowers on the tracks of a Parisian railway station. The engineer alerts his crew, but they apply the brake too late. The train slams into the platform, tearing a spectacular furrow in the landing and sending bystanders scrambling for cover. The engine plows through the lobby and into the glass façade, hurtling toward the avenue below.

The same child awakens from the dream of technological catastrophe to find himself safely in bed, under the vigilant gaze of a humanoid figure he calls the "automaton." The figure sits at a makeshift desk with pen in hand, its face a placid contrast to the mayhem of the previous scene. The boy and automaton live in an apartment inside the walls of Gare Montparnasse, following the family practice of maintaining the clocks. Traumatized by his father's death in a museum fire, the boy hides from public view, scavenging food from the depot and machine parts from a small toy store.

Life behind the walls is at once dreadful and enchanted, involving grimy stairwells, precipitous drops, and a nest of gears, plates, springs, and levers that connote danger and play in equal measure.

As our protagonist wakes to those surroundings, he at first finds comfort in the face of the mechanical man. It represents a bond with his father, the expert horologer who brought the machine home from the museum so they might repair it together. Yet the reparations remained incomplete at the time of the fire, and the child has proven unable to finish them alone. The automaton therefore languishes at its drafting desk, poised to compose a message it cannot deliver. The boy's relief upon encountering that familiar image gives way to grief, and then to mounting alarm. Rapidly and without explanation, the flaw in the automaton begins to infect the child himself, who unbuttons his shirt to find not flesh but cogwheels and metal ligature. Panic sets in as he morphs entirely into the machine, ducking and dodging as the innards of the station clock swarm his body. By now thoroughly imprisoned in his erstwhile sanctuary, the boy awakens a second time.

Thus runs a key sequence from *Hugo*, Martin Scorsese's meditation on the historical materiality of cinema. The protagonist is Hugo Cabret, an industrious, heartbroken child whose desire to fix the automaton parallels his yearning to reunite with his father. So strongly does he identify the two figures that he courts near-constant peril to obtain the requisite parts, risking the wrath of the station inspector and the toy maker alike. When the toy maker catches Hugo stealing from the shop, he forces the boy to empty his pockets, one of which contains a notebook with original blueprints for the automaton. First threatening to burn the notebook, the man later decides Hugo can earn it back through (closely supervised) labor behind the counter. Gradually, the boy becomes apprentice to the toy maker, who reveals himself to be an inventor and accomplished magician. The magician's goddaughter, a bibliophile and budding detective, takes interest in Hugo's notebook and his secret life behind the walls. As the children set out together to revitalize the automaton, they undertake an adventure that leads them through the history of *fin de siècle* moving pictures.

That adventure takes them through an illicit screening in a Parisian movie house, a visit to the "film academy library," and most crucially, back to the shopkeeper himself, whose talents as a craftsman and illusionist attest to his years as a moviemaker. The children begin to uncover that past by coaxing the automaton to life, whereupon it sketches an image from the 1902 short film *A Trip to the Moon* and then signs the name "Georges Méliès." The signature, Isabelle recognizes with astonishment, belongs to her godfather. She and Hugo commence investigating the coincidence, learning from the film library and historian René Tabard that Papa Georges once constructed an independent movie studio where he wrote, directed, and starred in the films. Like the actual Méliès, who made over 500 movies in Montreuil between 1896 and 1913, the character proves to be a trailblazer in science fiction cinema as well as film color and special effects (Fry and Fourzon 8).

When the sleuths reveal their discovery to Papa Georges, he shows distress at how World War I interrupted his work. He surmises that the realities of battle killed the cultural desire for fanciful narrative, preventing his audience from fully coalescing. He also laments the loss of many prints, which he sold to a company that subsequently melted them down for raw materials. Unhappily, those materials would later infuse such mass commodities as high-heel shoes, so that Méliès's films came in both literal and figurative senses to be trodden under foot. As Hugo and Isabelle's adventures aggravate old injuries, it takes encouragement from his wife (and onetime collaborator) Jeanne D'Alcy to reignite his pleasure in the memory of making movies. With further encouragement from Tabard, he assists in salvaging over eighty of the original films, all of which historians thought unrecoverable. Pivotal as is Méliès to resurrecting the films, the narrative's final act shows the currents of revitalization to run in both directions. The movies appear to track him down—as much as the other way around—and in the process they summon an audience that has lain dormant for decades.

As Méliès recounts his creative history, he describes the automaton as his most prized invention, a magnum opus that he considered lost along with his moving pictures. The mechanical man served in a sense as progenitor of Méliès's films, for when the Lumière brothers declined to sell him a movie camera, he constructed his own apparatus from the robot's spare parts. Thus the mechanical figure becomes metonymically linked with moviemaking. The many visuals of the figure's interior architecture become identified with flashbacks to the inventor's studio work, and the film's copious images of clockwork gradually align with behind-the-scenes production labor.

While the products of that labor invite the collective gaze, they also have a way of looking back. When Hugo awakens from his nightmare, he encounters that new materialist liveliness in the return stare of a supposedly inert contrivance. The extrahuman mixture of self-possession and penetrating address constitutes a key feature not just of *Hugo* but also of metafilm in general. And the metafilmic trope of "looking back" holds multiple forms of significance, all of which converge in Hugo's layered dream sequence.

First, the picture looks back at itself, invoking a precisely tuned interior that requires painstaking, unseen exertions to generate its effects. Second, the narrative looks back at cinema history, not just in the tale of Méliès's reemergence, but through intertextual engagement with such precursors as the Lumières' *Workers Leaving the Lumière Factory* (1895) and *Arrival of a Train at La Ciotat* (1896), and Edwin S. Porter's *The Great Train Robbery* (1903). Depicting Hugo as a steward of time, Scorsese depicts the enabling dimensions of history as well as its potentially stifling effects. Hugo and Méliès share Laurie Gries's desire for things to function smoothly, to flow in ways unencumbered by the cruelties of time. But Méliès intercuts that desire with awareness of how rhetorical flow might be co-opted by economic agencies, and he thereby shows a materialist consciousness of alienated labor. Third, the movie looks back at the audience, especially by means of the robot, who peers into the lens throughout the final frames. By clouding the boundary between intra- and extradiegetic space, this machine regard codes the film as a way of engaging in cultural analysis, with a particular focus on the audience's negotiation of psychic and sociopolitical violence.

Studying those reflexive techniques opens a fourth way of looking back, wherein we survey what has come before in our considerations of metafilmic rhetoric. Treating Scorsese's movie as an instance of multimodal theory recapitulates one of the book's core methodological precepts—that metafilm signals not just the self-consciousness of singular movies or even sensitivity to cinema history, but a concern with the contradictory politics of mediation. A variation on that concern is the fear that, to use DeLillo's phrasing in *Zero K*, "the world is being lost to the systems" (239), the clockwork swarming of the body via neoliberal economics. Worse yet, such alienation yields the mechanization of human relations, reifying structures of power and reducing social justice rhetorics to objects of commerce. From the genre commentary in *Funny Games* and *Ararat*, to the class critique in *Even the Rain*, on through the depiction of racist policing in *Fruitvale Station*, metaleptic cinema visualizes its susceptibility to corporate-capitalist co-optation while conveying misgivings about prospects for resistance.

Yet, whatever the misgivings, those same movies represent the medium as a means of unconventional thinking and defiant affect. Advancing ideas akin to those in Latour's *Reassembling the Social*, they describe and embody moving pictures as "mediators" that "assemble the collective" (240). Whether in the ambient intersubjectivity of *Magnolia* or the citizen videography of *Fruitvale Station*, mediators participate in the negotiation of traumas both singular and communal. The dialectic of danger and healing inheres in the histories embedded within *Ararat* and *Even the Rain* just as it inhabits the automaton. That figure signals how mediators elude human command, sometimes in ways that flout the designer's will or fracture the subject's sense of self. But it also serves, as startlingly as Aimee Mann's music or a magical realist storm surge, to bring fractured subjects into restorative relation.

Where cinema addresses its condition as a mediator that is enmeshed in systemic violence, organized counterpower, or more ambiguous forms of antagonism and mutuality, it performs the work of reflexive materialism. That work corresponds with other strands of materialism, whether Gries's "new" variant or Scott and Welch's critical approach, without settling comfortably into either epistemology. It acknowledges the mutability of visual rhetoric while situating production and circulation within relations of structural inequality; it amplifies the human struggle implicit in various forms of vibrant matter without dismissing the vitality of extrahuman being or indulging in fantasies of rational autonomy.

Granted, not all metafilms exhibit such leanings. The idea that "reflexive equals progressive," writes Stam, proves faulty "when applied too rigidly" (16). Much self-aware cinema proceeds primarily for comic or parodic effect while expressing world-weary genre familiarity, working to gratify the cinephile, or bringing out the continuities in an auteur's catalogue. Some of the movies in this book manifest those very impulses. But the foregoing investigations have addressed less conspicuous tendencies where multimodal storytelling and political rhetoric converge by dwelling on their own manufacture, delivery, and reception. The relevant movies do not just invite analysis as objects, but rather present themselves as things to think with, and things that aim to transform our feelings about visual culture. Such aims announce themselves when the image looks back, whether in the form of a mocking sociopath, a survivor of childhood abuse, a composing robot, or Haskell Wexler's camera.

REGARDING MATERIALITY

Images of cameras answering the viewer's gaze also appear in *Hugo*, and those images persistently evoke the automaton. As Méliès recounts his time as a filmmaker, he establishes a connection between the automaton and the movie camera, noting how one birthed the other under conditions of artistic exigency. The Lumières refused to sell him their cinematograph not out of proprietary insecurity, he suggests, but because they believed the technology would die due to lack of interest. Yet Méliès, who was smitten with their demonstrations of moving images and already involved in eliciting lifelike performances from inanimate things, sensed a different future for the camera. He therefore developed his own device and assembled a glass microcosm in which to compose with it. To clarify the complexity of such composing, Scorsese depicts Méliès participating in a range of production activities, including building sets, directing and rehearsing scenes with other actors, devising animatronics and pyrotechnics, shooting multiple takes, as well as splicing and editing film. Late in the story, Jeanne D'Alcy even suggests that she worked with him on tinting the frames, undertaking early experiments in movie color. *Hugo* identifies the automaton with such procedures partly by having Méliès construct the camera from its excess components, and partly by lingering on the android's clockwork interior, which comes to represent the mechanics of visual art.

With *Hugo*'s magnificent train wrecks, its investigations of the space behind the station walls, its robot that springs to life in the boy's dreams, its shots that soar over Paris, enter the Gare Montparnasse, and pass through throngs on the rail platform, Scorsese's film exhibits breathtaking movie magic while preserving the secrets behind it. But even as it honors the magician's oath, it draws attention to behind-the-scenes toil by dramatizing the activities in Méliès's studio, framing his pictures as the outcome of skilled collaboration. In that way, *Hugo* departs from the typical functioning of the mass commodity, which, in the Marxian sense, tends to veil its relationship to labor. Critics of political economy often ignore such self-conscious rhetoric, addressing cinema as a vein of capital rather than a medium for its analysis. While such attitudes are often warranted, to render them axiomatic oversimplifies movie politics. Stam makes the pertinent point in *Reflexivity in Film and Literature*:

> Too much of Marxist criticism, unfortunately, rather than clarifying the demystification process as it operates *within* art, has applied the strategy *to* art. . . . At its best art is itself, like Marxism, a critical instrument designed to lay bare the mechanisms of society even as it lays bare the devices of art. (209)

It is not only that *Hugo* aims to demystify the composing process rather than inviting Marxist interpretation, but rather that the practice of demystification involves a rhetorical merger between self-regard and illustration of social structures. The strategy of demystification entails the identification of work on the set with naturalized systems of manufacture and distribution. In advancing such as analysis, *Hugo* looks back at itself in ways that are relevant to all the movies in this book: on one hand, it casts film as a designed thing, the result of living labor that holds potential both to sustain its makers and undergo expropriation; on the other, it figures movies as expressions of multimodal agency, fusing photography, writing, drawing, painting, carpentry, and movement to envision alternative worlds.

The movie thereby embodies material rhetoric that conceptualizes and composes rather than serving as a static object of contemplation, and it thereby resists being ruled by the skeptical, occasionally pious textual analyst. Rita Felski announces the exhaustion of interpretive suspicion in *The Limits of Critique,* rejecting the idea that such detective work automatically aligns with the pursuit of social justice. She also claims that constant attention to the critical valences of texts means ignoring the other rhetorical work they perform. Taking Felski's cue, *Metafilm* takes this work to include imaginative historiography, sensory amplification, the fashioning of collective identity, the chronicling of media and technology development, and the experience of mourning—all of which *Hugo* exemplifies. Given this book's affinity for critical materialism, it gives sociopolitical analysis a prominent place in that litany of rhetorical labors. Although *Metafilm* parts ways with Felski on that score, it nevertheless codes cinema as agent rather than recipient of critical investigation.

Hugo insists from the outset on its contribution to materialist thought, focusing on the gears of the station clock, which swiftly align with a high-angle shot of Paris in motion, and more gradually with the motor of the automaton. By invoking the manual expertise that makes the illusion possible, the film prepares us to accept the continuity between Méliès's identities as builder and conjuror. *Hugo* also indirectly acknowledges its own design, which honors the work of not only Méliès and the Lumières but René Clair and Jean Renoir (Higgins 206). Like *Magnolia, Hugo* honors cinema's bygone era while taking full advantage of contemporary innovations in cinematography and special effects. Where Anderson extends the historiographic reach of his movie by capturing select images with an early twentieth-century Pathé camera, Scorsese dramatizes audience reactions to some of history's earliest short films. And where *Magnolia* gives us a dazzling amphibian storm, *Hugo* gives us the feel of a full-scale Parisian train station from the 1930s. The computer-generated effects in and around that station required the labors of Pixomondo studio workers in London, Stuttgart, Berlin, Shanghai, Beijing, Frankfurt, Burbank, Toronto, and Los Angeles ("Martin")—demonstrating how crucial the flows of neoliberal capital are to producing movies (and reproducing the idea of the auteur).

Scorsese's own history as a filmmaker enters into the film's rhetorical construction as well, especially in his signature dolly shots, darting camera movements, and first-person framing, all of which works to convey character psychology.[1]

As *Hugo* brings such processes into relief, it situates film labor within the splendor of Méliès's glass factory. There we see him engaged in creation, fashioning visions of undersea worlds and distant planets, teaching his actors how to inhabit those worlds, and inviting children (such as a young René Tabard) to witness the proceedings. Méliès even finds joy in the technical failures, reassuring the cast and repairing dysfunctional dragons with humor and efficiency. As an aging D'Alcy reflects on her involvement in the studio, she speaks lovingly of the movies themselves but even more passionately of the pleasure in making them.

For all its emphasis on those satisfactions, however, the movie also indicates the tenuous character of filmmaking, illustrating the bitter fortunes that await many of its adherents. The glass factory has an otherworldly quality, but remains a factory nonetheless, and its breakdown leaves employees stranded. Scorsese depicts the ruination of the studio in high-speed style, with months passing in seconds, the edifice withering as weeds and creeping vines reclaim the space. In a Burkean parallel that binds scene and agent, the destruction of Méliès's studio parallels his emotional collapse, which climaxes with the burning of a beloved prop from *A Trip to the Moon*—the very moon face the automaton draws when Hugo and Isabelle bring it back to life.

None of the pictures from earlier chapters shows so poignantly the foundering of an artistic career, though they all touch on the machinery of film production. *Magnolia* focuses on production by tying all of its character studies to the making of "What Do Kids Know?"—a television show whose participants' lives are secretly conjoined by histories of child abuse. Plunging behind the scenes of the show, with its contestant handlers, green room skirmishes, and celebrity host breakdowns, corresponds with a deep dive into family trauma. Both the television show and *Magnolia* itself generate crises of form that they negotiate by swerving from rhetorical commonplaces, one through a child's melodramatic monologue and the other through magical realism. Such swerving indicates a faith, however slender, that a destructive past might not determine things to come.

Ararat and *Even the Rain* also attempt to address troubled histories without allowing them to wreck the current moment, and in so doing, they visualize the apparatus of movie production. Egoyan gives particular consideration to tensions between scripting and art direction, asking whether transplanting Mt. Ararat to accentuate its iconicity constitutes artistic license or profane fabrication. He suggests that the affective needs of filmmakers inform practices of research and reenactment, shading the choices of varied composers, whether a celebrated director with a well-funded crew or a young man with a handheld digital camera. Bollaín similarly investigates how psychic commitments influence the decisions of producers, directors, stars, and so-called extras. In contrasting those commitments, *Even the Rain* works more vigorously than any text in this book to demystify socioeconomic divisions on-set. It illustrates a world where human subjects become "lost to the systems," indistinguishable from sandbags that stabilize light stands.

As the violence of the working arrangement parallels international resource inequalities, *Even the Rain* instantiates multimodal art performing materialist analysis rather than only proving susceptible to it. While not as overtly political as *Even the Rain*, *Hugo* also makes a materialist argument through carefully choreographed modal interchange. Scorsese's film derives in part from Brian Selznick's *The Invention of Hugo Cabret*, which mixes prose and hand-drawn images in ways that are themselves decidedly multimodal (Annett 173). As the movie looks back at its design, it emphasizes writing, photography, set construction, acting, choreography, sketch artistry, painting, and music. The celebration of interlocking modes announces itself early in the narrative: when cinematographer Robert Richardson's camera sweeps through the station, it lingers on James Joyce and Salvador Dalí drinking together while Django Reinhardt plays guitar with a small orchestra. The scene punctuates *Hugo*'s representation of cinema as a remediation of existing art forms.[2]

The automaton recapitulates that representation while drawing, writing, and acting on cue, incorporating all those activities into its imitation of life. This multiplicity recalls the "mixed and impure" history of cinema, which "did not only develop technically out of the magic lantern, the Daguerrotype, the phenakistoscope and similar devices . . . but also out of strip-cartoons, Wild West shows, automata, pulp novels, barn-storming melodramas, magic" (Wollen 153). In Wollen's account, the automaton figures as one of many material agents that collaborate in the development of movie culture; in Scorsese's film, the automaton serves as a metonym for the rest of the collective.

Mr. Cabret underscores the multimodal quality of the android by pointing out its wind-up structure and calling it the most sophisticated music box he has ever seen. The allusion to music as a constituent of movie rhetoric evokes a mode that is not merely decorative or ancillary but key to film's affective energy. Of the films in this book, *Funny Games* and *Magnolia* transmit that energy in the most distinctive ways, supporting Annett's argument that with multimodal texts, one mode can filter the rhetorical appeals of the others (173). Beginning with a musical game that reveals the cultural refinement of a vacationing family, *Funny Games* abruptly contradicts the initial vision of relaxed security with the bewildering thrash of Naked City. That music later reaffirms the reflexive character of the text when Paul claims it as a personal soundtrack, slipping the disc into a stereo system while hunting a terrified child. When Paul seizes the score as his own, the movie takes us into the territory of metadiegetic rhetoric, effacing the distinction between the sensory-material spheres of character and audience.

Magnolia disturbs that distinction in more sophisticated fashion by building Aimee Mann's songs into its ambient ecology. Not only do those songs influence how we process the visual mode, but they also give sensory materiality to the affective mesh in which the players are caught. Aurality articulates the collective in ways characteristic of Latour's mediators; to "follow the actors" and recognize their identification with each other, we must follow the music (*Reassembling* 240). When the characters sing along with seemingly extradiegetic tunes, and when they address the lens in ways that are alternately oblique and direct, *Magnolia* challenges our safe distance from the skein that envelops its mini-narratives. The picture collapses that distance by featuring characters who comment on the nature of cinema or question popular assumptions about narrative plausibility. It watches itself while demonstrating a penchant for reflexive listening, attending to how sound binds fictive subjects to each other while inviting audiences to join in the mix.

In listening to itself, metafilm highlights its constituent parts and the labor of assembling them. Yet this self-regard sometimes risks becoming mired in the synchronic. That risk involves divorcing trauma from the history in which it has festered, while extracting multimodal argumentation from the long-term commodification and co-optation of visual culture. Several of the filmmakers in this book confront those dangers by addressing them head-on within the diegesis. Such critical representations of reactionary reception practices may not be enough to stave them off, but it presses the audience not to settle for spectatorship as the limit of politics.

REGARDING HISTORY

In their desire not to repeat the violence of the past, numerous metafilms fixate on images of time. Some characters become preoccupied with clocks and relics, others reject artifacts that trigger harrowing memories, and still others exhibit both tendencies in a single narrative. In their occasionally contradictory regard for history, they aim to improve a specific set of material circumstances while nonetheless doubting the likelihood of change.

Méliès, who renounces cinema and secludes himself in a quiet section of the depot, lives in uncanny proximity to repressed materials. He builds and repairs toys in ways that evoke his movie magic; he exists without knowing it within close range of his automaton, which sits behind the walls of the station in the clock-tender's apartment. Exhibiting behaviors described by Cathy Caruth and Dominick LaCapra in their respective reflections on trauma, Méliès gravitates, as if against his own will, toward the scene of his psychic wound.

The films we have encountered feature catastrophic events that have a magnetizing effect on survivors, their loved ones, or future generations. Whether the movies depict families coping with the legacy of the Armenian Genocide, production crews addressing indigenous resistance to occupation, or a boy struggling with the loss of his parents, they emphasize the pull of unassimilated crises. Hugo shows the effects of that pull through his effort to fix the automaton and continue his father's practice of maintaining clocks. Both activities manifest the desire to resurrect the affect of security and wholeness, and both show how that desire becomes a prison. When the image of clockwork in the opening scenes merges with the image of Paris, all of which accentuates the boy's relative insignificance, the sequence hints how vast and overwhelming will be the effort to ameliorate trauma. Hugo mostly faces that situation with stoicism, though his frustration becomes clear when he finally gets the robot to compose for him, only to see it stop mid-message. The delay in composing, which he reads as the machine seizing up again, precipitates Hugo's own breakdown, whereupon he sobs to Isabelle that he will never be able to restore the android or his own life.

Similar attempts to engineer a technical solution to crisis occur in *Ararat* and *Even the Rain*. Saroyan and Raffi imagine the camera as a way to remedy the disorders of history, while Arshile Gorky probes the limits of visual rhetoric for treating psychic pain. The visual apparatus provides a medium whereby the painter can reach out to a distant time, yet when he touches the likeness of his absent mother he finds only the medium itself, denying access to the body it depicts. With *Even the Rain*, the problems of limited financing, unpredictable actors, and contemporary political upheaval all keep the director from capturing the trauma of Columbus's exploits during the so-called Age of Discovery. In one instance Sebastián faces resistance from actors who refuse to perform a scene on the grounds that its violence is too cruel to imagine, much less reenact. In his dedication to an idea of authenticity, the director proves insensitive to issues of local integrity and to the social movement coalescing before his eyes, all while ignoring the ideological continuities between his project and the Bolivian water wars.

By representing a traumatic past and simultaneously critiquing the effects of the representation, historiographic metafilm exposes a tension between generative memorialization and psychic stasis. Like Hugo, Raffi and Sebastián attempt to be good stewards of time, composing multimodal histories for purposes of attunement with the legacies of older generations. But also like Hugo, they risk entrapment by those very ambitions, as if lodged in the same clockwork they tend. The boy's confinement in the clock's space becomes especially resonant when juxtaposed with his memories of Mr. Cabret, which the automaton sets in motion like a movie reel:

> As Hugo looks at the machine and begins to reminisce, the darkness behind him is filled with the flickering blue light and unmistakable clatter of a phantom film projector. His eyes seem to gaze at an imagined screen. The flashback he "watches" depicts a montage of father and son fixing the automaton followed by visions of fire, a blaze that leaves the orphaned Hugo in his callous uncle's care. (Annett 174)

The memory brings a temporary affect of proximity while nonetheless marking a distance, which the unwanted "visions of fire" confirm. Méliès has learned to repress such visions, but must confront them when he discovers Hugo's notepad, with its flipbook-style animated automaton that turns to address its maker. "Ghosts," Méliès whispers upon encountering the familiar face. He then threatens to burn Hugo's book, which harbors things that not only refuse to be forgotten but also appear to reject their own lifelessness.

Those things not only trigger memory but invest it with a specific form. When Hugo remembers his father's death, he does so as an audiovisual montage accompanied by the sounds of a film projector and the feel of a screening room. When Méliès recollects the heyday of his studio along with its premature demise, we encounter an urgently sequenced montage once again, an elegantly crafted movie-within-the-movie. Such miniature films, Turim argues, have come to mediate memory beyond the space of the cinema, productively confusing the cinematic and psychological definitions of flashback (5). Whereas the narrative power of flashback rests largely in what Turim terms its "didactic character" (18) — which teaches characters and audiences how to interpret the diegetic present — the materialist vibrancy of the technique inheres in its gradual identification with cultural recall itself.

Méliès's robot embodies history's claim on Scorsese's focal characters. Long thought consumed by the fire that took Hugo's father, the automaton returns with a fury, evoking layers of loss—of career, of direction, and of the films themselves. *Hugo* conveys the loss of the movies with particular poignancy, creating a mix of visual and sonic cues to signal the force of the blow. As Méliès describes how financial distress led him to sell the pictures, we see the celluloid catch fire and begin to crumple. The liquid then gets poured into channels that flow into stiletto molds, one after another. Next we hear heels click in walking rhythm on the station floor as people pass the toy shop, echoing in what sounds like cavernous space, producing a cadence that resonates long after the sound dies away. The rhetorical modes conjoin in a lament of the movies' interchangeability with the image of the mass-produced commodity, as vital singularities drain into the assembly-line machinery of dead labor. The audiovisual arrangement of the scene constitutes a bitter rendering of worlds that are "being lost to the systems."

Those systems involve a contradictory mix of circulation and stasis. To return to Gries's favored metaphor, the celluloid literally "flows" into the mold of the heel, where its communicative flexibility hardens. It thus streams toward the cessation of rhetorical becoming. In a more general sense, the conversion of the pictures into undifferentiated commodities represents the movement of industrial capitalism, which subjugates what Marx calls the use value of designed things, or their capacity to fill the needs of living laborers, to an exchange value that abstracts things from rhetorical purpose while concealing their relation to embodied work.

As long ago as 2000, John Trimbur counseled studying rhetorical delivery by affiliating it with a specifically Marxian inflection of circulation (189–90). Since then, attention to circulation and delivery has broadened considerably, as manifested in the writings of Hariman and Lucaites; Sheridan, Ridolfo, and Michel; Gries, *Still*; Lynch and Rivers; and Rai. Their studies do not take the form that Trimbur might have envisioned, however, as they focus more on technologies of dissemination and practices of uptake than on the labor condensed within those phenomena. Much of the research replicates Latour's insight that if we want to understand human discourse, we must follow extrahuman mediators. Yet if we follow those mediators into history, we typically find undercompensated or otherwise exploited work.[3] Theorists of circulation give much space to the idea of multimodality, but limited consideration to how multimodal texts might themselves reflect on the circuit between their own production and delivery.

Without that reflection, considerations of rhetoric often focus on a single dimension of communication, whether the process of creation or the semiotics of design. Drawing on Marx, Trimbur describes such concentration, instructive as it might be, as indicating a "one-sided view of production" (190). By focusing on the film as commodity, *Hugo* tracks the "materialization of an underlying and contradictory process" that includes studio collaboration, outflow into the public, market valuation, and reception—or, to use the Marxian lexicon, "production, distribution, exchange, and consumption" (Trimbur 190). The contradictions of that process lie in the tensions between life-affirming cooperation and the reification of creative energy as merchandise, easily convertible into unrelated goods if that is where the demand exists. In specifying those contradictions, *Hugo* exemplifies Stam's idea of the "demystification process as it operates *within* art," bringing into view the cultural effects of war, the passing of cinema into the mold of the commodity, and the intersection of those tendencies with stories of personal and family hardship.

Those intersections reveal the porousness of boundaries between local, national, and international trauma. In *Hugo,* we learn not only that World War I interrupted Méliès's artistic labor, but also that Lisette's brother died at the Battle of Verdun, and that the station patrolman's war injury limits the use of his leg. Those losses converge with Hugo grieving the death of his parents and Isabelle recounting her own experience as an orphan. By sharing these ordeals with each other, the characters at once reveal the social nature of trauma and begin to mitigate its effects.

But not all such sharing is therapeutic or voluntary. In *Ararat,* for example, Raffi finds himself detained at the Canadian border on the condition that he account for his film canisters, and by extension his family's connection to the Armenian Genocide. Although his interrogator releases Raffi after determining that Turkish officers have duped the young man, the border investigation encapsulates the power hierarchy wherein oppressed subjects must seek validation from more privileged addressees. By using the interrogation as a structuring device for the drama, Egoyan gives us a way to think about the "distribution, exchange, and consumption" of his own picture, exposing the contradiction between the desire to relate suppressed histories and the fear of their co-optation. The emphasis on that contradiction coheres with the critical materialist attention to circulation, not as an absolute good or a necessary indicator of rhetorical vitality, but rather as part of the dynamic assemblage through which power reproduces itself.

Co-optation proceeds not only as narrative hijacking, however, but also as the harnessing of narrative to capital accumulation. Although *Fruitvale*

Station attempts to depict what Henry Jenkins calls "participatory culture" in pursuit of social justice, showing how camera phones can expose the racist abuse of police authority, certain dimensions of the film's marketing nevertheless reduce participatory culture to the logic of the sweepstakes. Like *Ararat*, *Fruitvale Station* discloses the operation of power, telling stories that interrupt authoritarian efforts to dictate the terms of the visual. And like *Ararat*, Coogler's movie endorses telling those stories in multiple modes, using portable technology to construct vernacular histories. Both pictures show how use value relents, in local but ominous ways, to systemic imperatives for exchange value.

The hegemony of those imperatives, and the related foreclosure of rhetorical becoming, may not be the central focus of any of the metafilms in this book. Yet all the movies either address commodification or find themselves uncomfortably caught within it. Whether in the instance of *Funny Games* refusing to adhere to genre conventions, *Ararat* questioning the good of its distribution, *Even the Rain* hinting at its own labor exploitation, or *Fruitvale Station* buying eye time for American Express, the pictures argue against the very conditions they exemplify.

Still, self-critique may not be enough. The metafilmic anxiety about rhetorical circulation stems from the idea that movies themselves do little to disrupt established power arrangements. They may constitute mediators within a dissident assemblage, but that assemblage must combine multiple, durable forms of life to intervene in the discourses the films portray. Whether the movies obstruct their reduction to bare exchange value depends on viewers' readiness to do more than watch. For all the pictures' attention to themselves and the histories in which they are embedded, their most penetrating look returns the gaze of the moviegoer, posing the question of what follows the act of reception.

REGARDING COLLECTIVES

Like looking back at history, looking back at the audience bears on the issue of rhetorical circulation. And like the forms of historical reflection undertaken by the films in this book, the return gaze contests the dominance of exchange value over use value. The films recognize, along with Richard Ohmann in *The Politics of Knowledge,* that the audience's attention may itself be transposed into the commodity form (175). However spirited the work of observing, it typically occurs amid commercial exigencies, whether in tweets, testimonials that help sell tickets and Blu-Ray discs, online reviews, fan fiction spin-offs, or book-length studies. None of the movies rejects those ways of responding, for to do so would mean shifting from self-critique to self-nullification. When the movies stare back at viewers, they defy interpretative practice as a predictable form of social reproduction, fixed and orderly as stiletto molds. Beyond challenging the routinization of response to cinematic rhetoric, some promote an activist orientation toward the troubles onscreen, as when *Even the Rain* affirms anticorporate demonstrations and *Fruitvale Station* documents Justice for Oscar rallies. By taking up such invitations, we participate in a convergence where various sorts of materiality join to resist their discrete commodification.

That convergence gives an activist inflection to Latour's idea of the collective, not just by locating agency in the cooperation of human and extrahuman actants but by situating that agency against neoliberal orthodoxy. Much new materialist theory pays little attention to neoliberalism, concentrating instead on how expressive memes replicate and transform themselves in ways that slip the grasp of traditional, speaking-writing rhetors. Whatever its faults, that approach has the virtue of decentering the autonomous, flesh-and-blood subject. Critical materialist theory, on the other hand, tends to see such decentering as a form of mystification, suggesting that if we look deeply into the history of vital objects we will find people vying for control. Deeply influenced by Marxism, such theory depicts that contest as a kind of death in life. So rather than observing how things come alive in the new materialist sense, Scott and Welch track how neoliberalism drains life from the labor that powers it. Chris Harman frames the problem nicely in *Zombie Capitalism*, attributing an "undead" state to banks during the 2007 recession but also to the global economic system, which he represents as "seemingly dead when it comes to achieving human goals and responding to human feelings, but capable of sudden spurts of activity that cause chaos all around"—chaos Harman associates with war, poverty, job instability, housing crises, and climate change (11–12). Several of the films in this book share that denunciation, with *Even the Rain* and *Hugo* providing especially clear indictments of capital's undead voracity.

Such films also demonstrate a belief in the suasive power of the nonhuman surround, be it in the affective vibrations of communications media, the embeddedness of history in things, the power of place to organize bodies and ideologies, or the refusal of rhetorical matter to accede to human design or expectation. Looking to discover the political economy of objects, reflexive materialism attempts to generate counter-hegemonic force without ever imagining itself free of the injustices it makes visible. It entails studying the movement of things—Gorky's photograph, Méliès's automaton, a BART station video—while situating those things within currents of imperialism and class reproduction. Sometimes such materialism involves an accusatory return gaze, charging U.S. viewers with complicity in violence overseas. Sometimes that gaze not only affiliates Western viewers with contemporary violence but also accuses them of failures of historical awareness, such that they participate unwittingly in the continued violation of traumatized subjects. In other instances, the return look charges spectators with temporary compassion, and thus with fleeting outrage toward clear, tangible forms of violence while ignoring the less obvious forms that structure social experience.[4] And where structural antagonism maps onto race rhetoric, the look enrolls audiences in a distributed effort to expose the discontinuities between law and justice.

That effort requires the interplay of a wide variety of mediators, from human bodies and public confrontations to wireless networks and the mass proliferation of screens. The film screen, in particular, produces only part of the enormous influence of visual culture, though certain kinds of cinema advance unexpectedly shrewd ways of participating in the posthuman collective. By enlisting the viewer in opposition to the commodification of the visual, the movies evoke the possibility of a circulation that eludes total regulation by exchange value.

In preserving inventive capacities against commercial reification, the collaboration of human and extrahuman rhetoric gives a novel coding to the idea of material correspondences, which we first encountered in chapter 3. There we tracked the conceptual linkage of varied substances, which became embroiled over the centuries in practices of imperialism, appropriation of resources, and forced or underpaid labor. Here similar substantive convergences are still at issue, while the emphasis changes to the political articulation of things in the interest of interrupting narratives of smooth progress. The films, which already connect copious modes and materials, generate agency by prompting a range of affective responses, including bodily distress at onscreen problems and a long-term determination to mitigate them. The work of the collective inheres not only in the articulation known as human solidarity (though such solidarity is indispensable to the process of sociopolitical transformation), but also in the correspondence of mediators that encompass and exceed people's diverse embodiment. Trimbur views such correspondence as embedded in a system of circulation that cannot be easily distinguished from commodification. But circulation, for all its service to capital, also constitutes the rhetorical engine for dissent.

The circulation of political metafilm participates, if only in a small way, in the creation of posthuman publics. Michael Warner associates the rhetorical construction of publics with "poetic world making," or the crafting of material correspondences among strangers (114). We should understand this poetry not just as the delivery of written and oral modes, but also as the shaping of resonant imagery, and—to return once more to Ahmed's ideas—the production of multimodal stickiness. We might think of that stickiness in two distinct but related ways: First, it signals the adhesive durability of rhetoric, its capacity to make a lasting mix of sensory impressions. Those impressions circulate not only in the memory of a particular film or communicative situation, but also in the ways later texts call up their predecessors to generate specific meanings.[5] Second, that stickiness refers to the social bonds that the poetic moment conjures. *Fruitvale Station* reaffirms the connections that were already forged on the BART platform in 2009, which gained strength in the intervening years due to such videographers as Diamond Reynolds, Feiden Santana, Ramsey Orta, Brandon Brooks, and Levi Frasier, as well as images from police body- and dash-cams. Those images contribute to the sometimes brutal poetics of world making, and they constitute rhetorical agents within the same collectives they help to assemble.

Maintaining movement cohesion also requires awareness of our habits of perception and communication, which often depend on a cluster of underlying contradictions—such as that between entertainment and social conditioning, progressive sentiment and repressive history, local security and transnational distress, meritocracy and oligarchy, postracial rhetoric and the relentless manifestation of structural racism. For Dana L. Cloud, one of the most urgent questions of materialist rhetorical theory is

> how people come to consciousness of the basic dynamism of society and collectively accrue a sense of shared identity and an intention to act out of and upon the fundamental antagonisms structuring society. . . . A revolutionary rhetoric is one that seizes on dialectical opportunities, and this practice might be captured productively in the Aristotelian concept of *kairos*. (299)

This kairotic seizing constitutes the basic desire of anticapitalist collectivism. But rather than locating decisive moments solely in human cognition, we might also consider the ways concrete antagonisms seize us. The agile, bustling environment offers up its own internal tensions as indicators of sociomaterial instability and as prompts toward more sustainable ontologies. The means through which we communicate, argues Michael Calvin McGee, structure our existing ontologies while tending to delimit possibilities for change: "Every 'speech' is in miniature a predictive model of the 'changes' which it recommends. Every 'speaker,' in other words, creates a picture of the world in the suggestion that 'audience' perceives reality through the terms and with the resources of 'speech'" (36). To extend McGee's point, sometimes a picture of the world emerges not through speech but through the pictorial mode itself, and more pertinent to the case at hand, through the timely meshing of images with speech, writing, sound, and motion.

Insofar as that multimodal assemblage establishes a filter through which audiences "perceive reality," it acts on us as much as we on it. By picturing some of the contradictions that structure the collective, it moves us in ways that more isolated modes may fail to do, making a densely embodied impression that, when replicated or remixed in still other forms, has potential for mnemonic and intersubjective stickiness. The assemblage adheres to our bodies even while circulating in the felt space between. Its kairotic appeal depends not on some fortunate discovery by the autonomous human subject, but rather on an ecology whose antagonisms are always in motion. The idea of variable antagonism captures the sense of Cloud's "social dynamism" while simultaneously signaling the conceptual significance of kairos for what Rickert calls ambient rhetoric. In ambient conditions the available means of communication encroach, coalesce, evolve, or swarm at the opportune time, but they never merely wait to be activated. To supplement Elkins's thinking, kairotic objects not only stare back, they reach out.

But even as the extrahuman world presses upon us, it does so without ready solutions to the problems it poses. The movies in these pages address us more explicitly than much material culture, and though their urgency is clear, the proper response is not. The pictures give us ways to see and feel while only hinting at ways to act on those perceptions. When Haskell Wexler turns his camera our way at the close of *Medium Cool*, for instance, he implies that there is work to be done yet stops short of defining it. He thus appropriates McLuhan's idea of the cool medium, the vehicle that requires our considered participation, and situates it precisely where McLuhan does not—in the experience of cinema. His film offers no assurances, however, that participation will yield welcome results. The journalist at the core of his narrative becomes more socially conscious as the story proceeds, but by the end he finds himself in critical condition while his companion lies dead. The crash that he filmed with such detachment at the outset returns with the force of tragedy; violence presents itself as not easily remedied but cyclical. *Funny Games* offers an even bleaker ending, with the Droog progeny entering a new house to prey on another unsuspecting family. As they survey the interior, John Zorn's vocals violate the calm just as they did in the opening sequence. Paul locks eyes with the viewer in a final freeze-frame.

Not all the movies lay such emphasis on traumatic recurrence, though most teach us to take a cautious approach to tidy resolutions. *Ararat* verges on such resolution with its unlikely reunions between Raffi and Ani, David and Philip. The film even leaves us with the gentle vision of an Armenian woman sewing a button onto a child's coat, capturing the tactile, textured character of the family bond. Yet that vision simultaneously calls up the losses suffered by Gorky and Saroyan, reminding us that where Raffi's father is concerned, nothing has been settled. Even though the scene is intimate and particular, it participates in a collective for whom resolution remains indefinitely suspended, and for whom that suspension becomes a way of life.

Whereas *Ararat* outlines the risks of narrating those ways of life to outsiders, *Even the Rain* probes the limits of outsiders' compassion. Sebastián shows initial concern for the economic concerns of his extras, but values his movie more; Costa risks his life to save Belén, but cannot commit to the long-term fight. In a moment of psychic contradiction, his most profound identification with Daniel coincides with his decision to leave Cochabamba. Shortly thereafter he contemplates a bottle of *yaku* even as the city around him dissolves from view. *Fruitvale Station* similarly suggests that long-term commitment, while in short supply, is precisely what is needed to combat racism, and specifies moviemaking as a vital contributor to that process. But the efficacy of citizen videography remains a troubled question given the co-optation of resistance and the backlash against antiracist movements during the 2016 U.S. presidential campaign. What that campaign made clear with its depictions of border walls, as well as its demonization of African American protest, targeting of Muslims, and slurs against women of many backgrounds and creeds, is that struggle by historically oppressed groups will continue to play itself out in the realm of the visual.

Paul Thomas Anderson and Martin Scorsese approach that realm as a space to dramatize the effects of psychic and social trauma, and to imagine (if not enact) the process of healing. That imagining typically comes to us saturated with ambivalence, affirming cinematic agency while anticipating further turmoil. Such tension occupies the final frames of *Magnolia* as Claudia, like Paul at the end of *Funny Games,* looks directly at the viewer. Where his look radiates menace, hers implies relief. After decades of repression and addiction, she appears to have discovered a trustworthy companion. After numerous appeals from the ambient environment, including television and radio broadcasts and a biblical cataclysm, the new lovers generate harmony from shared wounds. And yet in the same moment, the voice that most persistently endeavors to fashion collectivity among *Magnolia*'s disparate players brings a note of uncertainty to the conclusion. Rather than offering assurances, Aimee Mann raises a question: "Can you / save me / from the ranks / of the freaks / who could never love anyone?" To draw again on the work of Caruth, the film affirms healing correspondences between traumatized subjects, yet presents the possibility of lasting transformation as a query instead of an assertion. In a text that identifies unlikely events onscreen with unlikely events in viewers' lives, the image of relief arrives laced with doubt. By extension, it casts doubt on the collective's attunement to widespread experiences of injury and grief—an attunement that the narrative depicts as a species of miracle.

As we saw in chapter 4, Claudia accepts the miracle, as does the film itself with the narrator's claim that "these strange things happen all the time." It is nevertheless telling that Anderson locates agency at the juncture of melodrama and fantasy, and that Scorsese figures it as a sort of magic—the conjuror's most loved creation, which, after separation and dormancy, finds its way back to him. Agency circulates, disappears, and resurfaces, never belonging to human subjects, even (and perhaps especially) when they attempt to harness it within the commodity form. As the automaton stares back at us in the last moments of *Hugo*, it bears the gaze in multiple senses, at once receiving, holding, and producing it. It embodies the reciprocity of metafilm, watching as it is watched. And like *Magnolia*, it proffers a comforting ending even after the film questions the integrity of any assured resolution.

"Happy endings only happen in the movies," Méliès tells Hugo after chronicling his tempestuous film career. His words linger near the close of the film as the camera scans a party in the director's honor, settling briefly on Hugo performing magic tricks for a group of admirers. The film has taught us to expect such glad occurrences within the realm of the diegesis but to doubt their transferability to extradiegetic space. While the movie offers us a vision of reunion and regeneration, it casts our side of the lens as a world being lost to the systems—a world whose violence extends from the micropolitics of familial and sexual relationships to the macropolitics of empire and transnational capital.

Yet the emphasis on the reproduction of violence involves a certain contradiction. For all the metaleptic sophistication of *Hugo*, Papa Georges shows no awareness of being in a movie himself. For him, the return of the automaton and the rediscovery of his early films contravenes his sense of life outside the movies. What is more, movies throughout this book have troubled the hard distinction between the worlds on either side of the lens. In *Medium Cool*, we hear "Look out, Haskell, that's real!" as Wexler films the detonation of tear gas; in *Funny Games*, Paul addresses us as perpetrators of onscreen violence, influencing his actions with our genre-inflected viewing desires; in *Magnolia*, nurse Phil, a lively painting, and the narrator all counsel faith in the implausible; and in *Fruitvale Station*, images of the actual Oscar flow into his fictional representation just as the fictional representation of his daughter flows into images of the real Tatiana. There can be, it seems, no safe distance from depictions of trauma, but reciprocally, there exists no necessary chasm between viewers and images of principled headway.

The dialectic between visions of healing and those of systemic containment may appear to suggest an entropic inconsistency at the core of political metafilm. But in contrast to such perspectives, we do well to engage the dialectic as a reminder of continuing exigency. In an era of xenophobic presidencies, transnational attacks on the labor movement, the exoneration of racist vigilantes and police officers, as well as the repression of dissent and journalism, the precariousness of past social victories becomes distressingly plain. *Medium Cool* holds a startling relevance half a century later; *Fruitvale Station*'s urgency intensifies rather than diminishing with the passing years. Their kairotic appeal derives in part from attention to antagonisms between national rhetorics of democracy and embodied experiences of repression. The salience comes not only from their subject matter but also from insistence on the irresolution of systemic trauma and the necessary persistence of struggle.

Reflexive materialism locates the exigency for struggle in the layered character of sociopolitical discord, which Scott and Welch ably address in their reading of Kenneth Koch's poem "One Train May Hide Another." Rehearsing his emphasis on tracks lurking behind tracks, they contend that a fixation on conspicuous hazards may divert attention from more deeply embedded ones. The cinematic corollary may well be Hugo, frozen in place as the train approaches, bearing with it the loss of his parents, his purpose, and his home. He awakens to find the automaton watching curiously as if awaiting his next move. There is momentary relief. Then the boy inspects his body, looking down inside himself to find the metal bands and gear teeth, the coils, wheels, and pinions, the creeping of the systems, before awakening once more.

NOTES

NOTES TO THE INTRODUCTION

1. This form of contextualization aligns with the participatory character of McLuhan's concept of coolness. In *The Rhetoric of Cool: Composition Studies and New Media*, Jeff Rice interprets McLuhanesque "cool" as an "interactive system of pattern making that foregrounds connectivity" (35), and that enrolls participants in the creative co-construction of meaning.
2. Such praxis often sparks anxiety about voyeurism, the privilege of temporary compassion, and violent images being incorporated into public rhetoric in ways that lead to predictability and disregard. The films indict us for partaking in scenes of carnage, however confidently we claim analytical distance (Houck and Picart 172).
3. Michael Haneke, who figures prominently in chapter 1, represents the camera as a kind of shield against self-analysis in *Benny's Video* (1992) and *Code Unknown* (2000).
4. Stam locates a similarly materialist reflexivity in Jean-Luc Godard's *Tout Va Bien* (216).
5. Halbritter develops the idea of the life soundtrack (324) in his analysis of the Rolling Stones's music in *The Big Chill* (1983).
6. Anderson also examines such abuse in *Boogie Nights* (1997), *Punch-Drunk Love* (2002), and *There Will Be Blood* (2007). Drawing connections between these movies requires examining what Caroline Levine characterizes as network semiotics, which privilege associative epistemology over causal logic.

NOTES TO CHAPTER 1

1. Wenders won Best Director at Cannes for *Wings of Desire* (1987) and Moretti won the same award for *Dear Diary* (1993). Speck's *Funny Frames* (85) and Dargis's "*Amour*, a Wrenching Love Story, Wins at Cannes" report the directors' dislike for *Funny Games*.
2. See *Terministic* 3. While paying homage to Burke, he features the work of Barry Brummett, Bill Nichols, Anna Chisholm, and Ekaterina Haskins, who argue that viewers' identification with filmic situations demonstrates interpellation by ideological apparatuses and acceptance of well-worn narrative cues.
3. Wes Craven's *Scream* (1996) and Drew Goddard's *The Cabin in the Woods* (2011) express similar self-consciousness about audience expectations. But whereas those movies intensify narrative pleasure through comic irony, *Funny Games* defies that pleasure.
4. In an interview packaged with the *Benny's Video* DVD, Haneke contrasts the chilly palette of his first three movies with the warmth of television. Although he refers specifically to color scheme, the commentary overlaps productively with McLuhan's reflections on the temperature of delivery. McLuhan describes TV as a cool medium, but Haneke takes issue with that assumption, associating the device with a one-way cascade of affect rather than an invitation to interactivity. Like Wexler, Haneke affiliates cool rhetoric with cinema.
5. See Schumacher's *The Lost Boys* (1987) and Red's *Bad Moon* (1996) for examples of sensitive dogs in horror films.
6. I attribute the point about "eggy weggs" to Sarah Hanks, a fine writing teacher and a canny interpreter of Kubrick movies.
7. Dingo finds that such power consciousness has long informed the study of rhetorical circulation, citing the work of John Trimbur as an example. Studying communicative flows without attention to wealth inequality will prove misleading, she argues, for "rhetorical production and circulation *cannot* be separated from the political economy or the material conditions of writing" (16–17).
8. The movie thereby prefigures Rita Felski's case in *The Limits of Critique*, appropriating the labor of the detective-critic and contesting his privilege.
9. His opposition to a deterministic model of spectatorship informs his writing about Robert Bresson, whose films work by "reduction and omission" to engage the creativity of the addressee ("Terror" 573).
10. Such moments nudge us to consider Haneke's body of films as a fugue-like argument. *Funny Games* recalls *Benny's Video*, where Haneke also compares the ability to rewind and alter images with the capacity to control others' lives. The picture begins with Benny fixating on video of a pig slaughter, advancing and reversing the tape so as to witness the animal dying over and over, and even freezing the scene at the moment of maximum violence. The fixation culminates in a reenactment in which Benny steals the farmer's bolt gun and uses it to kill a newly made friend. The skills he acquires in his recording studio later permit him to monitor his parents when they discuss how to hide the crime. He uses the footage to charge them with the murder despite the measures they take to cover for him. Unflattering as Haneke can be toward his audience, he reserves his more scathing appraisals for those (like himself) who wield the camera.
11. Whereas early sequences of *Funny Games* evoke Kubrick's *A Clockwork Orange*, Schorschi's ingenuity in the face of terror calls up *The Shining*. If Schorschi's escape alludes to that of Danny Torrance, Paul's theme music parallels the maniacal Jack

Torrance's "Here's Johnny!"—surely among horror's most unnerving assertions of a villain's bad intentions.
12. Subdued cross-referencing invites attunement to small details, playing into what D. A. Miller depicts as the plight of the "too-close viewer" (22). In *Hidden Hitchcock*, Miller begins by noting the director's famous cameos in his own movies, and then proceeds to find his image in less obvious places—barely noticeable on a book cover in *Strangers on a Train*, for example, or (perhaps) wandering into the Mellon Gallery scene in the same film (31, 38). Given titles like *Caché* (*Hidden*) and *Funny Games*, it comes as little surprise that Haneke would also embed secrets within the visual field. But considering how firmly his films accentuate their sociopolitical dimensions, they confront the too-close viewer with a paradox. The texts demonstrate such self-referential tendencies that they compel us to dwell with them, to work through their enigmas and discover new ones through repeat viewings; yet they also hint at necessary action in the world beyond the movie screen. At once confounding for viewers and indicative of ethical vigilance, his work appears unsure of the efficacy of its critique and the prospect of audience uptake.
13. See Jorge Luis Borges's "The Analytical Language of John Wilkins" in *Other Inquisitions, 1937–1952*.
14. In a chilling intertext, the opening sequence of Egoyan's *The Sweet Hereafter* (1997) also features its central character entering a car wash. Whereas Haneke's picture generates claustrophobia with its creeping movement through the system, *The Sweet Hereafter* creates even deeper anxiety by having the car get stuck. The malfunctioning coincides with the driver's cell phone conversation with his estranged daughter. That broken relationship haunts the subsequent narrative, as he investigates a bus crash in a Canadian mountain town that killed most of the area's children.
15. See Gries, *Still 18*, where she attributes the critique of scholarly egoism to Marback.
16. John Carpenter's *Halloween* (1978) and Wes Craven's *A Nightmare on Elm Street* (1984) typify the "final girl" narrative.
17. See Lowenstein 7. Recent instances of this collapse include Ana Lily Amirpour's *A Girl Walks Home Alone at Night* (2014), Jennifer Kent's *The Babadook* (2014), and Osgood Perkins's *I Am the Pretty Thing That Lives in the House* (2016).
18. See Sontag 18, 88. Wendy Hesford's *Spectacular Rhetorics* also locates the presumption of safe distance in human rights discourse, arguing that "American nationalist rhetoric often assumes that all [human rights] violations take place elsewhere" (32–33).
19. The recurring names in Haneke's pictures invite comparison of how families disintegrate, as the films situate those breakdowns alongside traumas of imperialism, workplace alienation, nationalism, surveillance culture, screen fixation, child abuse, and children's cruelty to each other. To recall Levine's emphasis on network form, the web of names asks us to treat the films as interlinked forms of theory rather than texts with something to hide, something that only the savvy critic can uncover.
20. These forms of torture call to mind Pier-Paolo Pasolini's *Salò* (1975), which Haneke ranks as his fourth favorite film (BFI). The picture focuses on a group of World War II–era Italian libertines who gather victims into a stately home only to defile and murder them in theatrical fashion. The structure of *Funny Games* (Haneke's fourth feature film) summons that of the earlier movie, and the names of its killers echo the first name of Pasolini, who was himself murdered before *Salò* was released. Haneke provides no more psychological history for his villains than Pasolini does for his libertines.

NOTES TO CHAPTER 2

1. See Siraganian 134 and Parker 1047. What Parker sees as Egoyan's insistence on "intergenerational embrace" also enters into Saroyan's film, which dramatizes young people struggling to support suffering parents as well as parents reaching helplessly toward lost children.
2. Davis features the quoted passage from Burke's *Language as Symbolic Action* in her own *Inessential Solidarity* 33.
3. See Rai 174–75. She relies here on Pezzullo 9.
4. In his reflections on historical re-creation, Michael Bernard-Donals considers the possibility that memory sites "don't invoke or catalyze memory" of genocide "so much as they provoke *other* memories, and these other memories both *present* the event and also potentially *undo* that memory by betraying what can't be said" (16). *Ararat* shows the memory site provoking those other remembrances in multiple instances: Celia's recollections of her father, David's tensions with his son, Ali's childhood that does not cohere with Saroyan's narrative. Egoyan acknowledges the synecdochic rhetoric of the memory site, which activates mental images it cannot contain. But he also shows how those counter-memories perpetuate the Armenian Catastrophe, the displacement of post-exilic memory by the narcissism of audiences whose psychic investments lie elsewhere.
5. Historical documents by Clarence Ussher spell the name "Jevdet Bey," though the credits for *Ararat* read "Jevdet Bay." I use Egoyan's spelling to refer to the character in Saroyan's film, as distinct from the actual person.
6. See Romney 171 and Torchin 9 for discussions of Spielberg's translation of Holocaust testimony into spectacle.
7. Theriault describes the circumstances of Gorky's emigration in *Rethinking Arshile Gorky* (15). She observes that Gorky's ensuing work tended toward abstract experimentalism, as he experienced what Georgiana Banita describes as "an ambivalent relationship to figurative painting" (93). His simultaneous practice and suspicion of figurative representation make him an especially apt ally for Egoyan, who expresses a similar attitude toward mimetic film.
8. See *Inessential Solidarity* 21. Although Davis elegantly describes Burke's grounding of identity in multiple, sometimes clashing affinities, she challenges his idea of a biological individual that precedes discourse, and that engages in persuasion so as to overcome its original division from other subjects (23–25). She posits union as a constitutive condition rather than a frustrated aspiration.
9. *Ararat*'s tendency to trouble its protagonists' truths has led some viewers to reject the narrative as muddled. Reviewers regularly dislike the movie's didactic tone, finding that its lessons falter beneath the heft of Egoyan's self-consciousness (Dawson; Levy). Similar critiques commonly appear in reviews of metafilm. Detractors and enthusiasts alike note their overwhelming intricacies, calling them "academic," "over-ambitious," "clumsy," "convoluted," "incoherent," and "self-indulgent" while occasionally perceiving a certain condescension toward characters as well as audiences (Emerson; Gonzalez; "*Magnolia*"; Maslin; Thomas). At times, the movies merit the critique. But they also do necessary rhetorical work by prodding viewers' consciousness of historical violence and leaving them to consider next steps.
10. His attachment to his father may not signal absolute inertia, however. To return to Ahmed's thinking, melancholia may harbor its own quiet, internal movement insofar as political commitment undergoes transformation during repeat performance (187). Raffi acknowledges such mobility in a conversation with David late in the

movie. The border guard accuses him of making rash choices on the return from Armenia—acting out due to the trauma of "lost meaning." "I didn't lose meaning," Raffi replies. "It was more like the meaning of things changed." After he sees how cleanly the record of genocide has been expunged, the change may involve a more poignant identification with his father's historical perspective—a view situated a generation closer to the events of 1915 and yet no better able to resurrect geographical and architectural traces of the Catastrophe.

11. The Blanchot quotation appears in *The Historiographic Perversion* (10). In an intriguing turn in the same work, Nichanian also refuses to describe events in Armenia as genocide. He does so, however, from a position deeply opposed to the one adopted by Ali. Nichanian details how historians have demanded copious archival testimony to support the claim of genocide, yet argues that such testimony could never encompass the horror of what took place in Van during and after 1915. Insofar as the idea of genocide makes a commodity of unrepresentable violence, he finds it inadequate to a catastrophe that has not ended but continues in the form of denial.

12. The interrogation proceeds within a system of answerability that David takes to be natural and that Raffi lacks the resources to resist. Scott and Welch represent that system as an "economy of exchange values" that reflects the interlacing of transnational rhetorics with global capitalism, while helping to determine whose stories attain widespread circulation and whose remain muted ("One" 564).

NOTES TO CHAPTER 3

1. See Latour, "Berlin" 10. Bill Brown cites the same passage in "Thing Theory," though he distinguishes a "thing" from an "object" (3). As likely to be an idea as a concrete artifact, the signifier "thing" fuses loose generality with the ostensible precision of tangible materials. The tension between vagueness and the desire for certitude commands our attention, Brown observes, when objects "stop working for us: when the drill breaks, when the car stalls, when the windows get filthy, when their flow within the circuits of production and distribution, consumption and exhibition, has been arrested, however momentarily" (4). Although this chapter focuses on the consubstantiality of what Brown calls objects, it also concerns the thing-ness of varied valued substances—the way they cloud the border between physicality and abstraction.
2. Bollaín's partner Paul Laverty wrote the screenplay for *Even the Rain*. He meant it to be the first in a series of pictures based on Zinn's *A People's History of the United States*, all of which would be period films tied to specific chapters. When those plans collapsed, he kept working on the initial chapter and added the metafilmic layering that included the fictional filmmakers and the water wars (DP/30).
3. See Dobrin 67 and Hayles 2.
4. Perez derives these definitions from Smith's "Altered States: Character and Emotional Response in Cinema."
5. See *Grammar* 77–85 for a discussion of how changing the location or spatial circumference in which an act unfolds may change actors' (or audiences') interpretation of that act, along with the language they use to describe it.
6. The riot squads fired tear gas into crowds of dissenters, and one army officer killed the student Victor Hugo Daza with a rifle shot to the face (Assies 29–30; Finnegan).
7. The Cochabamban extras speak Quechua as their primary language.

8. See Dingo 9–10. David Karjanen also tracks how neoliberalism represents itself as common sense, citing James Aune's argument that "free market rhetoric has become the dominant framework for people to think and talk about economic forces in the post Cold War world where an unbridled global capitalism is deemed the 'natural' and 'superior' means of organizing any economy" (5). Studying a range of corporate rhetorics in U.S. and U.K. contexts, Karjanen finds that those rhetorics construct living wage ordinances as "natural disasters" insofar as they depart from market self-regulation (8).
9. See Hesford, "Global" 788 and Schell 168.
10. The rushes evince a visual style akin to Werner Herzog's *Aguirre, the Wrath of God* (1972) and *Fitzcarraldo* (1982). *Fitzcarraldo* is a suggestive intertext insofar as it features a European adventurer who exploits indigenous workers so as to erect an opera house in Peru. Bollaín confirms the connection to Herzog by recognizing *Aguirre* as an inspiration for Sebastián's aesthetic (DP/30).
11. Stam (155) finds such a proleptic strategy in Fellini's *8½* (1963) and Woody Allen's *Stardust Memories* (1980).
12. His leadership becomes apparent in his moderating of community debates, his public oratory, and his conflict with police. That conflict clarifies how human and extrahuman agents collaborate to transform the existing order, giving evidence for Gries's contention that "breakdowns, strikes, and political events are occasions in which the collective activity of visual things becomes highly visible and, thus, traceable" ("Dingrhetoriks" 303). Channeling Latour, she points out that during times of upheaval, "visual things, typically thought of as intermediaries, become overt, active mediators" (303). While Daniel already commands respect due to his ease with the bullhorn, televised imaged of officers bloodying his face work to strengthen his cause.

NOTES TO CHAPTER 4

1. Most family dysfunction in *Magnolia* develops in the context of the entertainment industry, with ambitious or already powerful fathers mistreating their children or using them for personal gain. Considering Anderson's at times difficult relationship with New Line Cinema, the film functions in part as a comment on the studio's parenting of the project. Anderson underscores the point in a documentary in which he and singer-songwriter Fiona Apple perform a skit about the making and reception of the picture. He plays the part of the studio while Apple stands in for the film. Anderson badgers her and forces her to dance, but the more she tries to please him, the angrier he becomes. He berates her for harboring ridiculous frogs and interminable speeches by Jason Robards, for being too long, too self-indulgent, "too fucking too." After several efforts to impress, she tries to flee. Finding no escape, she assumes the fetal position. The studio then decides that he loves her after all, though she's "no *Boogie Nights*." The skit aligns nicely with J. D. Connor's argument in *The Studios after the Studios: Neoclassical Hollywood (1970–2010)*, where he interprets much Hollywood fare since 1970 as allegory for battles between filmmakers and corporate financiers. Although not all the films in this book are Hollywood productions, many nevertheless fit Connor's schema by implicitly framing production companies as psychopaths, border guards, rapacious adventurers, or cruel fathers.
2. See Stilwell 187, 194. See also Kassabian (43–46), who outlines a different vocabulary for phenomena similar to those Stilwell describes. Citing the work of Earle Hagen, she develops an idea of "source scoring" that corresponds with Stilwell's theory of

"metadiegetic" music. Source scoring fuses "source music," which proceeds inside the narrative world, with the idea of "dramatic scoring," which accompanies the visuals yet exists outside the diegetic domain. Despite the elegance of Hagen's terminology, the advantage of the term "metadiegetic" lies in its complex associations: it refers to the liminal territory between intra- and extradiegetic music while also connoting the reflexive character of metaleptic rhetoric.

3. Jason Sperb attributes to *Magnolia* an "intensely affective logic," arguing that "it operates on an emotional level much more than a narrative one" (115). Rather than creating a hard distinction between narrative and affective rhetoric, however, we might instead attend to how those rhetorics become enmeshed.

4. It is unsurprising, when we think of *Magnolia* as a composed event, to learn that Mann's songs inspired the film and afforded root material for many of its scenes (Sperb 125). Although Sperb views some of those scenes as "hysterical" displays in a "rambling story," he hears Mann's songs as an organizing force (117, 126).

5. See Thompson and Biddle 6. Ahmed anticipates the insight by claiming that "some forms of stickiness are about holding things together. Some are about blockages or stopping things moving" (91).

6. Alain Badiou relates the sense of emergency in *Magnolia* to anxiety over the sustainability of "humanity" within a media structure that appears to permit connection while instead fostering intensified individuation. "It's a film that serves as a warning of urgency and that says: 'Make no mistake about it, what's at stake is the question of humanity itself; it's really under threat'" (187). With such concerns in mind, he reads the film's excesses—Frank's hyper-macho lecture to his followers, Linda's stormy denunciation of the pharmacists who question her drug prescriptions—as instances of both virtuoso acting and self-conscious glossiness (180–81, 188–89). Contrasting *Magnolia* with the plays of Eugene O'Neill and Tennessee Williams, Badiou suggests that their stagecraft often locates moments of catharsis in high-powered soliloquys by gifted actors. "Anderson's thesis," he argues, "is exactly the opposite. Performance, in the fictional sense, will be shown as the moment of greatest *alienation*, not at all as that of the resolution of truth" (185).

7. Haneke's *71 Fragments of a Chronology of Chance* performs a more sinister variation on the sociospatial network, as Viennese and Romanian strangers who travel seemingly divergent paths become enmeshed in a mass shooting near the film's end.

8. The idea of identification through sound harmonizes with prominent themes in *Rhetoric of Motives*. In Shannon Walters's reading of that text, rhetoric emerges as a "physical art" grounded in "a variety of nonverbal maneuvers beyond 'sheer words.'" She explains that "nonverbal and tactile elements are integral to his movement from traditional rhetorics of persuasion to rhetorics based on identification" (39). The nonverbal and tactile dimensions of Burke's idea make it particularly relevant to Walters's theory of a haptic rhetoric—one dedicated to touch as a form of communication. Aural rhetoric, while not necessarily departing from words, also makes meaning through nonverbal means. Such meaning emerges from vibrations that register not just in the ear but also in the torso and extremities.

9. Both Joanne Clarke Dillman and Sperb see the televisual thematics in *Magnolia* as providing clues to the film's rhetorical structure. Citing Dillman, Sperb claims that the movie "works as a televisual soap opera in cinematic form" (135–36).

10. Affective coordination tends to happen in unpredictable ways. As a form of identification, it enrolls subjects in what Kassabian specifies as "scenarios" rather than "single positions" (86). To clarify her point, Kassabian cites Sharon Willis's claim that "identification is not a state, but a process . . . it is likely to be mobile and intermittent rather than consistent." The "Wise Up" chorus connotes a period

of intense alignment between scenarios—though most of the characters remain unaware of their mutual interpellation. Some of them develop that awareness during the closing scenes of the film, however, supporting the idea of identification as a mobile process.

11. Observing how Stanley's maturity surpasses that of the other characters, Lane contends that he "not only knows more (intellectually and emotionally) than the surrounding adults; but he also anticipates the film's final 'catastrophe' and reacts openly without fear or question" (14). Such anticipation indicates Stanley's sensitivity to ambience, which he demonstrates by researching atmospheric disturbances before the frogs arrive.

12. *Magnolia* contributes to movie theory not only by exemplifying contemporary insights regarding aurality and affect, but also by commenting on the rhetoric of its own medium. It performs a variation on what W. J. T. Mitchell terms "picture theory," by which he means something different from theorizing with pictures or devising a system to describe their semiotic functioning. For Mitchell, the pictures themselves constitute ways of thinking.

13. See Badiou 187, 176. He suggests that tendencies toward unity in *Magnolia* generally proceed alongside countermovements. Jim and Claudia's romance develops in the shadow of her addiction and his failures at work; Stanley's brave confrontation with his father meets with quiet dismissal; in a sequence otherwise replete with forgiveness, Jimmy Gator meets a fiery end. As the film posits overlap between movie magic and psychic recovery, it hints that such magic is endangered. For Badiou, the danger concerns not just *Magnolia*'s character ensemble but also the sustainability of a certain idea of humanity. That Anderson holds such ambitions for his ensemble—that he thinks it a microcosm for humankind—finds affirmation in its encounter with a biblical plague (178).

14. Boyer's comments appear in "'Say Yes to Love, or Else Be Lonely': An Interview about Paul Thomas Anderson's *Magnolia*," where she and six other scholars discuss the film with Badiou. The interview appears in Badiou's *Cinema* (176–92).

NOTES TO CHAPTER 5

1. The idea of the postracial society achieved notoriety during the Obama presidency, figuring in cable news, radio, Internet discourse, and the scholarship of political scientists such as Wilbur C. Rich.
2. The public reversal of the monitoring gaze enacts a rhetoric of parrhesia, which Vorris Nunley and Gerard Hauser define as speaking frankly to unjust authority. Here speaking must be understood not strictly as orality but as fully embodied delivery.
3. To use Brinkema's formulation, the blackout constitutes the "form of the affect." That affect is, in one sense, extrapersonal, but it manifests in bodily form as revulsion, nausea, incredulity, dysphoric urgency. The seeming non-form of the visual caesura figures the traumatic rupture, which begs for explanation but frustrates narrative closure.
4. See Labrecque interview. Coogler suggests in another interview that the film lends weight to widespread stories of "people our age getting shot, being killed by each other and by the police. . . . But this time, we were witnesses to it. The video made all of us witnesses" (J. Rhodes).
5. However attentive we are to the distinctions among cases, we should not overlook the significance in Grant wearing a hoodie on the day of his death, three years before Trayvon Martin's hoodie drew George Zimmerman's attention. The garment would become an icon of the movement against racist policing, first representing

outrage over Martin's death and later figuring into "I Can't Breathe" and "Black Lives Matter" demonstrations. As the hoodie image flows through varied instances of public protest, it conveys what Gries names the "dynamic eventfulness" of iconic rhetoric (*Still* 8).

6. Turim describes the flashback as an affordance of film form, suggesting that although written and theatrical texts used such devices before the emergence of cinema, the term likely came to movies from mechanics and physics. While the word "flash" has long referred to small explosions, lightning, and sparking engines, Turim traces the "flash back" to early twentieth-century references to the misfiring of those engines, some of which burned up the vehicles in which they were housed. Borrowing from that machine context, people began referring to leaps backward in movie time as "flashbacks," which created the effect of transporting audiences in the film's "time machine" (3–4). She contends that after the term gained acceptance in "film criticism and screen writing," audiences began applying it in retrospective fashion to "similar techniques of narration in earlier poems, novels, and plays" (4).

7. For stories of police interfering with citizen camera work, see American Civil Liberties Union; Arsenault; Kelly; Meyer; Serna, "With." For information about the Texas and Arizona bills, see Campbell, "Texas"; Fischer; Woolf. Details about police confusing cameras with weapons appear in Campbell, "Deputies"; M. Wilson.

8. The Supreme Court attributes racial profiling only to conscious intention (Epp, Maynard-Moody, and Haider-Markel 6).

9. See Epp, Maynard-Moody, and Haider-Markel 92 and Jennifer Ritterhouse's *Growing Up Jim Crow*.

10. See Campaign Zero website. Candice Rai provides background in *Democracy's Lot*, explaining that broken windows theory requires addressing "relatively innocuous crimes" with "severity" to maintain a community's high self-concept and preempt "more serious criminal behavior and neighborhood deterioration" (155). The point is not to promote hypervigilant policing for its own sake, but rather to act as a deterrent. Campaign Zero counters that the practice leads to unnecessary confrontations, creating circuits of suspicion that poison the atmosphere of many communities.

11. Although hindrances to dialogue have particular prominence in the United States, Haneke finds them in Europe as well. In *Code Unknown*, he examines the racism of Parisian police while tying it to anti-immigrant sentiment: a young white man (Jean) casually drops trash in the lap of a Romanian woman sitting on the sidewalk; another young man of Malian heritage (Amadou) demands that he apologize. A fight ensues, and officers arrive on the scene to break it up. Amadou agrees to visit the police station to make a statement but refuses to be manhandled. The officers read his attempt at dialogue as resistance and subject him to violent restraint. The scene breaks at the point of highest tension, though we learn later that police beat and humiliated him before his release, and that authorities deported the woman he tried to defend.

12. Gries offers a mixed assessment of rhetors' efforts to imagine uptake in advance and thereby influence the circulatory process: "While authors and artists can attempt to account for rhetorical velocity by anticipating the third-party recomposition of their own work (Ridolfo and DeVoss 2009), they can never fully control where or how the things they produce will circulate" (*Still* 18).

13. Focusing on iconic photographs, they detail how pictures like Dorothea Lange's "Migrant Mother," Alfred Eisenstadt's "Times Square Kiss," and Nick Ut's "Napalm Girl" synthesize public affect while providing material for negotiating national selfhood.

14. Coverage of the respective cases appears in Chandler; Bellware; Serna, "No."

15. Green tracks the contradictions of docufiction to "early French cinema's aesthetic and conceptual scission between the Lumière brothers and Georges Méliès" (67), as the Lumières trained their lenses on everyday "actualities" and Méliès delved into fantasy and science fiction. Clear as those distinctions may seem, movie production tends to fuse the staged and the unstaged, the fantastic and the commonplace.
16. See Lipkin, *Real* 71. Turim also notes the flashback's historical association with an insider's view of past events, while observing how the term has acquired psychological connotations (5). In the case of traumatic flashback, certain kinds of sensory input trigger memories so vivid that they feel less like recalling than reliving. The video of Grant's shooting takes that phenomenon from an individual to a social scale, as the footage becomes a metonym for centuries of related killings.
17. History discloses itself through the process of mediation. This process ensures that "any attempt to render an event authentically will always be vexed by what cannot be integrated into history and memory, and by the impossibility of ever being able to point to an object or an image and to finally say, 'See? That's what happened. Understand?'" (Bernard-Donals 87).
18. Central Connecticut State University's Institute for Municipal and Regional Policy finds that police perception of a suspect's race has a dramatic effect on whether officers only threaten to use a Taser or actually fire one. Black men in Connecticut "were about three times more likely to be Tased than simply warned" by police. Latino men were over 40 percent more likely to be Tased, while white men had an equal chance of receiving a Taser warning or being fired upon (Wang).

NOTES TO THE CONCLUSION

1. See *Raging Bull* (1980) and *Goodfellas* (1990) for memorable examples.
2. Selznick's *The Invention of Hugo Cabret* begins with explicit remediation, inviting the reader to experience the opening drawings in cinematic terms. Instructing the reader to "picture yourself sitting in the darkness, like the beginning of a movie," the book features images that proffer an establishing shot and a slow zoom that moves through Paris and into the train station, leading to a close-up of Hugo. The use of film-style storyboarding techniques supports Bolter and Grusin's claim that remediation involves not just the appropriation and alteration of older media by newer forms, but the reverse as well (Selznick; Clement and Long).
3. In his description of Marx's theory of value, Chris Harman explains how machines that appear to perform in autonomous fashion, and thus generate profit without the exploitation of human work, are themselves the product of social ingenuity and embodied production (41).
4. In *Violence*, Slavoj Žižek distinguishes between overt brutality and ideological antagonism while describing a consistent relation between the two. He describes conspicuous violence as "subjective" and naturalized forms as "objective" or systemic. Liberal fixation on combating subjective violence, he suggests, defers confrontation with the objective variety.
5. *Ararat* evokes the representational strategies of *Schindler's List* so as to subvert them. *Magnolia* derives its renderings of broadcast media from Sidney Lumet's *Network*, and Anderson bases his structure of crisscrossing mini-narratives partly on Robert Altman's *Nashville*.

WORKS CITED

Adams, Dale, and Robert Kline. "The Use of Films in Teaching Composition." *College Composition and Communication*, vol. 1, no. 3, Oct. 1975, pp. 258–62.

Agee, James, and Walker Evans. *Let Us Now Praise Famous Men*. 1941. Boston: Mariner, 2001.

Ahmed, Sara. *The Cultural Politics of Emotion*. Routledge, 2004.

Aktan, Gündüz. "Why Cannot It Be?" *Hürriyet Daily News*, 9 Jan. 2002, www.hurriyetdailynews.com/h.php?news=why-can-not-it-be-2002-01-09. Accessed 14 Feb. 2017.

Allen, Woody, director. *Stardust Memories*. United Artists, 1980.

Alloway, Meredith. "*Fruitvale Station*: Interview Ryan Coogler." *The Script Lab*, 9 July 2013, thescriptlab.com/features/the-lists/2327-fruitvale-station-interview-ryan-coogler-. Accessed 2 June 2016.

Althusser, Louis. *Lenin and Philosophy and Other Essays*. Monthly Review P, 1971.

Altman, Robert, director. *Nashville*. Paramount, 1975.

American Civil Liberties Union. "ACLU Sues D.C. Police Officer for Stealing Citizen's Smartphone Memory Card." *ACLU*, 5 Sep. 2012, m.aclu-nca.org/docket/aclu-sues-dc-police-officer-for-stealing-citizen's-smartphone-memory-card. Accessed 7 June 2016.

Amirpour, Ana Lily, director. *A Girl Walks Home Alone at Night*. Vice, 2014.

Anderson, Paul Thomas, director. *Boogie Nights*. New Line Cinema, 1997.

———, director. *Magnolia*. New Line Cinema, 1999.

———, director. *Punch-Drunk Love*. Columbia Pictures, 2002.

———, director. *There Will Be Blood*. Paramount Vantage, 2007.

Annett, Sandra. "The Nostalgic Remediation of Cinema in *Hugo* and *Paprika*." *Journal of Adaptation in Film and Performance*, vol. 7, no. 2, 2014, pp. 169–80.

Arsenault, Chris. "US Police Smash Camera for Recording Killing." *Al Jazeera*, 21 June 2011, www.aljazeera.com/indepth/features/2011/06/201162114131825860.html. Accessed 7 June 2016.

Assies, Willem. "David versus Goliath in Cochabamba: Water Rights, Neoliberalism, and the Revival of Social Protest in Bolivia." *Latin American Perspectives*, vol. 30, no. 3, 2003, pp. 14–36.

Atton, Chris. *Alternative Media*. Sage, 2002.

Aune, James Arnt. *Selling the Free Market: The Rhetoric of Economic Correctness*. Guilford P, 2002.

Badiou, Alain. *Cinema*. Translated by Susan Spitzer. Polity, 2013.

Banita, Georgiana. "'The Power to Imagine': Genocide, Exile, and Ethical Memory in Atom Egoyan's *Ararat*." *Film and Genocide*, edited by Kristi M. Wilson and Tomás Crowder-Taraborelli, U of Wisconsin P, 2012, pp. 87–105.

Bazin, Andre. *What Is Cinema?* U of California P, 2005.

Beachler, Hannah. "S&A 2013 Highlights: Production Designing *Fruitvale Station*." *Indiewire*, 7 Jan. 2014, www.indiewire.com/2014/01/sa-2013-highlights-production-designing-fruitvale-station-162754/. Accessed 18 Feb. 2017.

Bellware, Kim. "No Indictment for Cop Who Fatally Shot 12-Year Old Tamir Rice." *Huffington Post*, 28 Dec. 2015, www.huffingtonpost.com/entry/tamir-rice-inductment_us_56818253e4b0b958f65a0909. Accessed 19 June 2016.

Benjamin, Walter. "The Work of Art in the Age of Mechanical Reproduction." *Illuminations*. Edited by Hannah Arendt. Translated by Harry Zohn. Schocken, 2007.

Bennett, Jane. *Vibrant Matter: A Political Ecology of Things*. Duke UP, 2010.

Berkan, İsmet. "Tartışılan Ararat," *Radikal*, 24 Dec. 2001, www.radikal.com.tr/veriler/2001/12/24/haber_24547.php. Accessed 13 Feb. 2017.

Berlant, Lauren. "The Subject of True Feeling: Pain, Privacy, and Politics." *Cultural Pluralism, Identity Politics, and the Law*, edited by Austin Sarat and Thomas Kearns, U of Michigan P, 1999, pp. 49–84.

Bernard-Donals, Michael. *Figures of Memory: The Rhetoric of Displacement at the United States Holocaust Memorial Museum*. State U of New York P, 2016.

BFI Film Forever. "How the Directors and Critics Voted: Michael Haneke." *Sight and Sound* Greatest Films Poll, 2002, old.bfi.org.uk/sightandsound/polls/topten/poll/voter.php?forename=Michael&surname=Haneke. Accessed 13 June 2016.

Biesecker, Barbara, and John Louis Lucaites, editors. *Rhetoric, Materiality, and Politics*. Peter Lang, 2009.

Bishop, Ellen, editor. *Cinema-(to)-Graphy: Film and Writing in Contemporary Composition Courses*. Heinemann, 1999.

Blakesley, David. "Defining Film Rhetoric: The Case of Hitchcock's *Vertigo*." *Defining Visual Rhetorics*, edited by Charles A. Hill and Marguerite H. Helmers, Lawrence Erlbaum Associates, 2004, pp. 111–34.

———. "Sophistry, Magic, and the Vilifying Rhetoric of *The Usual Suspects*." Blakesley, *Terministic Screen*, pp. 234–45.

———, editor. *The Terministic Screen: Rhetorical Perspectives on Film*. Southern Illinois UP, 2003.

Blümlinger, Christa. "Figures of Disgust." Translated by Peter J. Schwartz. Grundmann, *Companion*, pp. 147–60.

Bollaín, Icíar, director. *Even the Rain*. Morena Films, 2010.

Bolter, Jay David. *Writing Space: Computers, Hypertext, and the Remediation of Print*. Lawrence Erlbaum, 2001.

Bolter, Jay David, and Richard Grusin. *Remediation: Understanding New Media*. MIT P, 2000.

Bonnaud, Frédéric. "The Captive Lover—An Interview with Jacques Rivette." Translated by Kent Jones. *Senses of Cinema*, vol. 79, Sept. 2001, sensesofcinema.com/2001/jacques-rivette/rivette-2/. Accessed 29 Oct. 2017.

Bordwell, David. *Making Meaning: Inference and Rhetoric in the Interpretation of Cinema*. Harvard, 1991.

Borges, Jorge Luis. *Other Inquisitions, 1937–1952*. Translated by Ruth L. C. Simms. U of Texas P, 1975.

Borrowman, Shane, and Marcia Kmetz. "Divided We Stand: Beyond Burkean Identification." *Rhetoric Review*, vol. 30, 2011, pp. 275–92.

Brinkema, Eugenie. *The Forms of the Affects*. Duke UP, 2014.

Brooks, Brian. "Specialty Box Office: Fruitvale Station Is a Hit; Sundance Winner Opens with Parallels to Trayvon Martin Case." *Deadline*, 14 July 2013, deadline.com/2013/07/specialty-box-office-fruitvale-station-michael-b-jordan-trayvon-martin-540902/. Accessed 21 May 2016.

Brown, Bill. "Thing Theory." *Critical Inquiry*, vol. 28, no. 1, 2001, pp. 1–22.

Brownell, Brett. "*Fruitvale Station* and the Weinstein Company's Push for Social Justice." *Mother Jones*, 13 July 2013, www.motherjones.com/mixed-media/2013/07/fruitvale-station-weinstein-company-social-justice. Accessed 25 May 2016.

Brummett, Barry. *Rhetorical Dimensions of Popular Culture*. U of Alabama P, 1991.

Brunette, Peter. *Michael Haneke*. U of Illinois P, 2010.

Bruzzi, Stella. *New Documentary: A Critical Introduction*. Routledge, 2000.

Burke, Kenneth. *Attitudes Toward History*. U of California P, 1984.

———. *A Grammar of Motives*. 1945. U of California P, 1969.

———. *Language as Symbolic Action: Essays on Life, Literature, and Method*. U of California P, 1966.

———. *Permanence and Change*. 1935. U of California P, 1984.

———. *A Rhetoric of Motives*. 1950. U of California P, 1969.

Campaign Zero. www.joincampaignzero.org. Accessed 10 June 2016.

Campbell, Andy. "Deputies Shoot Man Recording His Neighbor's Arrest, Say They Thought Phone Was a Gun." *Huffington Post*, 15 Sep. 2015, www.huffingtonpost.com/entry/deputies-shoot-man-recording-arrest_us_55f86dd7e4b0e333e54b78f9. Accessed 7 June 2016.

———. "Texas Bill Would Make Recording Police Illegal." *Huffington Post*, 13 March 2015, www.huffingtonpost.com/2015/03/13/bill-recording-police-illegal_n_6861444.html. Accessed 7 June 2016.

Carpenter, John, director. *Halloween*. 1978. Anchor Bay Entertainment, 1997.

Caruth, Cathy. *Unclaimed Experience: Trauma, Narrative, and History*. Johns Hopkins UP, 1996.

Ceraso, Steph. "(Re)Educating the Senses: Multimodal Listening, Bodily Learning, and the Composition of Sonic Experiences." *College English*, vol. 77, no. 2, 2014, pp. 102–23.

Chandler, Adam. "No Indictment in NYPD Eric Garner Chokehold Case." *The Atlantic*, 3 Dec. 2014, www.theatlantic.com/national/archive/2014/12/eric-garner-grand-jury-no-indictment-nypd/383392/. Accessed 19 June 2016.

Chisholm, Ann. "Rhetoric and the Early Work of Christian Metz: Augmenting Ideological Inquiry in Rhetorical Film Theory and Criticism." Blakesley, *Terministic Screen*, pp. 37–54.

Chouliaraki, Lilie. "Ordinary Witnessing in Post-Television News: Towards a New Moral Imagination." *Critical Discourse Studies*, vol. 7, no. 4, 2010, pp. 305–19.

Cilento, Fabrizio. "*Even the Rain*: A Confluence of Cinematic and Historical Temporalities." *Arizona Journal of Hispanic Cultural Studies*, vol. 16, 2012, pp. 245–58.

Clark, Danae. *Negotiating Hollywood: The Cultural Politics of Actors' Labor*. U of Minnesota P, 1995.

Cleaver, Harry. *Reading* Capital *Politically*. 1979. AntiThesis, 2000.

Clement, Jennifer, and Christian B. Long. "*Hugo*, Remediation, and the Cinema of Attractions, or the Adaptation of Hugo Cabret." *Senses of Cinema*, no. 63, July 2012, sensesofcinema.com/2012/feature-articles/hugo-remediation-and-the-cinema-of-attractions-or-the-adaptation-of-hugo-cabret/. Accessed 29 Oct. 2017.

Cloud, Dana L. "The Materialist Dialectic as a Site of *Kairos*: Theorizing Rhetorical Invention in Material Social Relations." Biesecker and Lucaites, pp. 293–320.

Clover, Carol J. *Men, Women, and Chain Saws*. Princeton UP, 1993.

Coen, Joel, director. *Miller's Crossing*. Twentieth Century Fox, 1990.

Connerton, Paul. *The Spirit of Mourning: History, Memory, and the Body*. Cambridge UP, 2011.

Connor, J. D. *The Studios after the Studios: Neoclassical Hollywood (1970–2010)*. Stanford UP, 2015.

Coogler, Ryan, director. *Fruitvale Station*. Weinstein Co., 2013.

Cooper, Merian C., and Ernest B. Schoedsack, directors. *King Kong*. Radio Pictures, 1933.

Coppola, Francis Ford, director. *The Conversation*. Paramount, 1974.

Cram, Emily Dianne. "'Angie Was Our Sister': Witnessing the Transformation of Disgust in the Citizenry of Photography." *Quarterly Journal of Speech*, vol. 98, no. 4, 2012, pp. 411–38.

Craven, Wes, director. *A Nightmare on Elm Street*. 1984. New Line Home Video, 2010.

———, director. *Scream*. 1996. Dimension Home Video, 1998.

Cronenberg, David, director. *Videodrome*. Universal Pictures, 1983.

Dargis, Manohla. "*Amour*, a Wrenching Love Story, Wins at Cannes." *New York Times*, 12 May 2012, www.nytimes.com/2012/05/28/movies/amour-by-michael-haneke-wins-palme-dor-at-cannes.html. Accessed 29 Oct. 2017.

Dassanowsky, Robert von. *Austrian Cinema: A History*. McFarland, 2005.

Davis, Diane. *Inessential Solidarity: Rhetoric and Foreigner Relations*. U of Pittsburgh P, 2010.

Dawson, Tom. Review of *Ararat*. *BBC Movies*, 11 March 2003, www.bbc.co.uk/films/2003/03/11/ararat_2003_review.shtml. Accessed 29 Oct. 2017.

Debord, Guy. *The Society of the Spectacle*. 1967. Black and Red, 2000.

DeLillo, Don. *Zero K*. Scribner, 2016.

DeLuca, Kevin, and Joe Wilferth. Forward to *Enculturation*, vol. 6, no. 2, 2009, enculturation.net/6.2/foreword. Accessed 29 Oct. 2017.

Demme, Jonathan, director. *The Silence of the Lambs*. Orion Pictures, 1991.

DePalma, Brian, director. *Dressed to Kill*. Filmways Pictures, 1980.

Dillman, Joanne Clarke. "Twelve Characters in Search of a Televisual Text: *Magnolia* Masquerading as Soap Opera." *Journal of Popular Film and Television*, vol. 33, no. 3, 2005, pp. 142–50.

Dingo, Rebecca. *Networking Arguments: Rhetoric, Transnational Feminism, and Public Policy Writing*. U of Pittsburgh P, 2012.

Dobrin, Sidney I. *Postcomposition*. Southern Illinois UP, 2011.

DP/30: The Oral History of Hollywood. "*Even the Rain*: Director Icíar Bollaín," www.youtube.com/watch?v=oliHeIto8PM. Accessed 1 Nov. 2014.

Dreyer, Carl Theodor. *Day of Wrath*. Palladium, 1943.

Dyer, Richard. *Stars*. London: British Film Institute, 1979.

Ebert, Roger. Review of *Even the Rain*, directed by Icíar Bollaín. *RogerEbert*, 24 Feb. 2011, www.rogerebert.com/reviews/even-the-rain-2011. Accessed 16 Aug. 2014.

Eddy, Beth. *The Rites of Identity: The Religious Naturalism and Cultural Criticism of Kenneth Burke and Ralph Ellison*. Princeton UP, 2003.

Egoyan, Atom, director. *Ararat*. Miramax, 2002.

———. "In Other Words: Poetic License and the Incarnation of History." *University of Toronto Quarterly*, vol. 73, 2004, pp. 886–905.

———, director. *The Sweet Hereafter*. Ego Film Arts, 1997.

Elkins, James. *The Object Stares Back*. Simon and Schuster, 1996.

Elsaesser, Thomas. "Performative Self-Contradictions: Michael Haneke's Mind Games." Grundmann, *Companion*, pp. 53–74.

Emerson, Jim. Review of *Funny Games. RogerEbert,* 13 March 2008, www.rogerebert.com/reviews/funny-games-2008. Accessed 22 May 2013.

Epp, Charles R., Steven Maynard-Moody, and Donald P. Haider-Markel. *Pulled Over: How Police Stops Define Race and Citizenship.* U of Chicago P, 2014.

"Eric Garner Death: 76 Arrested at London Westfield Demo." *BBC,* 11 Dec. 2014, www.bbc.com/news/uk-england-london-30424338. Accessed 10 June 2016.

Esmeir, Samera. "On Making Dehumanization Possible." *PMLA,* vol. 121, no. 5, 2006, pp. 1544–52.

Feehan, Michael. "A Note on the Writing of *A Rhetoric of Motives*." *K. B. Journal: The Journal of the Kenneth Burke Society,* vol. 8, no. 1, Spring 2012, kbjournal.org/feehan_note_rhetoric_of_motives. Accessed 18 Feb. 2017.

Fellini, Federico, director. *8½.* Embassy, 1963.

Felski, Rita. *The Limits of Critique.* U of Chicago P, 2015.

Finnegan, William. "Leasing the Rain: The World Is Running Out of Fresh Water, and the Fight to Control It Has Begun." *The New Yorker,* 8 April 2002, www.newyorker.com/magazine/2002/04/08/leasing-the-rain. Accessed 12 May 2014.

Fischer, Howard. "Kavanagh Bill Would Ban Videos within 20 Feet of a Police Officer." *Arizona Capitol Times,* 7 Jan. 2016, azcapitoltimes.com/news/2016/01/07/kavanagh-bill-would-ban-videos-within-20-feet-of-a-police-officer/. Accessed 7 June 2016.

Flanagan, Richard. *The Narrow Road to the Deep North.* Vintage, 2015.

Fleckenstein, Kristie S. *Vision, Rhetoric, and Social Action in the Composition Classroom.* Southern Illinois UP, 2010.

Fry, Ron, and Pamela Fourzon. *The Saga of Special Effects: The Complete History of Cinematic Illusion, from Edison's Kinetoscope to Dynamation, Sensurround . . . and Beyond.* Prentice-Hall, 1977.

Fusco, Coco, and Brian Wallis, editors. *Only Skin Deep: Changing Visions of the American Self.* International Center of Photography, 2003.

Fuss, Diana. *Identification Papers.* Routledge, 1995.

Goddard, Drew, director. *The Cabin in the Woods.* 2011. Lionsgate, 2012.

Goldstein, Joseph, and Nate Schweber. "Man's Death after Chokehold Raises Old Issue for Police." *New York Times,* 18 July 2014.

Gonzalez, Ed. Review of *Funny Games. Slant,* 3 May 2006, www.slantmagazine.com/film/review/funny-games. Accessed 29 Oct. 2017.

Gorbman, Claudia. *Unheard Melodies: Narrative Film Sound.* Indiana UP, 1987.

Green, Jared F. "The Reality Which Is Not One: Flaherty, Buñuel, and the Irrealism of Documentary Cinema." Rhodes and Springer, pp. 64–87.

Gries, Laurie. "Dingrhetoriks." Lynch and Rivers, *Thinking,* pp. 294–309.

———. *Still Life with Rhetoric: A New Materialist Approach for Visual Rhetorics.* Utah State UP, 2015.

Grundmann, Roy, editor. *A Companion to Michael Haneke.* Wiley-Blackwell, 2010.

Guynn, William. *Writing History in Film.* Routledge, 2006.

Hagen, Earle. *Scoring for Films: A Complete Text.* Criterion Music, 1971.

Hallbritter, Bump. "Musical Rhetoric in Integrated-Media Composition." *Computers and Composition*, vol. 23, no. 3, 2006, pp. 317–34.

Haneke, Michael, director. *71 Fragments of a Chronology of Chance*. 1994. Palisades Tartan, 2009.

———, director. *Benny's Video*. 1992. Palisades Tartan, 2009.

———, director. *Caché*. Les Filmes du Losanges, 2005.

———, director. *Code Unknown*. MK2 Editions, 2000.

———, director. *Funny Games*. 1997. Palisades Tartan, 2006.

———, director. *Funny Games*. 2007. Warner Home Video, 2008.

———, director. *The Piano Teacher*. 2001. Kino, 2002.

———, director. *The Seventh Continent*. 1989. Palisades Tartan, 2009.

———. "Terror and Utopia of Form: Robert Bresson's *Au hasard Balthasar*." Grundmann, *Companion*, pp. 565–74.

———, director. *Time of the Wolf*. Les Filmes du Losanges, 2003.

———. "Violence and the Media." Grundmann, *Companion*, pp. 575–79.

Hariman, Robert, and John Louis Lucaites. *No Caption Needed: Iconic Photographs, Public Culture, and Liberal Democracy*. U of Chicago P, 2007.

Harman, Chris. *Zombie Capitalism: Global Crisis and the Relevance of Marx*. Haymarket, 2009.

Harrington, John. *The Rhetoric of Film*. Holt, Rinehart, and Winston, 1973.

Hart, Gail K. "Michael Haneke's *Funny Games* and Schiller's Coercive Classicism." *Modern Austrian Literature*, vol. 39, 2006, pp. 63–75.

Haskins, Ekaterina. "Time, Space, and Political Identity: Envisioning Community in *Triumph of the Will*." Blakesley, *Terministic*, pp. 92–106.

Hauser, Gerard A. *Prisoners of Conscience: Moral Vernaculars of Political Agency*. U of South Carolina P, 2012.

Hawhee, Debra. *Bodily Arts: Rhetoric and Athletics in Ancient Greece*. U of Texas P, 2004.

———. *Moving Bodies: Kenneth Burke at the Edges of Language*. U of South Carolina P, 2009.

Hayles, N. Katherine. *How We Became Posthuman: Virtual Bodies in Cybernetics, Literature, and Informatics*. U of Chicago P, 1999.

Hemmings, Clare. "Invoking Affect: Cultural Theory and the Ontological Turn." *Cultural Studies Review*, vol. 19, 2005, pp. 548–67.

Hennessy-Fiske, Molly. "A Sign for Sandra Bland: Signal Lane Change or Sheriff May Kill You." *Los Angeles Times*, 24 July 2015, www.latimes.com/nation/la-na-sandra-bland-sign-20150724-story.html. Accessed 10 June 2015.

Hersh, Seymour. "Torture at Abu Ghraib." *New Yorker*, 10 May 2004, www.newyorker.com/magazine/2004/05/10/torture-at-abu-ghraib. Accessed 29 Oct. 2017.

Herzog, Werner, director. *Aguirre, the Wrath of God*. Werner Herzog Filmproduktion, 1972.

———, director. *Fitzcarraldo*. Filmverlag der Autoren, 1982.

Hesford, Wendy S. "Global Turns and Cautions in Rhetoric and Composition Studies." *PMLA*, vol. 121, no. 3, 2006, pp. 787–801.

———. *Spectacular Rhetorics: Human Rights Visions, Recognitions, Feminisms*. Duke UP, 2011.

Higgins, Scott. "3D in Depth: *Coraline, Hugo,* and a Sustainable Aesthetic." *Film History*, vol. 24, no. 2, 2012, pp. 196–209.

Hirsch, Marianne. *Family Frames: Photography, Narrative, and Postmemory*. Harvard UP, 1997.

Hitchcock, Alfred, director. *Vertigo*. 1958. MCA/Universal Home Video, 1998.

Hopper, Dennis, director. *Easy Rider*, 1969. Columbia Pictures, 1999.

Horn, Dan and Hannah Sparling. "UC Report: Sam Dubose Shooting 'Entirely Preventable.'" *Cincinnati.com*, 14 Sep. 2015, www.cincinnati.com/story/news/2015/09/11/uc-release-new-dubose-shooting-report/72058718/. Accessed 10 June 2016.

Houck, Davis W., and Caroline J. S. Picart. "Opening the Text: Reading Gender, Christianity, and American Intervention in *Deliverance*." Blakesley, *Terministic*, pp. 163–89.

Jenkins, Henry. *Convergence Culture: Where Old and New Media Collide*. New York UP, 2006.

Joffé, Roland, director. *The Killing Fields*. Warner Bros., 1984.

Jones, Nicole. "Johannes Mehserle Released from Jail." *Oakland North*, 13 June 2011, oaklandnorth.net/2011/06/13/johannes-mehserle-released-from-jail/. Accessed 21 May 2016.

Karjanen, David. "Opposition to the Living Wage: Discourse, Rhetoric, and American Exceptionalism," *Anthropology of Work Review*, vol. 31, no. 1, 2010, pp. 4–14.

Kasdan, Lawrence, director. *The Big Chill*. Carson Productions, 1983.

Kassabian, Anahid. *Hearing Film: Tracking Identifications in Contemporary Hollywood Film Music*. Routledge, 2001.

Kaufman, Amy. "*Fruitvale* Starts Strong, May Benefit from Zimmerman Acquittal." *Los Angeles Times*, 14 July 2013, articles.latimes.com/2013/jul/14/entertainment/la-et-mn-fruitvale-station-box-office-zimmerman-acquittal-20130714. Accessed June 29 2016.

Keisner, Jody. "Do You Want to Watch? A Study of the Visual Rhetoric of the Postmodern Horror Film." *Women's Studies*, vol. 37, no. 4, 2008, pp. 411–27.

Kelly, Douglas A. *Accountability by Camera: Online Video's Effects on Police-Civilian Interactions*. LFB Scholarly Publishing, 2014.

Kent, Jennifer, director. *The Babadook*. Causeway Films, 2014.

Köksal, Özlem. "'Past Not-So-Perfect': *Ararat* and Its Reception in Turkey." *Cinema Journal*, vol. 54, no. 1, Fall 2014, pp. 45–64.

Kubrick, Stanley, director. *A Clockwork Orange*. 1971. Warner Brothers, 2001.

———, director. *The Shining*. 1980. Warner Brothers, 2000.

Kunzru, Hari. "Nowhere to Hide: Hari Kunzru Assesses the Films of Michael Haneke." *The Guardian*, 30 Oct. 2009, www.theguardian.com/film/2009/oct/31/michael-haneke-films-hari-kunzru. Accessed 4 July 2017.

Labrecque, Jeff. "Best of 2013: Michael B. Jordan and Ryan Coogler on Filming the Harrowing Tragedy of *Fruitvale Station*." *Entertainment Weekly*, 16 Dec. 2013, ew.com/article/2013/12/16/michael-b-jordan-fruitvale-station-ryan-coogler/. Accessed 25 May 2016.

LaCapra, Dominick. *Writing History, Writing Trauma*. Johns Hopkins UP, 2001.

Lane, Christina. *Magnolia*. Wiley-Blackwell, 2011.

Latour, Bruno. "The Berlin Key or How to Do Words with Things." *Matter, Materiality, and Modern Culture*, edited by P. M. Graves-Brown, Routledge, 2000, pp. 10–21.

———. *Reassembling the Social: An Introduction to Actor-Network-Theory*. Oxford UP, 2005.

———. *We Have Never Been Modern*. Harvard UP, 1993.

Lee, Chris. "Weinstein Co. Uses Social Justice Campaign to Promote *Fruitvale Station*." *Los Angeles Times*, 17 July 2013, articles.latimes.com/2013/jul/17/entertainment/la-et-mn-weinstein-co-uses-social-justice-campaign-to-promote-fruitvale-station-20130717. Accessed 21 May 2016.

Levine, Caroline. *Forms: Whole, Rhythm, Hierarchy, Network*. Princeton UP, 2015.

Levy, Emanuel. "*Ararat* (2002): Armenian Drama from Atom Egoyan." *Emanuel Levy Cinema 24/7*, 4 May 2010, http://emanuellevy.com/review/ararat-2002-1/. Accessed 29 Oct. 2017.

Lipkin, Steven N. *Real Emotional Logic: Film and Television Docudrama as Persuasive Practice*. Southern Illinois UP, 2002.

Lipkin, Steven N., Derek Paget, and Jane Roscoe. "Docudrama and Mock-Documentary: Defining Terms, Proposing Canons." Rhodes and Springer, pp. 11–26.

Lowenstein, Adam. *Shocking Representation: Historical Trauma, National Cinema, and the Modern Horror Film*. Columbia UP, 2005.

Lumet, Sidney, director. *Network*. United Artists, 1976.

Lumière, Auguste, and Louis Lumière. *Arrival of a Train at La Ciotat*. Société Lumière, 1896.

Lumière, Louis. *Workers Leaving the Lumière Factory*. Lumière, 1895.

Lynch, David, director. *Blue Velvet*. De Laurentiis Entertainment Group, 1986.

Lynch, Paul, and Nathaniel Rivers, editors. *Thinking with Bruno Latour in Rhetoric and Composition*. Southern Illinois UP, 2015.

"Magnolia." *Time Out*, 1999, www.timeout.com/london/film/magnolia. Accessed 29 Oct. 2017.

Mailloux, Steven. *Reception Histories: Rhetoric, Pragmatism, and American Cultural Politics*. Cornell UP, 1998.

Malcolm X Network. "Sam Dubose Traffic Stop by Officer Ray Tensing (Full Video of Body Cam Footage)." 29 July 2015, www.youtube.com/watch?v=kYINt6uNjAo. Accessed 10 June 2016.

Maloney, Edward, and Paul Miller. "*Rear Window*: Looking at Film Theory through Pedagogy." Bishop, pp. 32–44.

Malooley, Jake. "Haskell Wexler on the Criterion Collection Release of *Medium Cool*: Interview." *TimeOut Chicago*, 21 May 2013, www.timeout.com/chicago/film/haskell-wexler-on-the-criterion-collection-release-of-medium-cool-interview. Accessed 28 Nov. 2016.

Mann, Michael, director. *The Insider*. Buena Vista Pictures, 1999.

———, director. *Manhunter*. De Laurentiis Entertainment Group, 1986.

Marback, Richard. "Unclenching the Fist: Embodying Rhetoric and Giving Objects their Due." *Rhetoric Society Quarterly*, vol. 38, no. 1, 2008, pp. 46–65.

"Martin Scorsese's *Hugo*." *Computer Graphics World*, 5 Dec. 2011, www.cgw.com/Press-Center/In-Focus/2011/Martin-Scorseses-Hugo.aspx. Accessed 5 July 2017.

Marx, Karl. *Capital: Volume I: A Critique of Political Economy*. Penguin, 1992.

Maslin, Janet. "Entangled Lives on the Cusp of the Millennium." *New York Times*, 17 Dec. 1999, www.nytimes.com/1999/12/17/movies/film-review-entangled-lives-on-the-cusp-of-the-millennium.html. Accessed 20 Feb. 2017.

Massumi, Brian. *Parables for the Virtual: Movement, Affect, Sensation*. Duke UP, 2002.

———. *The Politics of Affect*. Polity, 2015.

Mazierska, Ewa. *European Cinema and Intertextuality: History, Memory and Politics*. Palgrave, 2011.

McGee, Michael Calvin. "A Materialist's Conception of Rhetoric." Biesecker and Lucaites, pp. 17–42.

McLuhan, Marshall. *Understanding Media: The Extensions of Man*. 1964. MIT P, 1994.

Menninghaus, Winfried. *Disgust: Theory and History of a Strong Sensation*. Translated by Howard Eiland and Joel Golb. State U of New York P, 2003.

Meyer, Robinson. "What to Say When the Police Tell You to Stop Filming Them." *The Atlantic*, 28 Apr. 2015, www.theatlantic.com/technology/archive/2015/04/what-to-say-when-the-police-tell-you-to-stop-filming-them/391610/. Accessed 7 June 2016.

Micciche, Laura R. *Doing Emotion: Rhetoric, Writing, Teaching*. Heinemann, 2007.

Miller, Carolyn. "Genre as Social Action." *Quarterly Journal of Speech*, vol. 70, no. 2, 1984, pp. 151–67.

Miller, D. A. *Hidden Hitchcock*. U of Chicago P, 2016.

Mirzoeff, Nicholas. *The Right to Look: A Counterhistory of Visuality*. Duke UP, 2011.

Mitchell, W. J. T. *Picture Theory: Essays on Verbal and Visual Representation*. U of Chicago P, 1994.

———. *Seeing through Race*. Harvard UP, 2012.

———. *What Do Pictures Want? The Lives and Loves of Images*. U of Chicago P, 2005.

Mitrovica, Andrew. "Mainstream Media Fashioned Post-Truth, Not Trump." *Aljazeera*, 9 Dec. 2016, www.aljazeera.com/indepth/opinion/2016/12/mainstream-media-fashioned-post-truth-trump-161208094807553.html. Accessed 10 Dec. 2016.

Moretti, Nanni, director. *Dear Diary*. 1993. Warner Home Video, 2008.

Nichanian, Marc. *The Historiographic Perversion*. Columbia UP, 2009.

Nichols, Bill. *Blurred Boundaries: Questions of Meaning in Contemporary Culture*. Southern Illinois UP, 2003.

Nunley, Vorris L. *Keepin' It Hushed: The Barbershop and African American Hush Harbor Rhetoric*. Wayne State UP, 2011.

Ohmann, Richard. *The Politics of Knowledge: The Commercialization of the University, the Professions, and Print Culture*. Wesleyan, 2003.

Oktay, Yakut. "'You're Not Going to Try and Change My Mind?': The Dynamics of Identification in Aronofsky's *Black Swan*." *K. B. Journal: The Journal of the Kenneth Burke Society*, vol. 10, 2014, kbjournal.org/oktay. Accessed 28 Feb. 2017.

Oliver, Kelly. *Witnessing: Beyond Recognition.* U of Minnesota P, 2001.

Padgett, Barry L. *Marx and Alienation in Contemporary Society.* Continuum, 2007.

Parker, Mark. "Something to Declare: History in Atom Egoyan's *Ararat.*" *University of Toronto Quarterly*, vol. 76, 2007, pp. 1040–54.

Pasolini, Pier Paolo, director. *Salò, or the 120 Days of Sodom.* 1975. Criterion Collection, 1998.

Pavis, Patrice. *Dictionary of the Theatre: Terms, Concepts, and Analysis.* Translated by Christine Shantz. U of Toronto P, 1998.

Perez, Gilberto. "Toward a Rhetoric of Film: Identification and the Spectator." *Senses of Cinema*, vol. 5, 2000, sensesofcinema.com/2000/society-for-cinema-studies-conference-2000/rhetoric2/. Accessed 28 Feb. 2017.

Perkins, Osgood, director. *I Am the Pretty Thing That Lives in the House.* Netflix, 2016.

Peucker, Brigitte. "Games Haneke Plays: Reality and Performance." Grundmann, *Companion*, pp. 130–46.

Pezzullo, Phaedra C. *Toxic Tourism: Rhetorics of Pollution, Travel, and Environmental Justice.* U of Alabama P, 2007.

Pflugfelder, Ehren Helmut. "Is No One at the Wheel? Nonhuman Agency and Agentive Movement." Lynch and Rivers, *Thinking*, pp. 115–34.

Porter, Edwin S., director. *The Great Train Robbery.* Edison Manufacturing, 1903.

———, director. *Life of an American Fireman.* Edison Manufacturing, 1903.

Price, Brian. "Pain and the Limits of Representation." *Framework: The Journal of Cinema and Media*, vol. 47, 2006, pp. 22–29.

Proctor, Russell F., II, and Ronald B. Adler. "Teaching Interpersonal Communication with Feature Films." *Communication Education*, vol. 40, no. 4, Oct. 1991, pp. 393–400.

Raengo, Alessandra. *On the Sleeve of the Visual: Race as Face Value.* Dartmouth College P, 2013.

Rai, Candice. *Democracy's Lot: Rhetorics, Publics, and Places of Invention.* U of Alabama P, 2016.

Rampell, Ed. "Oscar Winner Haskell Wexler, Hollywood's Perennial Progressive." *The Progressive*, 20 Jan. 2016, progressive.org/dispatches/oscar-winner-haskell-wexler-hollywood-s-perennial-progressive/. Accessed 28 Feb. 2017.

Ratcliffe, Krista. *Rhetorical Listening: Identification, Gender, Whiteness.* Southern Illinois UP, 2005.

Red, Eric, director. *Bad Moon.* 1996. Warner Home Video, 2000.

Rhodes, Gary, and John Parris Springer, editors. *Docufictions: Essays on the Intersection of Documentary and Fictional Filmmaking.* Macfarlane, 2006.

Rhodes, Joe. "A Man's Death, a Career's Birth: A Bay Area Killing Inspires *Fruitvale Station.*" *New York Times*, 28 June 2013, www.nytimes.com/2013/06/30/movies/a-bay-area-killing-inspires-fruitvale-station.html. Accessed 21 May 2016.

Rice, Jeff. *The Rhetoric of Cool: Composition Studies and New Media.* Southern Illinois UP, 2007.

Rice, Jenny Edbauer. "The New 'New': Making a Case for Critical Affect Studies." *Quarterly Journal of Speech*, vol. 44, no. 2, Apr. 2008, pp. 200–212.

Rich, Wilbur C. *Recognition, Critics, and the Nation-State.* Routledge, 2013.

Rickert, Thomas. *Ambient Rhetoric: The Attunements of Rhetorical Being.* U of Pittsburgh P, 2013.

———. "The Whole of the Moon." Lynch and Rivers, *Thinking,* pp. 135–50.

Rickman, Alan, director. *The Winter Guest.* Fine Line Features, 1997.

Ridolfo, Jim, and Dànielle Nicole DeVoss. "Composing for Recomposition: Rhetorical Velocity and Delivery." *Kairos: A Journal of Rhetoric, Technology, and Pedagogy,* vol. 13, no. 2, 2009, kairos.technorhetoric.net/13.2/topoi/ridolfo_devoss/index.html. Accessed 28 Feb. 2017.

Ritterhouse, Jennifer. *Growing Up Jim Crow: How Black and White Southern Children Learned Race.* U of North Carolina P, 2006.

Roberts, James. "On Rhetorical Bodies: *Hoop Dreams* and Constitutional Discourse." Blakesley, *Terministic,* pp. 107–24.

Romney, Jonathan. *Atom Egoyan.* British Film Institute, 2003.

Ross, Murray. *Stars and Strikes: Unionization of Hollywood.* Columbia UP, 1941.

Ryan, Mike. "Ryan Coogler, *Fruitvale Station* Director, Defends His Controversial Scene." *Huffington Post,* 12 July 2013, www.huffingtonpost.com/2013/07/12/ryan-coogler-fruitvale-station_n_3580960.html. Accessed 25 May 2016.

"Samuel Dubose: Body-Camera Video Shows 360 Degree View of Police Killing." *The Guardian,* 30 July 2015, www.theguardian.com/us-news/video/2015/jul/30/body-cameras-officers-samuel-dubose-shooting-video. Accessed 10 June 2016.

Santaolalla, Isabel. *The Cinema of Icíar Bollaín.* Manchester UP, 2012.

Schell, Eileen E. "Gender, Rhetorics, and Globalization: Rethinking the Spaces and Locations of Women's Rhetorics in Our Field." *Teaching Rhetorica: Theory, Pedagogy, Practice,* edited by Kate Ronald and Joy S. Ritchie, Heinemann, 2006, pp. 160–74.

Schenker, Andrew. Review of *Even the Rain,* directed by Icíar Bollaín. *Slant,* 14 Feb. 2011, www.slantmagazine.com/film/review/even-the-rain. Accessed 28 Feb. 2017.

Schilb, John. *Rhetorical Refusals: Defying Audiences' Expectations.* Southern Illinois UP, 2007.

Schrader, Paul, director. *The Comfort of Strangers.* Skouras Pictures, 1990.

Schumacher, Joel, director. *The Lost Boys.* 1987. Warner Home Video, 1998.

Scorsese, Martin, director. *Goodfellas.* Warner Bros., 1990.

———, director. *Hugo.* Paramount Pictures, 2011.

———, director. *Raging Bull.* United Artists, 1980.

———, director. *Taxi Driver.* Columbia, 1976.

Scott, Tony, and Nancy Welch. "One Train Can Hide Another: Critical Materialism for Public Composition." *College English,* vol. 76, no. 6, July 2014, pp. 562–79.

———. "Tony Scott and Nancy Welch Respond." *College English,* vol. 77, no. 6, July 2015, pp. 586–89.

Selfe, Cynthia L. "The Movement of Air, the Breath of Meaning: Aurality and Multimodal Composing." *College Composition and Communication,* vol. 60, 2009, pp. 616–63.

Selznick, Brian. *The Invention of Hugo Cabret.* Scholastic P, 2007.

Serna, Joseph. "No Criminal Charges for CHP Officer Seen Punching Woman in Video." *Los Angeles Times*, 3 Dec. 2015, www.latimes.com/local/lanow/la-me-ln-chp-punching-video-marlene-pinnock-charges-20151203-story.html. Accessed 19 June 2016.

———. "With Smartphones Everywhere, Police on Notice They May Be Caught on Camera." *Los Angeles Times.com*, 21 Apr. 2015, www.latimes.com/local/lanow/la-me-ln-feds-probe-video-phone-in-south-gate-20150421-story.html. Accessed 7 June 2016.

Sheridan, David M., Jim, Ridolfo, and Anthony J. Michel. *The Available Means of Persuasion: Mapping a Theory and Pedagogy of Multimodal Public Rhetoric*. Parlor P, 2012.

Shipka, Jody. *Toward a Composition Made Whole*. U of Pittsburgh P, 2011.

Silverstone, Roger. *The Message of Television: Myth and Narrative in Contemporary Culture*. Heinemann, 1981.

Singer, Bryan, director. *The Usual Suspects*. 1995. MGM Home Entertainment, 2001.

Siraganian, Lisa. "Telling a Horror Story, Conscientiously: Representing the Armenian Genocide in Atom Egoyan's Films." Tschofen and Burwell, pp. 133–56.

Smith, Brad W., and Malcolm D. Holmes. *Race and Police Brutality: Roots of an Urban Dilemma*. State U of New York P, 2008.

Smith, Kyle. "*Fruitvale Station* Is Loose with the Facts about Oscar Grant." *Forbes*, 25 July 2013, www.forbes.com/sites/kylesmith/2013/07/25/fruitvale-station-is-loose-with-the-facts-in-an-effort-to-elicit-sympathy-for-oscar-grant/. Accessed 29 Oct. 2017.

———. "*Fruitvale Station* Tells Some, Omits Some." *New York Post*, 12 July 2013, nypost.com/2013/07/12/fruitvale-station-tells-some-omits-some/. Accessed 25 May 2016.

Smith, Murray. "Altered States: Character and Emotional Response in Cinema." *Cinema Journal*, vol. 33, 1994, pp. 34–56.

Sontag, Susan. *Regarding the Pain of Others*. Picador, 2003.

Speck, Oliver C. *Funny Frames: The Filmic Concepts of Michael Haneke*. Continuum, 2010.

Sperb, Jason. *Blossoms and Blood: Postmodern Media Culture and the Films of Paul Thomas Anderson*. U of Texas P, 2013.

Spielberg, Steven, director. *Jaws*. Universal Pictures, 1975.

———, director. *Minority Report*. Dreamworks, 2002.

———, director. *Schindler's List*. Universal Pictures, 1993.

Springer, John Parris, and Gary Rhodes. Introduction. Rhodes and Springer, pp. 1–9.

Stam, Robert. *Reflexivity in Film and Literature: From Don Quixote to Jean-Luc Godard*. Columbia UP, 1992.

Stanton, Robert. "Video Shows That Traffic Stop of Woman Who Died in Texas Jail Escalated Quickly." *Reuters*, 22 July 2015, www.reuters.com/article/us-usa-texas-death-idUSKCN0PV1XM20150722. Accessed 10 June 2016.

Stilwell, Robynn J. "The Fantastical Gap between Diegetic and Nondiegetic." *Beyond the Soundtrack: Representing Music in Cinema*, edited by Daniel Goldmark, Lawrence Kramer, and Richard Leppert, U of California P, 2007, pp. 184–202.

Stumm, Bettina. "Witnessing Others in Narrative Collaboration: Ethical Responsibility beyond Recognition." *Biography*, vol. 37, no. 3, 2014, pp. 762–83.

Tatko-Peterson, Ann. "*Fruitvale Station* Criticized for Fictional Scene, Marketing Tied to George Zimmerman Trial." *Mercury News*, 12 July 2013, www.mercurynews.com/

2013/07/12/fruitvale-station-criticized-for-fictional-scene-marketing-tied-to-george-zimmerman-trial/. Accessed 21 May 2016.

Theriault, Kim S. *Rethinking Arshile Gorky.* Pennsylvania State UP, 2009.

Thomas, Rob. "The Exploitation Story Never Ends in *Even the Rain.*" *Capital Times,* 5 May 2011, host.madison.com/entertainment/movies/reviews/article_6fe0e6f6-3b68-5345-8108-112ef6ff69fc.html. Accessed 29 Oct. 2017.

Thompson, Marie, and Ian Biddle. "Introduction: Somewhere between the Signifying and the Sublime." *Sound, Music, Affect: Theorizing Sonic Experience.* Edited by Marie Thompson and Ian Biddle. Bloomsbury, 2013.

Torchin, Leshu. *Creating the Witness: Documenting Genocide on Film, Video, and the Internet.* U of Minnesota P, 2012.

Torner, Evan. "Civilization's Endless Shadow: Haneke's *Time of the Wolf.*" Grundmann, *Companion,* pp. 532–50.

Trier, Lars von, director. *Dancer in the Dark.* Fine Line Features, 2000.

Trimbur, John. "Composition and the Circulation of Writing." *College Composition and Communication,* vol. 52, no. 2, 2000, pp. 188–219.

Tschofen, Monique, and Jennifer Burwell, editors. *Image and Territory: Essays on Atom Egoyan.* Wilfrid Laurier UP, 1997.

Turim, Maureen. *Flashbacks in Film: Memory and History.* Routledge, 1989.

Verstraten, Peter. *Film Narratology.* Translated by Stefan van der Lecq. U of Toronto P, 2009.

Villanueva, Victor, Jr. *Bootstraps: From an American Academic of Color.* National Council of Teachers of English, 1993.

Villarejo, Amy. *Film Studies: An Introduction.* Routledge, 2013.

Vitagraph Films Distribution. "*Even the Rain* Filmmakers Juan Gordon and Icíar Bollaín on How Not to Exploit Extras in Bolivia," www.youtube.com/watch?v=qGWJ6rpD0_c. Accessed 1 Nov. 2014.

Walker, Janet. *Trauma Cinema: Documenting Incest and the Holocaust.* U of California P, 2005.

Walters, Shannon. *Rhetorical Touch: Disability, Identification, Haptics.* U of South Carolina P, 2014.

Wang, Hansi Lo. "Who Gets Tased? First Statewide Study Reveals Racial Disparities." *NPR,* 30 June 2016, www.npr.org/2016/06/30/483829855/who-gets-tased-first-statewide-study-reveals-racial-disparities. Accessed 2 July 2016.

Warner, Michael. *Publics and Counterpublics.* Zone, 2002.

Wenders, Wim, director. *Wings of Desire.* 1987. MGM/UA Home Entertainment, 2003.

Wexler, Haskell, director. *Medium Cool.* Paramount Pictures, 1969.

Wheatley, Catherine. *Michael Haneke's Cinema: The Ethic of the Image.* Berghan, 2009.

Wheeler, Duncan. "*También la lluvia/Even the Rain* (Icíar Bollaín, 2010): Social Realism, Transnationalism and (Neo-)colonialism." *Spanish Cinema, 1973–2010: Auteurism, Politics, Landscape and Memory,* edited by Maria M. Delgado and Robin Fiddian, Manchester UP, 2013, pp. 239–55.

Wicks, Ulrich. "Studying Film as Integrated Text." *Rhetoric Review*, vol. 2, no. 1, Sept. 1983, pp. 51–62.

Willis, Sharon. *High Contrast: Race and Gender in Contemporary Hollywood Films.* Duke UP, 1997.

Wilson, Emma. *Atom Egoyan*. U of Illinois P, 2009.

Wilson, Mark D. "SAPD: 2nd Officer Was Present at Time of Fatal Shooting of Unarmed Antronie Scott." *My San Antonio*, 10 Feb. 2016, www.mysanantonio.com/news/local/article/Antroine-Scott-SAPD-fatal-shooting-6820794.php. Accessed 7 June 2016.

Wittgenstein, Ludwig. *Philosophical Investigations.* Translated by G. E. M. Anscombe. Macmillan, 1953.

Wolfe, Cary. *What Is Posthumanism?* U of Minnesota P, 2010.

Wollen, Peter. *Signs and Meaning in the Cinema.* Indiana UP, 1972.

Woolf, Nicky. "Arizona State Senator Proposes Bill to Restrict Recording Videos of Police." *The Guardian*, 11 Jan. 2016, www.theguardian.com/us-news/2016/jan/11/arizona-state-senator-john-kavanagh-recording-police-video. Accessed 7 June 2016.

Worsham, Lynn. "Going Postal: Pedagogic Violence and the Schooling of Emotion." *JAC*, vol. 18, no. 2, 1998, pp. 213–45.

Wurmitzer, Gabriele. "'What Goes without Saying': Michael Haneke's Confrontation with Myths in *Funny Games*." *New Austrian Film*, edited by Robert von Dassanowsky and Oliver C. Speck, Berghan, 2011, pp. 166–76.

Zacharek, Stephanie. "A Shivery, Understated Tension Runs throughout *Fruitvale Station*." *Village Voice*, 10 July 2013, www.villagevoice.com/film/a-shivery-understated-tension-runs-through-fruitvale-station-6438851. Accessed 20 June 2015.

Zinn, Howard. *A People's History of the United States.* 1980. HarperPerennial, 2005.

Žižek, Slavoj. *Violence.* Picador, 2008.

INDEX

8½ (Fellini), 164n11
71 Fragments of a Chronology of Chance (Haneke), 37–38, 165n7

Adams, Dale, 9
Adler, Ronald B., 9
affect, 2, 8, 11, 19–20, 22, 24, 34–36, 38–39, 41–43, 45, 47, 49, 51–54, 57, 60, 68, 70, 75, 88–110, 116–19, 124–26, 130, 136, 140, 145–48, 152, 160n4, 165n3, 165n10, 166n12, 166n3, 167n13
Agee, James, 12–13, 16. See also *Let Us Now Praise Famous Men*
Aguirre, the Wrath of God (Herzog), 164n10
Ahmed, Sarah, 19, 60, 96, 154, 162n10, 165n5
Aktan, Gündüz, 62
alienation, 5, 16, 21, 31, 46–47, 49–50, 52, 55–56, 59, 61, 63, 68, 73–75, 95, 105, 109, 140, 161n19, 165n6

Allen, Woody, 164n11. See also *Stardust Memories*
Alloway, Meredith, 128
Althusser, Louis, 34
Altman, Robert, 168n5. See also *Nashville*
ambient rhetoric, 2, 38, 79, 92, 98–99, 103, 106–7, 109, 140, 146, 155–56, 166n11
ambiguities of substance, 71, 73, 76, 78, 86–87, 89
American Civil Liberties Union, 167n7
American exceptionalism, 43–47, 161n18
Amirpour, Ana Lily, 161n17. See also *A Girl Walks Home Alone at Night*
Amour (Haneke), 44, 161n1
analepsis, 15, 56, 119
Anderson, Paul Thomas, 19–20, 90–110, 117, 140, 143–44, 146, 156–58, 159n6, 162n8, 164n1, 165nn3–4, 165n6, 165n9, 166nn12–14, 168n5. See also *Boogie Nights*; *Magnolia*; *Punch-Drunk Love*; *There Will Be Blood*

185

Annett, Sandra, 145–46, 148
anticlimax, 36–40
Ararat (Egoyan), 18–20, 49–69, 140–41, 144–45, 147–48, 150–51, 156, 161n1, 162n4, 162n6, 162nn8–9, 163n11, 168n5
Aristotle, 8, 154–55
Armenian Genocide, 18, 49–69, 147, 150
Arrival of a Train at la Ciotat, (Lumière brothers), 140
Arsenault, Chris, 167n7
Artist and His Mother, The (Gorky), 55–56
Assies, Willem, 80, 163n6
Atton, Chris, 116
attunement, 10, 77, 84, 92, 99–103, 105–6, 120, 130, 133–35, 148, 157, 161n12
Aune, James Arndt, 163n8
aural rhetoric, 6, 14, 19, 26–27, 29, 37, 82, 90–110, 112, 115–17, 145–46, 149, 165n8, 166n12
automata, 137–39, 141–45, 147–49, 152–53, 157–58

Babadook, The (Kent), 161n17
Badiou, Alain, 110, 165n6, 166nn13–14
Bad Moon (Red), 160n5
Banita, Georgiana, 54–56, 59, 162n7
Bazin, André, 40
Behrens, Laurence, 9
Bellware, Kim, 167n14
Benjamin, Walter, 47
Bennett, Jane, 2, 29, 32–33, 35
Benny's Video (Haneke), 37, 42, 44, 159n3, 160n4, 160n10
Bergman, Ingmar, 43
Berkan, İsmet, 62–63
Berlant, Lauren, 66–67
Bernal, Gael García, 78, 81
Bernard-Donals, Michael, 162n4, 168n17
Biddle, Ian, 96, 99, 102, 165n5
Big Chill, The (Kasdan), 159n5
Bishop, Ellen, 9
Bitzer, Lloyd, 8
Black Lives Matter, 122, 166n5

Blakesley, David, 10–11, 14, 22, 25–26, 50, 68, 70, 160n2
Blanchot, Maurice, 65, 163n11
Bland, Sandra, 118, 122
Blue Velvet (Lynch), 90
Blümlinger, Christa, 42
Bollaín, Icíar, 19, 70–89, 145, 156, 163n2, 164n10. See also *Even the Rain*
Bolter, Jay David, 33, 168n2
Boogie Nights (Anderson), 159n6, 164n1
Bordwell, David, 22, 101
Borges, Jorge Luis, 38, 161n13
Borrowman, Shane, 59
Boyer, Élisabeth, 110, 166n14
Brecht, Bertolt, 17
Bresson, Robert, 43, 160n9
Brinkema, Eugenie, 88, 166n3
"broken windows" policing, 122, 167n10
Brooks, Brandon, 154
Brooks, Brian, 112, 133
Brown, Bill, 163n1
Brownell, Brett, 114, 134
Brummett, Barry, 160n2
Brunette, Peter, 22, 34, 40
Bruzzi, Stella, 112
Buhler, Jim, 94
Burke, Kenneth, 10, 18, 22, 25–26, 31, 50–52, 58–59, 63, 68–71, 74–79, 81, 86–87, 89, 91, 99, 102, 117, 125, 128, 132, 144, 160n2, 162n2, 162n7, 162n8, 163n5. See also ambiguities of substance; identification; motive; scene-act ratio; terministic screen
Burwell, Jennifer, 59
Butler, Judith, 46

Cabin in the Woods, The (Goddard), 160n3
Caché (Haneke), 38, 44, 161n12
Campaign Zero, 122, 167n10
Campbell, Andy, 167n7
Carpenter, John, 40, 161n16
Caruth, Cathy, 56, 100, 103, 105, 119, 147, 157
Castile, Philando, 118

INDEX

cellular phones, 19–20, 127, 111–36, 161n14
Ceraso, Steph, 117, 125
Chandler, Adam, 167n14
Chisholm, Anna, 160n2
Chouliaraki, Lilie, 116, 133
Cilento, Fabrizio, 80
circulation, 3–4, 7–10, 18, 20, 23–24, 30, 33, 45–46, 83, 97, 113–14, 116–18, 120, 124, 126, 132–34, 136, 141, 149–51, 153–55, 157, 160n7, 163n11, 167n12
citizen journalism, 16, 113, 115–16, 120, 133, 136, 158
Clair, René, 143
Clark, Danae, 83–84, 86
Cleaver, Harry, 74–75
Clement, Jennifer, 168n2
Clockwork Orange, A (Kubrick), 28–29, 35, 39, 155, 160n11
Cloud, Dana, 154–55
Clover, Carol J., 39
Cochabamba, 19, 70–71, 80–82, 84, 87–88, 156, 163n7
Code Unknown (Haneke), 159n3, 167n11
Coen, Joel, 93
collectives, 5, 11–12, 15, 19–20, 22, 31, 51, 53, 56, 58–60, 68, 72–73, 83, 89–90, 95–96, 99, 101, 109, 115, 117, 119, 127–28, 130, 135, 137, 139–40, 143, 145–46, 151–58, 164n12
Columbus, Christopher, 19, 70–71, 73, 77–81, 84–85, 88, 147
Comfort of Strangers, The, 101
commodities, 4, 7–8, 12, 15, 24, 30, 47, 54, 70, 74–75, 80, 83, 114, 126, 134–35, 139, 142, 146, 149–53, 157, 163n10
complexes of visuality, 45, 47
Connerton, Paul, 62, 64
Connor, J. D., 164n1
Conversation, The (Coppola), 90
Coogler, Ryan, 19–20, 111–36, 151, 156–58, 166n4
cool media, 5–8, 10, 155, 159n1, 160n4
Cooper, Merian C., 93. See also *King Kong*

Coppola, Francis Ford, 90. See also *The Conversation*
Cram, Emily Diane, 117, 127
Craven, Wes, 40, 160n3, 161n16. See also *A Nightmare on Elm Street; Scream*
critical materialism, 1, 4, 7–8, 10, 16, 20, 30, 64, 67, 72, 77
Crucible, The (Miller), 75

D'Alcy, Jeanne, 139, 142, 144
Dalí, Salvador, 145
Dancer in the Dark (Trier), 90
Dargis, Manohla, 160n1
Dassanowsky, Robert von, 44
Davis, Diane, 58, 162n2, 162n8
Dawson, Tom, 162n9
Day of Wrath (Dreyer), 75–77
Daza, Victor Hugo, 163n6
Dear Diary (Moretti), 160n1
Debord, Guy, 15. See also spectacle
DeLillo, Don, 137, 140
DeLuca, Kevin Michael, 7, 23
Demme, Jonathan, 93–94. See also *The Silence of the Lambs*
DePalma, Brian, 92. See also *Dressed to Kill*
DeVoss, Dànielle Nicole, 167n12
Diaz, Melonie, 114
Diderot, Denis, 6
Dillman, Joanne, 99, 165n9
Dingo, Rebecca, 82–83, 160n8
disgust, 42, 46
Dobrin, Sidney I., 72–73, 163n3, 163n8
docufiction, 111–14, 122, 126, 130, 167n15
documentary, 2, 9, 20, 81, 112–15, 117, 119–20, 125, 127–28, 130, 164n1
Dressed to Kill (DePalma), 92
Dreyer, Carl Theodor, 75–77. See also *Day of Wrath*
Dubose, Samuel, 118, 122
Dyer, Richard, 83

Easy Rider (Hopper), 15–16
Ebert, Roger, 86

Eddy, Beth, 58, 63
Egoyan, Atom, 18, 49–69, 161n14, 162n1, 162n4, 162n7, 162nn9–10, 163n12. See also *Ararat*; *The Sweet Hereafter*
Eisenstadt, Alfred, 167n13
Elkins, James, 11–12, 16, 155
Elsaesser, Thomas, 44
Emerson, Jim, 162n9
Encinia, Brian, 122
Eno, Brian, 98
Epp, Charles R., 121–22, 124, 167nn8–9
Esmeir, Samera, 130
Evans, Walker, 12–13, 16. See also *Let Us Now Praise Famous Men*
Even the Rain (Bollaín), 19–20, 70–89, 112, 134, 140–41, 144–45, 147, 151–53, 156, 163n2
excess, 28, 34–35, 42, 52, 101–2, 106, 114, 132, 165n6
extradiegetic rhetoric, 13, 19, 26, 87, 92–96, 98, 108, 112, 115, 140, 146, 157, 165n2

Fairey, Shepard, 7
fantasy, 157, 167n15
Feehan, Michael, 81
Fellini, Federico, 164n11. See also *8½*
Felski, Rita, 143, 160n8
fetishization, 45, 61, 74, 79
Finnegan, William, 163n6
Fischer, Howard, 167n7
Fitzcarraldo (Herzog), 164n10
Flanagan, Richard, 1–2, 17
flashbacks, 56, 104, 119–20, 130, 139, 148, 167n6, 168n16. See also analepsis
Fleckenstein, Kristie, 135
fourth wall, 6, 11, 14, 19, 29–33, 102
Fourzon, Pamela, 139
Frasier, Levi, 154
Freud, Sigmund, 60
Fruitvale Station (Coogler), 19–20, 111–36, 140, 150–52, 154, 156–58
Fry, Ron, 139
Funny Games (Haneke), 18–48, 140, 146, 151, 155–56, 158, 160n1, 160n3, 160nn10–12, 160n20

Funny Games (U.S.) (Haneke), 43–48
Fusco, Coco, 121
Fuss, Diana, 51

Garcia, Mannie, 7
Garner, Eric, 118, 122, 128
genre, 18, 22–24, 26–28, 30–37, 39–40, 42–43, 52, 101, 126, 140–41, 151, 158. See also docufiction; fantasy; horror; melodrama, science fiction
Girl Walks Home Alone at Night, A (Amirpour), 161n17
Godard, Jean-Luc, 17, 19, 159n4. See also *Tout Va Bien*
Goddard, Drew, 160n3. See also *The Cabin in the Woods*
Goldstein, Joseph, 122
Gonzalez, Ed, 162n9
Goodfellas (Scorsese), 168n1
Gorbman, Claudia, 96–97
Gordon, Juan, 87
Gorky, Arshile, 50, 55–57, 68, 147, 152, 156, 162n7. See also *The Artist and His Mother*
Grant, Oscar, 111–36, 154, 166n5, 168n16
Grant, Tatiana, 127–29, 134, 158
Grant, Wanda, 125, 127–29, 133
Great Train Robbery, The (Porter), 112, 140
Green, Jared F., 112, 126, 167n15
Gries, Laurie, 2–4, 7–8, 10, 21, 23–24, 26–27, 29, 31, 33, 35, 39, 42, 44, 53, 57, 67, 72, 117–19, 123, 126, 132–33, 140–41, 149, 161n15, 164n12, 166n5, 167n12
Grundmann, Roy, 36, 47–48
Guynn, William, 52

Hagen, Earl, 164n2
Haider-Markel, Donald P., 121–22, 124, 167nn8–9
Halbritter, Bump, 19, 90–91, 109, 159n5
Halloween (Carpenter), 161n16
Haneke, Michael, 17, 21–48, 140, 146, 151, 155–56, 158, 159n3, 160n1, 160nn3–4, 160nn9–12, 160nn19–20, 161n12, 165n7, 167n11. See also *71 Fragments of a Chronology of Chance*; *Benny's*

Video; Caché; Code Unknown; Funny Games; The Piano Teacher; The Seventh Continent; Three Paths to the Lake; Time of the Wolf
Hariman, Robert, 5, 118, 127, 149, 167n13
Harman, Chris, 152, 168n3
Harrington, John, 9
Harris, Eric, 118–19
Hart, Gail K., 42–43
Haskins, Ekaterina, 160n2
Hauser, Gerard, 46, 166n2
Hawhee, Debra, 52, 55, 117
Hayles, N. Katherine, 73, 163n3
Haze, Jonathan, 13
Hemmings, Clare, 96
Hennessy-Fiske, Molly, 122
Hersh, Seymour, 46
Herzog, Werner, 164n10. See also *Aguirre, the Wrath of God; Fitzcarraldo*
Hesford, Wendy, 46, 66–67, 83, 100, 103, 113, 129–30, 161n18, 164n9
Higgins, Scott, 143
Hirsch, Marianne, 66. See also postmemory
Hitchcock, Alfred, 10, 161n12. See also *Strangers on a Train; Vertigo*
Holmes, Malcolm D., 123
Hopper, Dennis, 15–16. See also *Easy Rider*
Horn, Dan, 122
horror, 26–28, 32–34, 36–37, 40, 42–43, 158
hot media, 5–6, 10–11
Houck, Davis W., 156n2
Hugo (Scorsese), 76–77, 137–58
hypermediacy, 33, 40, 42

I Am the Pretty Thing That Lives in the House (Perkins), 161n17
identification, 5, 10–11, 16, 18–19, 22–23, 25–27, 29–31, 33, 42, 46–47, 49–53, 55–59, 61, 63, 67–71, 73–77, 79, 81, 84–89, 91–94, 96–97, 99, 102–3, 105–6, 112–13, 117–18, 126–30, 134, 138–39, 142, 146, 148, 156–57, 160n2, 163n1, 162n10, 165n8, 165n10
immediacy, 33, 40, 42, 116, 120

"Inna-Gadda-Da-Vida" (Iron Butterfly), 94
Insider, The (Mann), 93
intradiegetic rhetoric, 13, 19, 86, 92–94, 98, 108, 112, 117, 140
Invention of Hugo Cabret, The (Selznick), 145, 168n2
Iron Butterfly, 94. See also "Inna-Gadda-Da-Vida"

Jaws (Spielberg), 92
Jenkins, Henry, 151
Joffé, Roland, 93. See also *The Killing Fields*
Jones, Nicole, 111
Jordan, Michael B., 114, 134
Joyce, James, 145

kairos, 154–55, 158
Karjanen, David, 45, 163n8
Kasdan, Lawrence, 159n5
Kassabian, Anahid, 92, 96, 98, 164n2, 165n10
Kaufman, Amy, 133
Kavanagh, John, 120
Keisner, Jody, 39
Kelly, Douglas A., 123, 167n7
Kent, Jennifer, 161n17. See also *The Babadook*
Killing Fields, The (Joffé), 93
King Kong (Cooper and Schoedsack), 93
King, Rodney, 118, 133
Kline, Robert, 9
Kmetz, Marcia, 59
Koch, Kenneth, 158
Köksal, Özlem, 62–63
Kony 2012 (Russell), 8
Kubrick, Stanley, 28–29, 35, 160n6, 160n11. See also *A Clockwork Orange; The Shining*
Kunzru, Hari, 44

labor ethics, 11, 18–19, 71–75, 77–78, 81–86, 140, 142–44, 149, 151–53, 158
Labrecque, Jeff, 111, 127, 166n4
LaCapra, Dominick, 60, 119, 147

Lane, Christina, 96–97, 100–101, 104–5, 166n11
Lange, Dorothea, 167n13
Latour, Bruno, 2, 12, 22, 54, 57, 60, 70, 105, 127–28, 137, 140, 146, 149, 152, 163n1, 164n12. *See also* collective
Laverty, Paul, 163n2
Lee, Chris, 112, 133, 135
Let Us Now Praise Famous Men (Agee and Evans), 12–13, 16
Levine, Caroline, 159n6, 161n19
Levy, Emanuel, 162n9
Life of an American Fireman (Porter), 112
Lipkin, Steven N., 130, 168n16
Lomis, Erik, 133, 135
Long, Christian B., 168n2
Lost Boys, The (Schumacher), 160n5
Lowenstein, Adam, 43, 161n17
Lucaites, John Louis, 5, 118, 127, 149, 167n13
Lumet, Sidney, 168n5. *See also Network*
Lumière, Auguste Marie Louis Nicolas, 139–41, 143, 167n15. *See also Arrival of a Train at la Ciotat; Workers Leaving the Lumière Factory*
Lumière, Louis Jean, 139–41, 143, 167n15. *See also Arrival of a Train at la Ciotat; Workers Leaving the Lumière Factory*
Lynch, David, 90. *See also Blue Velvet*
Lynch, Paul, 60, 149

magical realism, 104, 106, 109, 141, 144
Magnolia (Anderson), 19–20, 90–110, 117, 140, 143–44, 146, 156–58, 162n9, 164n1, 165nn3–4, 165n6, 165n9, 166nn12–14, 168n5
Mailloux, Steven, 32
Malcolm X Network, 177
Maloney, Edward, 9
Malooley, Jake, 14
Manhunter (Mann), 94
Mann, Aimee, 91, 94–104, 106, 109–10, 141, 146, 157, 165n4, 165n10. *See also* "Momentum"; "Save Me"; "Wise Up"
Mann, Michael, 93. *See also The Insider; Manhunter*

Marback, Richard, 161n15
Martin, Trayvon, 20, 57, 111–12, 114, 119, 124, 132–33, 135, 166n5
Marx, Karl, 74, 113, 142, 149–52, 168n3
Maslin, Janet, 162n9
Massumi, Brian, 11, 31
Maynard-Mooney, Steven, 121–22, 124, 167nn8–9
Mazierska, Ewa, 54
McGee, Michael Calvin, 8, 154–55
McLuhan, Marshall, 5–8, 155, 159n1
mediated mourning, 18, 49–69, 119–20, 126–29, 133, 136, 143
Medium Cool (Wexler), 1–17, 135, 141, 155, 158
Mehserle, Johannes, 111–12, 115–16, 118, 125, 128, 131–33
Méliès, Georges, 138–44, 147–50, 152, 157, 167n15
melodrama, 54, 56, 59, 68, 90, 100–101, 114, 131, 144–45, 157
Menninghaus, Winfried, 42
Mesa, Sophina, 115, 123–25, 127
metadiegetic rhetoric, 19–20, 92, 94, 96, 99–100, 102, 108–9, 117, 146, 164n2
metalepsis, 11, 18, 36, 42, 51, 140, 157, 165n2
Meyer, Robinson, 167n7
Micciche, Laura R., 19, 91, 95–96
Michel, Anthony J., 149
Miller, Arthur, 75
Miller, Carolyn, 27
Miller, D. A., 161n12
Miller, Paul, 9
Miller's Crossing (Coen), 93
mimesis, 6, 13, 23–24, 67, 101, 131, 162n7
Minority Report (Spielberg), 20
Mirzoeff, Nicholas, 45, 113, 115–16, 122, 136. *See also* complexes of visuality; right to look
Mitchell, W. J. T., 30–31, 124–25, 136, 166n12
Mitrovica, Andrew, 17
Molière, 6
"Momentum" (Mann), 91, 94–100, 103, 106, 109

Moretti, Nanni, 21, 31, 160n1. See also *Dear Diary*
motive, 68–69, 79
multimodal rhetoric, 6, 12, 16, 20, 23, 29, 32, 69, 88, 92, 113–14, 117–18, 125–26, 136, 140–41, 143, 145–46, 148–49, 154–55

Naked City, 26, 37, 146, 156
Nashville (Altman), 168n5
Neal, Ariana, 134
neoliberalism, 8, 73, 82–83, 85, 114, 126, 134, 140, 143, 152, 163n8
neorealism, 40, 42
Network (Lumet), 168n5
new materialism, 2–3, 6–7, 16, 20–21, 23, 31, 38, 61, 72–74, 83, 113, 118, 133, 139, 152
Nichanian, Marc, 49–50, 63–68, 163n11
Nichols, Bill, 160n2
Nightmare on Elm Street, A (Craven), 161n16
Nilsson, Harry, 91, 97
Nunley, Vorris, 166n2

object-oriented ontology, 2, 29
Ohmann, Richard, 151
Oktay, Yakut, 70, 74
Oliver, Kelly, 130
O'Neill, Eugene, 165n6
Orta, Ramsey, 154

Padgett, Barry L., 74
Paget, Derek, 130
Pantaleo, Daniel, 122
Parker, Mark, 162n1
parrhesia, 166n2
participatory culture, 151
Pasolini, Pier Paolo, 43, 161n20. See also *Saló*
Perez, Gilberto, 70–71, 75–77, 80, 84, 163n4
Perkins, Osgood, 161n17. See also *I Am the Pretty Thing That Lives in the House*
Peucker, Brigitte, 41

Pezzullo, Phaedra, 53, 162n3
Pflugfelder, Ehren Helmut, 105
Piano Teacher, The (Haneke), 38
Picart, Caroline J. S., 159n2
Pinnock, Marlene, 128
police violence, 13–15, 17, 19–20, 111–36, 158
posthumanism, 16, 72, 153
postmemory, 66
postracial society, 113, 154, 166n1
post-truth, 17
Price, Brian, 35
Proctor, Russell F., II, 9
prolepsis, 15
publics, 15, 19, 33, 92, 109, 115–16, 153–54
Punch-Drunk Love (Anderson), 159n6

racism, 18, 111–36
Raengo, Alessandra, 120–21, 124–25, 132–33, 136
Raging Bull (Scorsese), 168n1
Rai, Candice, 28, 34, 36, 53, 88, 91, 101, 149, 162n3, 167n10
Ratcliffe, Krista, 31
realism, 31, 36, 41. See also neorealism
reception of film, 9, 11, 16, 20, 23, 29, 32, 35, 44, 62–63, 67, 69, 77, 83–89, 101, 113–14, 116, 126, 141, 146, 150–51, 164n1
Red, Eric, 160n5. See also *Bad Moon*
reflexive materialism, 1–25, 32–35, 41, 45, 50–51, 64, 67, 73, 82–84, 90, 94, 99, 101–3, 109, 112–13, 126, 133, 135–36, 140–42, 146, 152, 158, 159n4, 165n2
Reinhardt, Django, 145
remix, 7–8, 23, 27, 113, 145, 155
Renoir, Jean, 43, 143
Reynolds, Diamond, 154
rhetorical refusal, 18, 24, 30–33, 35, 39, 42–43, 46–48
Rhodes, Gary D., 112
Rhodes, Joe, 112, 128, 166n4
Rice, Jeff, 159n1
Rice, Jenny, 11
Rice, Tamir, 118, 128
Rich, Wilbur C., 166n1

Richardson, Robert, 145
Rickert, Thomas, 2, 42, 54, 60, 79, 92, 98–99, 103–4, 106–7, 109, 155
Rickman, Alan, 93. See also *The Winter Guest*
Ridolfo, Jim, 149, 167n12
right to look, 113, 115–17
Ritterhouse, Jennifer, 167n9
Rivers, Nathaniel, 60, 149
Rivette, Jacques, 35
Roberts, James, 11
Rolling Stones, 159n5
Romney, Jonathan, 162n6
Roscoe, Jane, 130
Ross, Murray, 83
Ryan, Mike, 114

Saló (Pasolini), 161n20
Sanchez, Danny, 120
San Fernando Valley, 91
Santana, Feiden, 154
Santaolalla, Isabel, 78
"Save Me" (Mann), 110, 157
scene-act ratio, 75, 77
Schell, Eileen, 83, 164n9
Schenker, Andrew, 86
Schilb, John, 18, 24, 31–32, 34. See also rhetorical refusal
Schindler's List (Spielberg), 54, 162n5, 168n5
Schoedsack, Ernest B., 93. See also *King Kong*
Schrader, Paul, 101. See also *The Comfort of Strangers*
Schumacher, Joel, 160n4. See also *The Lost Boys*
Schweber, Nate, 122
science fiction, 139, 167n15
Scorsese, Martin, 76–77, 137–58, 168n1. See also *Goodfellas*; *Hugo*; *Raging Bull*; *Taxi Driver*
Scott, Antronie, 120
Scott, Tony, 1, 4, 8, 23, 29, 51, 64, 67, 74, 113–14, 116, 119, 126, 141, 152, 158, 163n12
Scott, Walter, 118–19

Scream (Craven), 160n3
Selfe, Cynthia, 95
Selznick, Brian, 145
Serna, Joseph, 167n7, 167n14
Seventh Continent, The (Haneke), 37–38
Sheridan, David M., 149
Shining, The (Kubrick), 160n11
Shipka, Jody, 54
Silence of the Lambs, The (Demme), 93–94
Singer, Bryan, 10, 107
Siraganian, Lisa, 162n1
Smith, Brad W., 123
Smith, Kyle, 114, 131–32
Smith, Murray, 76, 163n4
Sontag, Susan, 43, 161n18
Sparling, Hannah, 122
special effects, 139, 142–44
Speck, Oliver C., 29, 35, 43–45, 47, 160n1
spectacle, 15, 37, 66, 128, 135, 162n6
Spencer, Octavia, 133
Sperb, Jason, 165nn3–4, 165n9
Spielberg, Steven, 30, 54, 162n6. See also *Jaws*; *Minority Report*; *Schindler's List*
Spivak, Gayatri, 66
Springer, John Parris, 112
Stam, Robert, 5, 13, 16–17, 19, 29, 84, 101–2, 141–42, 150, 159n4, 164n11
Stanton, Robert, 122
Stardust Memories (Allen), 164n11
Sterling, Alton, 118
Stilwell, Robyn J., 92–94, 99, 117, 164n2
Strangers on a Train (Hitchcock), 161n12
Stumm, Bettina, 130
Sweet Hereafter, The (Egoyan), 161n14

Tatko-Peterson, Ann, 112, 131
Taxi Driver (Scorsese), 76–77
television, 3, 5, 8, 24, 30, 37–38, 41, 43, 45, 62, 106–7, 109, 116, 144, 156–57, 160n4, 164n12, 165n9
Tensing, Ray, 122
terministic screens, 10, 86
There Will Be Blood (Anderson), 159n6
Theriault, Kim S., 162n7
Thomas, Rob, 162n9

Thompson, Kristin, 101
Thompson, Marie, 96, 99, 102, 165n5
Thorpe, Geoffrey, 80
Three Paths to the Lake (Haneke), 42
Till, Emmett, 133
Time of the Wolf, (Haneke), 44
Torchin, Leshu, 162n6
Torner, Evan, 44
Tout Va Bien (Godard), 159n4
trauma, 4, 11, 13, 17–20, 41–43, 45, 55–56, 59–60, 65–66, 90–92, 95, 100–102, 104, 106, 108, 110, 119, 129–30, 137, 140, 144, 146–48, 150, 153, 156–58, 161n19, 162n9, 166n3, 168n16
Trier, Lars von, 90. See also *Dancer in the Dark*
Trimbur, John, 149–50, 153, 160n7
Trip to the Moon, A (Méliès), 138, 144
Tschofen, Monique, 59
Turim, Maureen, 56, 148, 167n6, 168n16. See also flashbacks

Usual Suspects, The (Singer), 10, 107
Ut, Nick, 167n13

Van, Turkey, 49, 63
Verstraten, Peter, 19, 92–93, 101
Vertigo (Hitchcock), 10
Videodrome (Cronenberg), 30
Villalba, Jason, 120
Villanueva, Victor, 82
Villarejo, Amy, 84
viral rhetoric, 8, 10, 33, 46, 51, 72, 83, 113, 117–18, 120, 133

Walker, Janet, 62
Walters, Shannon, 99, 102–3, 165n8
Wang, Hansi Lo, 168n18
Warner, Michael, 153–54

water wars, 19, 70–71, 73, 80–81, 148, 163n2
Weinstein Company, 20, 114, 126, 133–35
Welch, Nancy, 1, 4, 8, 23, 29, 51, 64, 67, 74, 113–14, 116, 119, 126, 141, 152, 158, 163n12
Wenders, Wim, 21, 23, 31, 160n1. See also *Wings of Desire*
Wexler, Haskell, 1–17, 141, 155, 158, 160n4. See also *Medium Cool*
Wheatley, Catherine, 22, 37, 40
Wheeler, Duncan, 86
Wicks, Ulrich, 9
Wilferth, Joe, 7
Williams, Tennessee, 165n6
Willis, Sharon, 165n10
Wilson, Emma, 54, 61
Wilson, Mark D., 167n7
Wings of Desire (Wenders), 160n1
Winter Guest, The (Rickman), 93
"Wise Up" (Mann), 91, 99–104, 106, 109, 165n10
witnessing, 66–67, 111–36
Wittgenstein, Ludwig, 125
Wolfe, Cary, 72
Wollen, Peter, 3, 9, 17–18
Woolf, Nicky, 167n7
Workers Leaving the Lumière Factory (Lumière brothers), 140
Worsham, Lynn, 34
Wurmitzer, Gabriele, 44

Zacharek, Stephanie, 128
Zimmerman, George, 111–12, 118, 132–33, 135, 166n5
Zinn, Howard, 70, 79–80, 163n2
Žižek, Slavoj, 168n4
Zorn, John, 26, 156. See also Naked City

www.ingramcontent.com/pod-product-compliance
Lightning Source LLC
Chambersburg PA
CBHW020737230426
43665CB00009B/471